W9-CRJ-233

# THE
# LOST PILLARS
## OF
# ENOCH

"Churton revisits the history of mankind and approaches its attempts to deal with the invisible since the dawn of times with a unique mastery. This book is not only of great erudition but could also be the start of a future global spiritual movement of the digital age."

THOMAS JAMET, AUTHOR, LECTURER, AND COMMUNICATION SPECIALIST

"Humanity's near-manic obsession with lost and rediscovered wisdom is the basis for nearly all esoteric philosophy and practice. Taking the ancient myths and histories as his guide, Churton provides us not only with an interpretation of Enoch and the various ideas around the 'known-and-lost-wisdom dichotomy' as they have shaped our views across history, he also gives us a means of shaping and entering the future. It is a future quickly coming upon us, wherein the Pillars of Enoch once again are a depository of the collective wisdom of the past and the guide for a humanity seeking to understand itself and, like Enoch, 'walk with God.'"

MARK STAVISH, AUTHOR OF *EGREGORES*

"This ambitious book traces the antediluvian origin of the spiritual wisdom hymned in the Book of Enoch. Churton explores the path of this unifying truth through the teachings of the mystery traditions that have served to initiate humanity ever since. Of central concern to this thesis is that the dichotomy between science and spirit is false. Truth is the unifying bond that excludes only error. The breach between science and religion is an artificial construct that serves to hinder understanding. I highly recommend this book."

JAMES WASSERMAN, AUTHOR OF
*THE TEMPLARS AND THE ASSASSINS*
AND *THE MYSTERY TRADITIONS*

# THE
# LOST PILLARS
## OF
# ENOCH

## When Science and Religion Were One

## TOBIAS CHURTON

Inner Traditions
Rochester, Vermont

Inner Traditions
One Park Street
Rochester, Vermont 05767
www.InnerTraditions.com

Text stock is SFI certified

Copyright © 2021 by Tobias Churton

All rights reserved. No part of this book may be reproduced or utilized in
any form or by any means, electronic or mechanical, including photocopying,
recording, or by any information storage and retrieval system, without permission
in writing from the publisher.

Cataloging-in-Publication Data for this title is available from the Library of Congress

ISBN 978-1-64411-043-0 (print)
ISBN 978-1-64411-044-7 (ebook)

Printed and bound in the United States by Lake Book Manufacturing, Inc.
The text stock is SFI certified. The Sustainable Forestry Initiative® program
promotes sustainable forest management.

10 9 8 7 6 5 4 3

Text design by Priscilla Baker and layout by Debbie Glogover
This book was typeset in Garamond Premier Pro with Nocturne Serif and
Columbia Serial used as display typefaces

To send correspondence to the author of this book, mail a first-class letter to the
author c/o Inner Traditions • Bear & Company, One Park Street, Rochester, VT
05767, and we will forward the communication, or contact the author directly at
**tobiaschurton.com**.

# Contents

# PART THREE

## PARADISE REGAINED?

# PREFACE

# Provenance

In the fall of 2018, Professor Gabriele Boccaccini of the University of Michigan kindly invited me to deliver a paper to the "Enoch Seminar" conference, to be held in Florence in June 2019. The invitation was fortuitous. Researching a paper for specialists in the ancient Book of Enoch transformed a longstanding idea about a book on "religion for the future" into something more epic, vital, and universal. Looking again into the enigmatic world of the Book of Enoch opened my eyes to new perspectives on how our species has approached the origins of human knowledge, religion, and civilization. That old esoteric conceit that at the beginning of civilization *science and religion were one* struck me again, not so much as a lament for the past but as a picture for the future. An ancient idea arose in all its grandeur: before the Flood, humankind possessed pristine knowledge, and that knowledge, enlivened by conscious intuition, was passed down to the worthy in fragments, whence it may be recovered.

This book describes the amazing voyage of how this idea has plowed through the waves of recorded history.

## A Note about the Timing of This Book

Days before I began editing this manuscript, my family's house was hit by a flood precipitated by Storm Dennis, whose tempest hit the UK on February 17, 2020. As if being made temporarily homeless was not woeful enough, then, even as we attempted to make good the damage, the world was hit by the coronavirus, spread from China by every modern amenity. Now we may all feel intimately the kind of reality shock that made so many cultures in the distant past relate legends of a great natural cataclysm, a story familiar to Judeo-Christian tradition as the Great Flood and the story of Noah and his ark. Presuming, doubtless rightly, that so much that was precious was lost in that flood, or for all we know, series of floods, a story developed that vital knowledge that had been discovered before the Flood had been inscribed on pillars to survive the coming catalclysm. *One of the pillars survived.* In time, the construction of the pillars was ascribed to Enoch, hero of the Book of Enoch, a man who, according to Genesis, never died but was taken directly to heaven. The story, or myth, of the pillars marks the beginning of this book's journey.

While we may wonder today just what *we* might wish inscribed on pillars designed to testify to our knowledge before an obliterating catastrophe, I should like to suggest that if we make a start in attending seriously to what has been believed to have come down to us already in fragments from the distant past, we may yet find ourselves able to avoid the worst of what may yet come, much of which, it appears, is the product of our species' own deliberate fault, the product of our political and social weakness, our spiritual confusion, and our unethical unwillingness to apply knowledge in a mature manner when it exists. He who does not confront facts will be haunted by phantoms. In the words with which I concluded my first-ever attempt at a history of the world, aged eleven: "Knowledge is the prize we strive to win." We need knowledge, and we need to act on it.

I offer my heartiest thanks to Jon Graham, Ehud Sperling, Jeanie Levitan, Mindy Branstetter, Erica Robinson, Eliza Burns, and Ashley Kolesnik at Inner Traditions International for turning a rare idea into concrete reality.

PART ONE

❧❧❧

# THE
# LOST PILLARS
# IN
# ANTIQUITY

# ONE

# Saving Knowledge
# from Catastrophe

*The World's First Archaeological Story*

Our investigation begins with a little-known story about the origins of knowledge—little known, but not without influence, and arguably the world's first-ever story of *archaeology*. Jewish historian Flavius Josephus wrote it down in the 80s of the first century CE, which is about fifty years after his countryman Jesus was crucified.

A guest of the Flavian imperial dynasty in Rome (hence "Flavius"), Josephus hoped his history—*The Antiquities of the Jews*—would help Greek-reading Romans better appreciate Jewish people. This was timely. Thousands of Jewish warriors had been slaughtered during the previous two decades by imperial troops confronted with religiously motivated zealots trying to overthrow Roman jurisdiction. Having joined the rebels himself in the war's early stages, Josephus shrewdly submitted to Rome, proclaiming that Roman general Vespasian fulfilled the East's widespread expectation of a savior. When Vespasian established the Flavian dynasty as emperor in 69 CE, Josephus was rewarded.

Josephus wanted Romans to see that not all Jews were persistent rebels, nor were they habitually addicted to crazy beliefs. On the contrary, Josephus's ancestors were, by Roman standards, rational people maintaining comprehensible traditions, supported by respectable

Fig. 1.1. Josephus (37–100 CE),
a romanticized engraving

ancient texts compiled long before Roman history began. Confident in his mission, Josephus believed that by presenting Jewish history, he was preserving truth for all humanity because Jewish history took *everyone* back to the beginning.

The progeny of the first human being is described by Josephus in *Antiquities'* second chapter: Adam was not only the Jews' ancestor; he was the Romans' ancestor too.

The human race, however, got off to a bad start. Adam's son Cain fathered a line of wicked reprobates, tainted by Cain's outrageous murder of his pious brother, Abel. Fortunately, Adam and Eve produced a third son, Seth. Seth fathered a lineage distinguished by respect for God and honorable conduct toward God's creatures: virtues rewarded by access to knowledge of higher things. Josephus describes the higher things in terms of awareness of God, farsighted inventiveness, and knowledge of astronomy.

They also were the inventors of that peculiar sort of wisdom which is concerned with the heavenly bodies, and their order.

And that their inventions might not be lost before they were sufficiently known, upon Adam's prediction that the world was to be destroyed at one time by the force of fire, and at another time by the violence and quantity of water, they made two pillars, the one of brick, the other of stone: they inscribed their discoveries on them both, that in case the pillar of brick should be destroyed by the flood, the pillar of stone might remain, and exhibit those discoveries to mankind; and also inform them that there was another pillar of brick erected by them. Now this remains in the land of Siriad to this day.[1]

Josephus's compelling image of antediluvian pillars is unique. Nowhere does it appear in the Hebrew Bible. In the Bible, pillars generally receive more bad press than good because Hebrew prophets perennially associated them with idolatry. We don't know whence Josephus obtained his pillars story, or—and this is important—what the original story may have *lost* in Josephus's rather casual telling of it. I say this because Josephus's history frequently glosses over what non-Jews might find difficult. His pillars story utilizes his distinctive style of ameliorative, urbanely philosophical apologetic. For example, Josephus does not labor the point that conflagrations of fire and water were horrific punishments sent by an outraged deity determined to exterminate humanity—and practically everything else on earth. Josephus may have suspected that such an emphasis might offend his Gentile audience with the whiff of unrestrained or fanatical vengeance, and he knew very well that it was apocalyptic predictions of an imminent end of the world in favor of a national savior that had recently motivated Jewish zealots to rise against Rome. Such activities left Jews suspect, and heavily taxed, with Rome commandeering the old temple taxes even after Jerusalem's temple ceased to exist.

In his rational, universalized account, Josephus's pillars (or stelae) of brick and stone were erected to preserve discoveries that would otherwise have disappeared in the event of cataclysms, with survivors denied knowledge of them. Josephus emphasizes educative benefit to all human beings. He was aware that predictions of terrestrial deluges were not confined to Jews. Educated Romans knew Greek philosopher Plato's account in the *Timaeus,* written in about 360 BCE, of how the great isle of Atlantis sank beneath unforgiving waves. In Plato's account, an Egyptian priest informs the Greek Solon that Egypt had avoided vastations by flood that ruined other countries thanks to blessed geography and intelligent management of the Nile. Thus, in Josephus's narrative, Adam's predictions of water and fire deluges reveal Adam as wise soothsayer rather than unstoical fire-and-brimstone prophet. And, to add a sign of good faith—and a reminder that it was real history about real things the historian was attempting to convey—Josephus added an intriguing codicil: *one of the Sethite pillars could still be found.*

Given what Josephus says about the stone pillar being the likeliest to survive a flood, it was presumably the stone pillar that remained in "Siriad." That God felt compelled to destroy human beings by water is presented by Josephus as proper punishment invited by provocation: all but Noah and his immediate kin had turned wicked, hell-bent on destruction. God would replace rotten seed with a purified race. Romans understood the necessity for imposing punitive measures upon any who failed to honor divine power, so Josephus was able to tiptoe the tightrope by showing that the Jews' God likewise favored order, austere justice, and respectful honor and that God's punishments, though severe, were nonetheless just, emblematic of an incorruptible judge of humankind. Indeed, the God of Genesis might be compared to stark Roman power as typified in a famous speech Roman historian Tacitus attributed to enemy Caledonian chieftain Calgacus: "They make a desert, and call it peace."*

---

*According to Tacitus (ca. 56–ca. 120 CE), the speech was made at almost precisely the time Josephus was writing and refers to the Battle of Mons Graupius in Scotland in 83 or 84 CE; Tacitus, *Agricola*, 29–38.

## THE NEPHILIM

Josephus's rationalizing of what he took to be Moses's account of early human history (Genesis) is evident in the way he handles the Flood's buildup. Look at the Genesis account (6:1–8, King James Version). It shows distinct signs of having been edited or censored, possibly because of its curiously ambiguous, potentially disturbing contents.

And it came to pass, when men began to multiply on the face of the earth, and daughters were born unto them,

That the sons of God saw the daughters of men that they were fair; and they took them wives of all which they chose.

And the Lord said, My spirit shall not always strive with man, for that he also is flesh: yet his days shall be an hundred and twenty years.

There were giants in the earth in those days; and also after that, when the sons of God came in unto the daughters of men, and they bare children to them, the same became mighty men [Hebrew: *gibborim*] which were of old, men of renown.

And God saw that the wickedness of man was great in the earth, and that every imagination of the thoughts of his heart was only evil continually.

And it repented the Lord that he had made man on the earth, and it grieved him at his heart.

And the Lord said, I will destroy man whom I have created from the face of the earth; both man, and beast, and the creeping thing, and the fowls of the air; for it repenteth me that I have made them.

But Noah found grace in the eyes of the Lord.

Here are the rudiments—or fragmentary remains—of a story first amplified (or reconstructed) in the apocalyptic Book of Enoch (ca. second to first century BCE). In our own time also, the story has provoked speculation, such that its peculiar "nephilim" (translated uncertainly in the King James Bible as "giants," from the the Septuagint's *gigantes*) have attracted multiple interpretations, unsurprising given the difficulties of the passage. It is unclear in Genesis whether a direct relationship exists between "giants" and "later" baleful copulations attributed to sons of God with daughters of men. It is often assumed that giants resulted from sons of God impregnating mortal women.

A son of God, in this context, is widely understood from other biblical sources to mean an angel (Hebrew *malach* = messenger), native to heavenly realms, functioning amid a host as spiritual governors of the stars (or the stars themselves; see Job 38:7), joined thereby to human destiny. Attempts to rationalize this Genesis myth have, however, led to seeing "sons of God" rather as Seth's righteous descendants, those who still "walked with God" (as Enoch did), until overcome by lust for the daughters of men. On this interpretation, the "daughters of men" referred to Cain's female descendants, so that it was mixing of Cainite and Sethite blood that corrupted humanity and provoked the Flood crisis.*

Genesis then gives us abbreviated references to a time when there were "giants" on the earth. The sense, however, is obscured by the statement that they continued after the sons of God fell upon the women and were directly or indirectly connected with the offspring deriving from sons of God and daughters of men.

---

*This view appears in the Ethiopic version of the apocryphal Jewish Book of Jubilees, which work, dated circa 160–150 BCE (though possibly much older) is generally considered to have based its account of giants and fallen angels on the Book of Enoch, though this reliance is not absolutely certain. A terrestrial view of lustful Sethites descending upon the charms of Cainite women was also one most acceptable to Christian writers such as Sextus Julius Africanus, John of Chrysostom, Augustine of Hippo, Ephrem the Syrian, and the authors of the Clementine literature. Jewish scholar Simeon bar Yochai (died ca. 160 CE) also rejected the idea that holy angels quit heaven in pursuit of human lusts. Angels, being immortal, were considered asexual, so sexual lust and procreation amid the angelic host seemed absurd to many pious commentators. Consider Luke 20:35–37, "But they which shall be accounted worthy to obtain that world, and the resurrection from the dead, neither marry, nor are given in marriage: Neither can they die any more: for they are equal unto the angels; and are the children of God, being the children of the resurrection." Consider also Matthew 22:30, in which the resurrected are in this respect "like angels in heaven."

Compiled from at least five sources perhaps some two to three centuries after Genesis was assembled, the Book of Enoch understood the "giants" as evil offspring of miscegenation between women and angels (called "Watchers"). There seems to be a residue of mythological material *behind* the Genesis passages about "mighty men, which were of old, men of renown," a description with no negative connotation about it, partly supported by a rare appearance of the Hebrew nephilim in a myth, or legend, alluded to in Ezekiel 32:37.

> And they shall not lie with the mighty that are fallen [nephilim] of the uncircumcised, which are gone down to hell with their weapons of war: and they have laid their swords under their heads, but their iniquities shall be upon their bones, though they were the terror of the mighty in the land of the living.

Here, mighty warriors are fallen. While this translation might suggest that *nephilim* refers to fallen angels or souls, the Ezekiel passage seems to refer to men who had attacked Jews, and thus been trapped in the underworld (a theme perhaps adopted by the Book of Enoch regarding punishment of the Watchers). The "warrior" interpretation might have affected the Septuagint's Greek translation of *nephilim* as "gigantes" (giants), implying a hero mythology Greco-Egyptians would have understood, for Greece's mythic heroes—such as Perseus and Theseus—often had mixed divine and human parentage. Genesis may originally have intended *nephilim* to indicate the fallen status of sons of God who had left heaven—or a former blessed state—out of lust for daughters of men, while subsequently, with the "mighty men of renown" theme, engendering an etiological myth rooted in some now vanished reference to an ancient heroic, if bloodthirsty (Cainite?) warrior class. If nothing else, these questions highlight that the Hebrew Bible does not always display plain sense, at least to us.

Josephus offers his own spin on all this in *Antiquities,* chapter 3. He liberally smooths the rough edges of the biblical account with calm reasonableness. Recognizing this, we may realize that his Sethite pillars story may have lost something important in his retelling; that is, Josephus's narrative may obscure a now lost mythic progenitor.

Now this posterity of Seth continued to esteem God as the Lord of the universe, and to have an entire regard to virtue, for seven generations; but in process of time they were perverted, and forsook the practices of their forefathers; and did neither pay those honors to God which were appointed them, nor had they any concern to do justice toward men. But for what degree of zeal they had formerly shown for virtue, they now showed by their actions a double degree of wickedness, whereby they made God to be their enemy. For many angels of God accompanied with women, and begat sons that proved unjust, and despisers of all that was good, on account of the confidence they had in their own strength; for the tradition is, that these men did what resembled the acts of those whom the Grecians call giants. But Noah was very uneasy at what they did; and being displeased at their conduct, persuaded them to change their dispositions and their acts for the better: but seeing they did not yield to him, but were slaves to their wicked pleasures, he was afraid they would kill him, together with his wife and children, and those they had married; so he departed out of that land.

Using a pseudepigraphical tradition of Noah pleading with the giants, and reference to familiar Greek giant legends, Josephus ironed out any problems in the narrative that might have caused a Gentile to shake his head on account of suspected credulity, save that stubborn aspect of the story referring to "many angels" joining themselves to human beings. Perhaps Josephus was familiar with the Book of Enoch Watchers story, but was wary of its apocalyptic character. Nevertheless, while intercourse twixt angel and human female was rare in the normal course of things, analogous combinations were familiar to Greek and Roman mythology.

⁓⊚⊙⊙⁓

So, Josephus's account of the pillars stands with little mythological coloring and a practical rationale. Seth's descendants had knowledge, and intended it to benefit all of humanity, taking intelligent, logical steps to preserve it from disaster, even when no obvious signs existed that disaster was imminent. They showed wisdom. And the proof of it, Josephus says, could still be seen, should readers choose to investigate further.

## WHERE COULD JOSEPHUS'S SURVIVING PILLAR BE FOUND?

Josephus's history was translated into English by mathematician William Whiston (1667–1752), sometime friend and colleague of the illustrious Isaac Newton. Whiston's Anglicized expression for where the pillar could be still found (in Josephus's day) was "the land of Siriad." In his footnote to the word, Whiston takes *Siriad* to mean "Syria," and, to push the Syria location further, informs his readers that Josephus confused "Seth" with the ancient Egyptian king Sesostris (Greek form of Senusret; possibly Senusret III, ca. 1862–1844 BCE). Familiar with references to stelae erected by Sesostris from book 2 (chapters 102–3, 106) of the *Histories* of Greek chronicler Herodotus (ca. 484–425 BCE), and ever keen to offer magisterial scientific explanations, Whiston puts his two and two together. This is Herodotus's account of conqueror Sesostris's pillars, referred to by Whiston in his footnote.

> Passing over these, therefore, I will now speak of the king who came after them, Sesostris. This king, said the priests, set out with a fleet of long ships from the Arabian Gulf and subdued all the dwellers by the Red Sea, till as he sailed on he came to a sea which was too shallow for his vessels. After returning thence back to Egypt, he gathered a great army (according to the story of the priests) and marched over the mainland, subduing every nation to which he came. When those that he met were valiant men and strove hard for freedom, he set up pillars in their land whereon the inscription showed his

own name and his country's, and how he had overcome them with his own power; but when the cities had made no resistance and been easily taken, then he put an inscription on the pillars even as he had done where the nations were brave; but he drew also on them the privy parts of a woman, wishing to show clearly that the people were cowardly. Thus doing he marched over the country till he had passed over from Asia to Europe and subdued the Scythians and Thracians. . . . As to the pillars which Sesostris, king of Egypt, set up in the countries, most of them are no longer to be seen. But I myself saw them in the Palestine part of Syria, with the writing aforesaid and the women's privy parts upon them. Also there are in Ionia two figures of this man carven in rock, one on the road from Ephesus to Phocaea, and the other on that from Sardis to Smyrna. In both places there is a man of a height of four cubits and a half cut in relief, with a spear in his right hand and a bow in his left, and the rest of his equipment answering thereto; for it is both Egyptian and Ethiopian; and right across the breast from one shoulder to the other there is carven a writing in the Egyptian sacred character, saying: "I myself won this land with the might of my shoulders." There is nothing here to show who he is and whence he comes, but it is shown elsewhere. Some of those who have seen these figures guess them to be Memnon, but they are far indeed from the truth.[2]

If Herodotus knew of people who had misidentified the pillars, it was easy for Whiston to consider Josephus likewise mistaken. Besides, the pillars spoken of by Herodotus, like the one to which Josephus referred, could still be seen—and may be so today. One is at Karabel in Turkey, the other on the Nahr al-Kalb's south bank, northeast of modern Beirut, Lebanon.

Unfortunately, Herodotus was also mistaken.

The relief by the Nahr al-Kalb ("Dog River") was once one of three celebrating victories secured by Pharaoh Ramesses II (ca. 1279–1213 BCE), *not* Sesostris. Another relief there commemorates

Fig. 1.2. William Whiston (1667–1752)

Fig. 1.3. *Nahr al-Kalb inscriptions;*
engraving by Louis-François Cassas, 1799

Assyrian king Esarhaddon's seizure of Memphis in 671 BCE. Herodotus's other "pillar" between Sardes and Smyrna, in the pass of Karabel, also has no claim to Sesostris's campaigns. It is a carving of King Tarkasnawa of Mira, vassal of the mighty Hittites. Had Whiston been better acquainted with ancient Syria's archaeology, he might also have referred to one of the obelisks from the still-extant Temple of Obelisks in what was once Byblos, Lebanon.

Fig. 1.4. The rock relief Karabel, visited by Charles Texier in 1839

Whiston, however, was himself mistaken.

Whiston's error probably derives from partial reliance upon the Latin version of Josephus's *Antiquities,* first printed by learned humanist and publisher, Johann Froben (1460–1527). On page 7 of chapter 4 of Froben's version of *Flavii Josephi Opera* (1524), we find that Josephus's surviving Sethite pillar was still extant "in terra Syria," which is Syria, unequivocally. However, the principal surviving Greek version of Josephus's *Antiquities* has the following Greek phrase for the pillar's whereabouts: *kata tēn gēn Seirida.*[3] The Greek *Seirida* has apparently been taken by a Latin translator of the Greek original as being either an error for, or variant of, "the land of Syria." In Greek there is all the difference between an upsilon (as in S*u*ria or the English "Syria") and vowels epsilon and iota (*ei*). The Greek "-ida" or "-da" ending of Seirida normally denotes a grouping or collective identity.

The meaning of the Greek "Seirida" almost certainly comes from *seirios,* which means "scorcher": the Greek name given to the Dog Star, Seirios (Latin *Sirius,* the nose of constellation Canis Major—the Great Dog), the star so eminently vital to the Egyptians for the timing of the Nile's annual life-giving inundation, anciently plotted (ca. 3000 BCE) in relation to the heliacal rising of Sirius, when the star returned at dawn in July (now August), after some seventy days' obscurity in the daytime sky.

The word *scorcher* probably came from the very hot ("dog") days of summer when Sirius and the sun rose together, or else from Sirius's uniquely exceptional luminosity (it may even have appeared as red in ancient Egypt). Therefore, the Greek phrase *kata tēn gēn Seirida* means "in the Siriusite land"; that is, among the Sirius worshippers: Egypt and/or Kush (today Sudan and northern Ethiopia). Perhaps religious propriety, that is to say Jewish horror at anthropomorphic polytheism, prevented Josephus from referring directly to the Gentile goddess of Sirius, Sopdet (Greek *Sothis*). "Seirida" would be a familiar name for Egyptian culture, notably in keeping with the astronomical theme of Josephus's pillars paragraph.

As well as the astronomy of flooding, Sopdet-Sothis was also identified with Isis, fertility goddess and fount of wisdom, and we may wonder whether such an identification may have had something to do with what was in Josephus's mind when he chose to indicate the stele's location while, perhaps unintentionally, obscuring it. Unsurprisingly, Sopdet was also identified with the dog-headed god Anubis, guardian of mysteries and the gates of death, whose terrors Isis traditionally overcame. Sopdet-Sothis-Isis was, anyway, the key divinity to a beneficent flooding, astronomically predicted. This link may give us a clue to what the stele referred to by Josephus may once have, or still, stood for.*

Sopdet-Sirius's summertime rising marked the Egyptian new year return of light and life. Egypt's fertility was directly joined to the visible presence of Sirius—and in Josephus's time, Egypt was known as the Roman Empire's granary. Rome had the circuses, but Egypt had the bread, and the bread came thanks to Sirius.

It now seems clear that Whiston combined the Latin and Greek words and came up with an English blend, or compromise: *Siriad,* which to his mind, especially a mind informed—or misinformed— by Herodotus, must have meant Syria, a suitably biblical setting for a Sethite pillar. This being the most likely case, we can probably see why Josephus did not simply say "Syria." While doubtless observing a scholarly translator's reticence at superseding his text, Whiston nonetheless misled those who followed him.

We must look to Egypt.

---

*Sirius was of course revered in places other than Egypt. Called "Tishtriya" in Persia's Zoroastrian *Zend-Avesta,* Sirius is made overseer of all stars by the Supreme God, Ahura Mazda (*Khorda Avesta* III 44), with responsibility to defeat the demon of drought by the blessing of rain. When the Zoroastrian Supreme God wishes to punish human evil, Tishtrya is required to provide the requisite flood; while in ancient Babylon, Sirius was on occasion included in a dominant place in lists of planets. Nevertheless, in the Roman Empire of the period, "Seirida" would almost certainly indicate Egyptian culture. In one Egyptian inscription, for example, Isis's home is called plainly "Seirias gē" (*gē* = land) while Isis herself is directly associated with the Nile as "Neilōtis" or "Seirias" (feminine form of *Seirios*) with the Nile in context called "Seirios."[4] We shall presently mention another relevant appearance of the "Seiriad" name in another work with specific reference to Egypt. See page 24.

# TWO

# "Sethites" in Egypt?

It may surprise readers that we have no way of knowing specifically where the authors of Genesis—or Josephus himself—thought the ante-diluvian leaders of the human race lived. The created world—at least as people of antiquity knew it—was their oyster, so to speak, and Josephus believed that when Seth appeared, there was no place called Egypt—or Judaea for that matter. According to Moses (Genesis's supposed author), the world's geographically diffused population, originally sharing one language and religion, derived from Noah's children, Ham, Shem, and Japheth. Certainly, Josephus was aware that the "Promised Land" had no meaning until promised to Abraham. Following Genesis, Abraham is placed by Josephus in northern Mesopotamia (described anachronistically as "Chaldaea"), on the Euphrates side, around Harran or Padan-Aram, and somewhere called "Ur," which I strongly suspect refers to the region of Urartu, the biblical "Ararat," in what is now the Turkish, Syrian, and Iraqi borderland. Like the Mitanni royalty who ruled Urartu until Assyrian invasion in the thirteenth century BCE, Abraham also enjoyed important links—possibly diplomatic and/or military—with Egypt's royal house, being on speaking terms with the pharaoh.

Perhaps Josephus knew of the Egyptian belief, rooted to Egypt's south in the kingdom of Kush, that life first appeared at the Jebel-Barkal ("Holy Mountain" in Arabic) by the Kushite capital, Napata (now Karima, Sudan), where the ruins of a temple to Amun still stand and a stele was erected to commemorate Kushite king Piye's victory over Egypt during his reign (744–714 BCE; the stele is now in Cairo). Perhaps Josephus did not, but I think he may have experienced awkwardness in dismissing Egyptian claims familiar to Romans from the *Timaeus* that Egypt held the most ancient records since it had avoided— thanks to divinely ordered inundations of the Nile—many deluges that periodically wrecked both valley and mountain people at sundry periods elsewhere. In circa 360 BCE, Plato has an Egyptian priest say this to Solon, a Greek visitor:

> Now this has the form of a myth, but really signifies a declination of the bodies moving in the heavens around the earth, and a great conflagration of things upon the earth, which recurs after long intervals; at such times those who live upon the mountains and in dry and lofty places are more liable to destruction than those who dwell by rivers or on the seashore. And from this calamity the Nile, who is our never-failing savior, delivers and preserves us. When, on the other hand, the gods purge the earth with a deluge of water, the survivors in your country are herdsmen and shepherds who dwell on the mountains, but those who, like you, live in cities are carried by the rivers into the sea. Whereas in this land, neither then nor at any other time, does the water come down from above on the fields, having always a tendency to come up from below; for which reason the traditions preserved here are the most ancient.[1]

Egyptian status in matters of antiquity was well attested, and Josephus himself had frequent cause to refer to Egyptian historical records for helpful material. For example, a chief source for his work *Against Apion* was one "Manetho," native of Sebynnetos in the Nile Delta, described in the *Book of Sothis* attributed to him as "high priest and scribe of the sacred shrines of Egypt . . . dwelling at Heliopolis," city of Re.[2] Apparently active in the late third century BCE during the reign of Ptolemy II Philadelphus (282–229 BCE), it is obvious from Josephus's borrowings that he knew more of Manetho's works than

Fig. 2.1. Jebel-Barkal, Hathor Columns, Temple of Mut

Fig. 2.2. Jebel-Barkal (Holy Mountain);
photo by Lassi Hu

Fig. 2.3. Pyramids at Jebel-Barkal

survive today.* We have only extracts from writings attributed to Manetho included in other men's work: references from historian and geographer Julius Africanus (160–240 CE) reported by Christian Bishop Eusebius (263–339 CE) and quotations from otherwise lost works by Eusebius and others made in compendious form (the *Chronographia*) by Palestinian monk and chronicler George "Syncellus"† (died 810 CE). Achieving ecclesiastical office in Constantinople during the Byzantine period, Syncellus's commitment to reading and writing has bequeathed us an otherwise lost story to tell.

What Syncellus drew from Manetho's works bears directly on attempts to locate the source and perhaps original context of Josephus's allegedly extant pillar of wisdom. A significant problem remains, however. While we have relevant passages supposedly drawn from a larger work by Manetho (*Aegyptiaca*), written to impress Greeks with Egypt's antiquity, and a shorter work on a prophetic dating system based on Egyptian dynasties (the *Book of Sothis*), extracts from the former work vary in detail, while the *Book of Sothis* has a number of different pharaonic dynasty entries to that of *Aegyptiaca* sources. This leads us to suppose that the *Book of Sothis* might be a later work—later than Josephus, anyway. It may have been tampered with by later sources using Manetho's name to lend spurious authority to forgery and propaganda. Most scholars accept that the letter from Manetho to Ptolemy II Philadelphus, which introduces the *Book of Sothis,* was not Manetho's work, despite its pertinence to our investigation. Unfortunately, we cannot regress in time to check what other sources were available to unknown manipulators of Manetho's reputation.

Nevertheless, let us hear George Syncellus's own introduction to Manetho:

---

*See *Against Apion,* book 1, 14, where "Manetho" identifies the Hebrews with the "Hyksos," "shepherd kings" who built Avaris and temporarily dominated Egypt, being later ejected by King Amenophis.

†The title Latinized as "Syncellus" comes from the Greek for "cell mate" and was given to an office of confidant and adviser to a senior Orthodox cleric.

It remains now to make brief extracts concerning the dynasties of Egypt from the works of Manetho of Sebennytus. In the time of Ptolemy Philadelphus he was styled high priest of the pagan temples of Egypt, and [*Note!*] wrote from inscriptions *in the Seriadic land* [my italics; the Greek is "en tēi Sēriadikēi gēi"], traced, he says, in sacred language and holy characters by Thoth, the first Hermes, and translated after the Flood . . . in hieroglyphic characters. When the work had been arranged in books by Agathodaemon, son of the second Hermes [Hermes Trismegistus] and father of Tat, in the temple-shrines of Egypt, Manetho dedicated it to the above King Ptolemy II Philadelphus in his *Book of Sothis,* using the following words: Letter of Manetho of Sebennytus to Ptolemy Philadelphus.

> To the great King Ptolemy Philadelphus Augustus* Greeting to my lord Ptolemy from Manetho, high-priest and scribe of the sacred shrines of Egypt, born at Sebennytus and dwelling at Heliopolis. It is my duty, almighty king, to reflect upon all such matters as you may desire me to investigate. So, as you are making your researches concerning the future of the universe, in obedience to your command I shall place before you the Sacred Books which I have studied, written by your forefather, Hermes Trismegistus. Farewell, I pray, my lord King.

Such is his account of the translation of the books written by the second Hermes. Thereafter Manetho tells also of five Egyptian tribes which formed thirty dynasties.[3]

It is clear that Syncellus has not received his basic information about the "second Hermes" (Trismegistus) and of his relatives

---

*"Augustus"—Greek *sebastos*—was an anachronistic title for the alleged period of composition of the letter.

Agathodaimon, Tat, and antediluvian deity Thoth from the allegedly forged letter, nor from the *Book of Sothis* that follows it. If this information was originally Egyptian, or came from Manetho himself from before or around Josephus's time, we must ask: *Was Josephus's account of the Sethite pillars a Jewish version of a Greco-Egyptian legend about Thoth's hieroglyphic inscriptions written before the Flood, and afterward transcribed by the second Hermes? Who took the basic story from whom?* Does Josephus's Sethite story conflate Seth, or descendant of Seth, with Thoth (with the biblical Enoch conflated with the "second Hermes," Hermes Trismegistos), or did Egyptians produce *their own* version from out of, or indeed *to counter,* a Jewish myth, with Thoth and Hermes Trismegistos as Egyptian heroes, progenitors of civilization? The issue is crucial to our question.

A competitive scenario is not unlikely. Aggressive competition existed in the first century, and presumably before that time, between rival claims for the antiquity of the Jews, and for the primacy of Egyptian history and religion, doubtless stimulated by the Hebrew scriptures having been translated into Greek, in Egypt, around the time a *Book of Sothis* and *Aegyptiaca* were allegedly composed by Manetho, apparently, at Heliopolis. Heliopolis's temple complex's native name, by the way, was *Iwnw,* which means . . . "The Pillars." We may have here a root idea for Josephus's surviving pillar in the "Sēiriadic" land.

The contention that Josephus was unaware of a relevant Thoth or Hermes Trismegistos story before he wrote about the Sethite stelae could be made from two principal points. First, we cannot be sure that Syncellus's "Manetho" source account of Thoth and Hermes was available, or had even been written, when Josephus composed his history (Josephus makes no mention of it in *Against Apion*). Second, the least ambiguous surviving evidence for a Hermes pillars story comes *after* Josephus, when, in the second or third centuries CE (though some scholars tolerate an earlier date, with pre–first century CE Egyptian antecedents) an important series of philosophical and religious tracts appeared in Egypt whose spiritually liberating gnosis (knowledge) was ascribed to

Hermes Trismegistos, accompanied by Agathodaimon, Tat, Asklēpios, and King Ammon. The "Hermetic" tract titled *Korē Kosmou* describes Hermes making tablets, whence the Hermetic books derived.* It is possible then that Syncellus's Hermetic cast list derives from *after* Josephus and was itself amalgamated with the idea of an antediluvian preservation of knowledge *derived from Josephus,* but we simply cannot be sure, frustrating as this doubtless is to our tidy minds. Oh, for a time machine!

In favor of Manetho's claim to a primary account (a pre-Josephus Egyptian pillars story), we do know that the god Hermes bore the epithet "three times great" as early as June 172 BCE, the title having been found on an ostraca discovered in the late sixties at Sakkara. It refers to the management of the ibis cult at Memphis's necropolis, close to Heliopolis. It was written by cult official Hor of Temenesi, son of Harendjiotef, devotee of Thoth, later of the nome (administrative area) of Sebennytos. According to John Ray's *Archive of Hor* (1976), Hor calls on Hermes in colloquial Demotic in terms rendered in Greek on another ostraca as *megistou kai megistou theou megalou Hermou,* "great and great the great god Hermes" (Hermes being the Greek name for the Egyptian god Thoth, creator, Egyptians held, of writing, magic, and other mysteries).[4]

As for Egyptian–Jewish competition, Josephus himself entered the fray when defending *Jewish* history and probity by attacking Apion's legacy. A Hellenized Egyptian grammarian who had used writings attributed to Manetho to favor Egyptian claims to greatest antiquity, Apion (20 BCE–45 CE) rudely denigrated Jewish claims, stimulating a conflict that enflamed anti-Jewish sentiments in Rome. Emperor Claudius would expel Jews from Rome some time between 41 and 53, allegedly for messianic agitations, while Claudius's predecessor, Tiberius, had expelled Egyptian ritualists, as well as Jews from Rome. A reference in "Manetho" to Jews being descended from "lepers," for example, stimulated Josephus to attack aspects of Manetho's historical work as well (namely in *Against Apion,* bk. 1, 27, where Manetho is accused of "arrant

---

*See page 63.

lies"). In this context, works attributed to Manetho had propaganda value and would be tampered with by sectarian interests, accounting in part for variant details in different Manetho (or pseudo-Manetho) sources. Such conflict only complicates matters further.

If Josephus *did* know the story of an antediluvian Thoth inscribing wisdom in hieroglyphs that after the Flood were transcribed from inscriptions into books by Hermes Trismegistos, then it is almost certain that Josephus would have assumed the Egyptian account not only *hijacked Jewish traditions* but also was in spirit and name contrary to those traditions—and mischievously so. This would include the pious account of Sethite science in Genesis, delivered, as Josephus supposed, anciently to Moses—the truth-dedicated Moses himself having escaped the duplicitous land of Sirius worshippers by signal divine agency (the Exodus). Indeed, such a scenario might well account for the rather vague way Josephus writes of the "descendants of Seth" distinguishing themselves in inventing astronomy, a particular distinction claimed by Egyptians for their own Thoth-Hermes. It might also account for Josephus's designation of the pillar being still extant in "Seiriad," an authentic phrase quite possibly taken originally from works attributed to Manetho, which by sundry routes was transmitted to George Syncellus's time intact. It should also be grasped that the very existence of "Egypt" would have been seen by Josephus as postdiluvian, its population descended from Noah and its language postdating the Tower of Babel in Shinar (Genesis 11:1–9).

The pillars story did not of course appear in Genesis, so even if Josephus *did* get the rudiments of it from an Egyptian source, it would be logical of him to, as it were, "translate it back" into what he must have truly believed to have been its authentic setting among descendants of Adam, free of Manetho's idolatrous lists of gods and "spirits of the dead" who, according to the Egyptian's account, used to govern Egypt, and afterward, through allegedly divine pharaohs whose failings as mere mortals—and whose reliance on the Hebrew wisdom of such as Joseph and Moses—invited ridicule in Hebrew scripture. In other words, if Josephus saw "Thoth" in the context of progenitor of wisdom, he would very likely have thought "Seth" or Seth's enlightened progeny, for Josephus was conscious of the move among Jews (including himself) to use Egyptian records to flesh out, and substantiate universally, Jewish history. Indeed, by similar motives, "Manetho"-Syncellus's account of Hermes Trismegistos would be used by Christian chronographers to date Noah's Flood in relation to Egyptian dynastic history considered extracted from Manetho's *Aegyptiaca*. It is likely that Josephus would have regarded Sethite astronomers as beings that Egyptian priests probably confused with, or corrupted into, Egyptian gods, Thoth among them. Josephus would never have seriously entertained the reverse proposition, which to numerous commentators in our own time seems the more appealing option, ancient Egyptian science being considerably more manifest to our senses than Josephus's Sethite science. Josephus's history was intended, among other things, to correct what he considered past misconceptions; it stood, Josephus believed, on the authority of the righteous lawgiver Moses, servant of the one true God who justified the existence of the Jewish people. And if this point is insufficiently emphatic, one need only consult Josephus's extraordinary account of Abraham's relations with Egypt in book 1, chapter 8 of *Antiquities* to see his position clearly.

> He [Abraham] communicated to them [the Egyptian priests] arithmetic, and delivered to them the science of astronomy; for, before Abram came into Egypt, they were unacquainted with those parts of learning; for that science came from the Chaldaeans into Egypt [via Abraham and before him, Seth's progeny], and from thence to the Greeks also.[5]

*The Greeks also*—that throws in the Romans too! In other words, any inscription, stele, or text to be found in Egypt concerning astronomy and arithmetic ought to be considered indebted to the patriarch Abraham's visit to Egypt with beautiful wife Sara, whom pharaoh especially coveted but could not possess. If an ancient pillar was venerated for wisdom in "Seiriad" (and there must have been numerous competitors for the dignity), then, in Josephus's view, one was looking at the legacy of Seth's inventive lineage, a special skein joined to the first Adam and blessed by God: an example to all who subsequently strayed from true religion and science, for according to Jewish traditions, Egyptians, like all Gentiles, had been hostile to Jews because Gentiles anciently deviated from the path ordained to those who "walked with God," of whom the most remarkable, Genesis informs us, was Enoch, to whom we must now turn to learn why the antediluvian pillars have at sundry times borne his name, a transposition involving one of the most influential conflations of cross-cultural identity ever recorded, with a vital bearing on the subsequent history of religion and science, extending even to our own disquiets.

# THREE
# Enoch and Hermes
## *Guardians of Truth*

The earliest reference we have to Adam's great-great-great-grandson, Enoch, is in Genesis, chapter 5, in which the Sethite lineage is delineated to the time of the Flood survivors. Compiled in the sixth or fifth century BCE, we cannot tell whence Genesis's data for Adam's lineage derived. The name Enoch in Hebrew is חנוך; that is chet, nun, vav, kaf, which produces English sounds like ChNOK, where the "Ch" sound is exhaled sharply from the back of the throat. The name is thought to mean "dedicated," or even "initiated," in the sense of training. According to Genesis, Enoch shared his name with a son of wicked Cain, though why this might be will probably remain unknown. In any event, you might say the bearer of this name was a man with a mission.

The Sethite line of descent up to Noah goes as follows (I have added in parenthesis the number of years each is said to have lived): Adam (800), Seth (912), Enos (905), Cainan (910), Mahalaleel (895), Jared (962), Enoch (365), Methuselah (969), Lamech (777), and Noah (950). The first thing we notice is that Enoch's tenure of earthly existence is by far the least, at 365 years. The second is that Enoch's entry at Genesis 5:22–24 contains biographical information about him not given to his kin.

And Enoch walked with God after he begat Methuselah three hundred years, and begat sons and daughters: And all the days of Enoch

27

were three hundred sixty and five years: *And Enoch walked with God: and he was not; for God took him.* [my italics]

Subsequent Jewish tradition took that last line—if it was not surmised already—to mean that Enoch did not die in any conventional sense; rather, he was so close to God (he "walked with God") that at the relatively young age of 365 he was taken from the earth and brought directly to eternal life. One is reminded of the adage that those whom the gods love die young, but Enoch apparently did not suffer death. Before we outline aspects of the extraordinary literature that Enoch's "special relationship" with God subsequently entailed for him, and for angelic- and humankind, we might note that Enoch's time on earth may not simply reflect his being "taken young" but may well involve something else that might have linked him to that wisdom Josephus relates as the invention of the "descendants of Seth."

Three hundred and sixty-five is of course the number of days in the solar year, and we know that people who subsequently held traditions of Enoch in great esteem emphatically asserted the primacy of the solar over the lunar year. A remarkably high number of Enochic fragments (from the Book of Enoch and other related works) were discovered in Aramaic among the so-called Dead Sea Scrolls (primarily circa second–first century BCE), formerly preserved by a group or groups who regarded adherence to the solar year as a religious duty. The Pharisees of Jesus's time were no less equally adamant that it was the lunar year that secured divine approval.

The Book of Enoch specifically recognizes solar computation as divine. Indeed, the book contains within it a "Book of the Courses of the Heavenly Luminaries" (chapters 72–82), which gives in precise detail the relation of the sun to our earthly days. Its account of the moon emphasizes the "loss of days" involved over periods in lunar computation, while exalting the solar year for its long maintenance of regularity of days. It computes an accurate solar year at, interestingly,

364 days.* This is the kind of "astronomical wisdom" that Josephus was probably referring to as that inscribed on his antediluvian stelae.

Was there an Egyptian aspect to the dating issue?

There was. We have mentioned the *Book of Sothis,* attributed to Manetho. The work is also known as the "Cycle of Sothis" because its account of dramatic events occurring through the procession of Egyptian dynasties reflects the "Sothis cycle" dating system. This cycle refers to a period of 1,461 civil years of 365 days each. Within that cycle (also known as a "Canicular period"—referring to Sirius), the 365-day year "loses" sufficient time that the next new year begins at Sirius's heliacal rising. The Sothic year, then, is the time it takes for Sirius to appear to return to the same position in relation to the sun. A remarkable thing about dating the year's start with the heliacal rising of "Sothis"—that is to say, Sirius (or Sopdet†)—is that it produces the same length of days (365) as a solar year, and that, almost exactly as in our solar year, there is a one-day displacement over four years (with the Sothic year about a minute longer than a solar year). The cosmic interplay of the sun and Sirius was deemed highly significant to Egyptian astronomy—where religion and science were one—even though it took until 22 BCE for the Egyptians to include leap years, their system being so conservatively attached to a civil year of a time-honored 365 days, sunup to sunup.

Now, the Book of Enoch was still current when Josephus was being educated (in the 40s and 50s CE), though there is a possibility he may have eschewed it for its messianic, apocalyptic content and

---

*This is because it starts the year on the first day of the week, with a 31-day month to end each of four seasons, with the remaining months being 30 days, which gives eight months of 240 days, and four months of 31 days, adding up to 364. For our 365-day calendar to work we have to add a day every four years (a leap year) because our solar year is exactly 365.2422 days, so in calendrically depriving ourselves a quarter day each year, we "add" the day back, as it were, every four years.

†The goddess's name means the "sharp one," or, literally, "triangle," which may refer to the stunning Winter Triangle, the stellar triangle formed by Betelgeuse in Orion, Procyon in Canis Minor, and Sirius in Canis Major.

uncompromising assertion of the falling of the "mighty from their seat" by direct intervention of God's angels in world affairs on behalf of the righteous. On the other hand, we know that Josephus admired the mystical Essenes, and Enoch I may have been dear to them, for Josephus mentions Essenes had books of "angels." Certainly, had he a mind to, he would have found much in it—had he considered its contents genuine— to flesh out the astronomical legacy of Seth's descendants, though its contents may well have put the wind up Josephus's intended audience, had Gentiles read the Book of Enoch in the raw.

In chapter 75 of the book, the angel Uriel shows the heavens-dwelling Enoch how the four intercalary days are generated (the four seasonal markers of thirty-one days in the Enoch system) by the "heads of the thousands" who rule over the stars, and how they are involved in the setting of seasons (verse 7) and the "coming forth" of the stars "corresponding to their number." Enoch is witnessing a kind of celestial computer, full of startling energies, expressed in visionary language. The chapter ends (verses 8–9), remarkably, in what might be a striking reference to Sirius, brightest star in the heavens (if, that is, the sun is not intended).

> And I saw chariots in the heaven, running in the world, above those portals in which revolve the stars that never set. *And one is larger than all the rest,* and it is that that makes its course through the entire world. [my italics]

It should be noted that there is no certain Hebrew word for the star Sirius in the Hebrew Bible. Perhaps "she" was too strongly associated with Egypt's pantheon. If the solar year tradition, associated in the first century with parties of Sadducees (or Zadokites), derived ultimately from Egyptian sources, that provenance might account for hypothetical reservation regarding Sirius's significance, or otherwise. It might be further noted that, like Saint Paul, Josephus claimed a Pharisaic education, and he may also have been taught resistance to a solar calendar, and therefore found the Book of Enoch impious. Anyhow, in Enoch, the one that is "larger than all the rest" seems to have a correspondingly great influence in the world, though not so great as the sun's.

Now, the Book of Enoch does not include any direct reference to Enoch being responsible for antediluvian stelae constructed to survive deluges of water and fire. There is, however, much in it that would, and did, serve to expand on the idea of an Enoch creating monuments to astronomical knowledge.

Chapter 81 of the Book of Enoch indicates that Enoch gains much of his learning of heavenly luminaries from "heavenly tablets." These are situated in the heavenly realms, not on earth, and while an undoubted resonance with Josephus's story may be discerned, there is an even stronger parallel with the Egyptian story related by Syncellus about Thoth and Hermes Trismegistos attributed by Syncellus to Manetho. Chapter 81:1–3 of the Book of Enoch begins:

And he [Uriel] said unto me:
"Observe, Enoch, these heavenly tablets,
And read what is written thereon,
And mark every individual fact."

And I observed the heavenly tablets, and read everything which was written [thereon] and understood everything, and read the book of all the deeds of mankind, and of all the children of flesh that shall be upon the earth to the remotest generations.

Having praised the Lord, Enoch is transported to earth by "seven holy ones" with the words: "Declare everything to thy son Methuselah, and show to all thy children that no flesh is righteous in the sight of the Lord, for He is their Creator. One year we will leave thee with thy son, till thou givest thy (last) commands, that thou mayest teach thy children and record [it] for them, and testify to all thy children; and in the second year they shall take thee from their midst."

Chapter 82:1–3 begins with Enoch addressing his son Methuselah.

And now, my son Methuselah, all these things I am recounting to thee and writing down for thee, and I have revealed to thee everything, and given thee books concerning all these: so preserve, my son Methuselah, the books from thy father's hand, and [see] that thou deliver them to the generations of the world.

I have given Wisdom to thee and to thy children [And thy children that shall be to thee], That they may give it to their children for generations, This wisdom [namely] that passeth their thought. And those who understand it shall not sleep, but shall listen with the ear that they may learn this wisdom, And it shall please those that eat thereof better than good food.

So, having seen the heavenly tablets, Enoch the scribe writes down in *books* what he has seen, that the knowledge may save those who learn and abide by pious knowledge, that they may avoid the worst of imminent judgment upon the unrighteous.* Now this doubtless alludes in the first instance to the Flood sent by God in Genesis, but it also stands for a judgment believed by the book's authors to be imminent when the book first appeared.†

This combination of reading sacred tablets followed by committal to writing in books almost precisely mirrors the account Syncellus attributed to Manetho, of divine Thoth inscribing cosmic knowledge in Egyptian temples, later committed to books by Thrice Great Hermes

---

*The apocryphal Jewish text the Book of Jubilees (ca. 160–150 BCE, a copy found at Qumran has been dated ca. 100 BCE), possibly taking its lead from the Book of Enoch, or similar textual tradition, asserts that it was Enoch who invented writing (an invention, note, that in Egyptian mythology belonged to Thoth-Hermes): "he [Jared] called his name Enoch. And he was the first among men that are born on earth who learnt writing and knowledge and wisdom and who wrote down the signs of heaven according to the order of their months in a book, that men might know the seasons of the years according to the order of their separate months. And he was the first to write a testimony and he testified to the sons of men among the generations of the earth" (Jubilees 4:17–18).

†Some parts, particularly chapters 12–36, may come from as early as the third century BCE, but of the remainder, most appears to have been composed between the second and first centuries BCE, with a possibility of additions made in the early first century CE.

("the second Hermes") after the Flood.* Indeed, we are again faced with the question, if, that is, there *was* a "lifting" of a story from one work to another: *Who took from whom?* For while it may be that Josephus could have been aware of an Egyptian version of a stele construction or "inscription-to-book" story, it is equally possible that enterprising Greco-Egyptians took congenial elements of the Enoch story and "Hermeticized" its revelatory framework into cooler, more Platonic oases, shorn of incomprehensible Jewish apocalypticism (Greek fragments of Enoch have been found in Egypt). Such, in the context of cultural competition and cross-cultural syncretism in Greco-Egyptian Egypt, is hardly unthinkable, and it is undoubtedly the case that practically explicit resonance with Genesis has long been recognized in "Poimandrēs," the Hermetic philosophical corpus's first tractate— generally dated well after the Book of Enoch and Josephus.

Influence from Enoch in the Hermetic (Trismegistos) mythology has not, I think, been suspected before, but it might yet prove a significant key to understanding one motive for composition of at least some of the tracts.

And this question brings us very naturally to one of the mysteries of history; that is, how it came to be that by the ninth century CE, Hermes and the biblical and extra-biblical Enoch were identified as *one figure,* to whom the writing down of antediluvian or primal sacred wisdom was a crucial element of his (or their) function.

## TRACING THE MYTH

Arguably the earliest evidence for conflation of Hermes and Enoch appears in the work of Egyptian alchemist Zosimos of Panopolis. Dwelling at Akhmim (the Egyptian Apu, or Khent-Min—the Greek Pan—and Greek Chemmis) in Upper Egypt during the late third and

---

*Syrian Neoplatonist Iamblichus, in his *de mysteriis* (8.1.260–1; ca. 300 CE) records that Hermes wrote 20,000 books, or "according to Manetho," 36,555. By Iamblichus's time, texts attributed to Hermes on spiritual philosophy, astrology, alchemy, and magic could be numbered in a few tens only, though their influence was considerable.

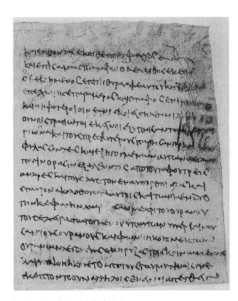

Fig. 3.1. Eighth- or ninth-century manuscript of the Gospel of Peter found at Akhmim, 1886

early fourth centuries, Zosimos inhabited "Gnostic territory." Indeed, excavating Akhmim in 1886, Urbain Bouriant recovered from a monk's grave a fourth-century Greek manuscript of the Book of Enoch's "Book of the Watchers," along with two eighth- or ninth-century manuscript apocrypha: the Gospel of Peter and the Apocalypse of Peter.

Zosimos was enthusiastic about the Hermetic philosophical tracts, particularly *Corpus Hermeticum* IV. This tract provided Zosimos with gnostic spiritual rationales for his otherwise practical alchemy. We are again indebted to the collection of George Syncellus for preserving this fragment from Zosimos's ninth book (eighth in the Syriac tradition),[1] called *Imouth** in which Zosimos writes to the lady Theosebeia, possibly an alchemical pupil.

> The Holy Scriptures, that is the books, say, my lady, that there is a race of demons who avail themselves of women. Hermes also mentioned this in his *Physika,* and nearly every treatise, both public and

---

*This name is understood in the Hermetic tract *Korē Kosmou* as referring to Asklēpios, pupil of Hermes. See page 23.

esoteric, made mention of this. Thus the ancient and divine scriptures said this, that certain angels lusted after women, and having descended taught them all the works of nature. For this reason they fell into disgrace, he [Hermes?] says, and remained outside heaven, because they taught mankind everything wicked and nothing benefiting the soul. The same scriptures say that from them the giants were born. So theirs is the first teaching concerning these arts [*Chemeu*]. They called this book *Chēmeu,* whence also the art is called Alchemy [namely, *chēmeia*], and so forth.[2]

The context is one of the alchemist showing Theosebeia how knowledge of dyeing techniques, so significant to Egypt's wealth, involves the activity of demons, because its secrets require astrology to ascertain proper times for an operation's performance (Panopolis manufactured fine textiles). Hence Zosimos refers to demons and angels (inconsistently) who brought knowledge that would otherwise have been denied. That knowledge, though of ambiguous origin, included alchemy, and coming from above required elevation of mind to employ the knowledge properly, lest ruin ensue; alchemical processes should be kept secret. Zosimos's story's ultimate source is almost certainly the account of the Watchers in the Book of Enoch bringing dangerously advanced sciences to humankind while lusting after human women. Zosimos regards the book's account as "holy scripture" whose contents he had also recognized in a tract attributed to Hermes Trismegistos known as *Physika.* By the late third century at least, no one could tell for sure whether a root story of the preservation of antediluvian knowledge brought from heaven involved the Hebraic Enoch, or the Egyptian Hermes.

Given the energy expended on the myths of Enoch and Hermes Trismegistos in late antiquity, and when we observe how their functions as divine scribes and all-knowing initiators into secrets of science and spiritual salvation were practically identical, it should not surprise us to learn that by the ninth century, long after Egypt had fallen to

Islamic conquest, the "Sabians" of Harran—who took Hermes as their prophet and his writings as their scripture—understood Hermes and Enoch as being identical. Identifying Agathodaimon with Seth, Hermes and Enoch were further conflated with the Qur'an's "Idris," thus bringing Sabian beliefs under Islamic toleration, which required of permitted believers faith in one God and final judgment.

The most brilliant astrologer of Baghdad's Abbasid court, Abu Ma'shar Ja'far ibn Muhammad ibn 'Umar al-Balkhi (787–886), confirms this, identifying "Harranian" sage Hermes not only with Enoch, but also with the Iranian "Adam," Kayumarth. Abu Ma'shar declares in his *Book of the Thousands:*

> The name Hermes is a title, like Caesar or Khusrau. Its first bearer, who lived before the Flood, was he whom the Persians call Abanjhan, the grandson of Jayumart [Kayumarth], the Persian Adam; and he whom the Hebrews call Khanukh [Akhnukh; i.e., Enoch], whose name in Arabic is Idris. The Harranians call upon his wisdom [declare his prophethood].[3]

Several centuries later, Andalusian magistrate Ṣā'id al-Andalusī (1029–1070) in writing about nations that respected learning in his *Ṭabaqāt al-'Umam* ("Categories of Nations," 39.7–16), quoted Abu Ma'shar: "This Hermes the Hebrews called Enoch . . . was first to predict the Flood, expecting a heaven-sent catastrophe to assail the earth in the form of fire or water. That being so, and afraid science and the arts would vanish, he constructed Upper Egypt's temples and pyramids."

Explicit identification of Enoch as constructor of the antediluvian pillars, or stelae, is evident in the *Palaea Historica,* a collection of texts about the Hebrew Bible preserved from pre-Christian times and from Christian apocrypha.

> Concerning Enoch. Enoch was born and became a good and devout man, who fulfilled God's will and was not influenced by the

counsels of the giants. For there were giants (on earth) at that time. And Enoch was translated (to heaven) by God's command, and no one saw [how] his removal [happened].

Concerning Noah. In the days when the giants were around and did not want to glorify God, a man was born whose name was Noah, who was devout and feared God, and like Enoch he was not influenced by the giants' counsels. . . .

. . . When the giants heard that the righteous Noah was building an ark for the Flood, they laughed at him. But Enoch, who was still around, was also telling the giants that the earth would either be destroyed by fire or by water. And the righteous Enoch was doing nothing else but sitting and writing on marble (tablets) and on bricks the mighty works of God which had happened from the beginning. For he used to say: "If the earth is destroyed by fire, the bricks will be preserved to be a reminder [for those who come after] of the mighty works of God which have happened from the beginning; and if the earth is destroyed by water, the marble tablets will be preserved." And Enoch used to warn the giants about many things, but they remained stubborn and impenitent, nor did they want to glorify the Creator, but instead each [of them] walked in his own will of the flesh.[4]

Scholar Andrei A. Orlov has made interesting observations about the account of Enoch in *Palaea Historica*.

Unlike the Sethites in Josephus's account, Enoch does not try to preserve only one facet of the prediluvian knowledge, astronomical or calendar, but attempts to save the totality of the celestial knowledge, as it was commanded to him by the Lord in some Enochic accounts. Just as in 2 Enoch* he writes about everything

---

*The Second Book of Enoch (II Enoch), also called the "Slavonic Enoch" and "The Secrets of Enoch" (sometimes dated to the late first century CE) is not to be confused with the Book of Enoch, or "I Enoch," that we have been discussing.

that happened before him. In contrast to the Sethites' account, the *Palaea* does not mention the name of Adam. In the Sethites' "two stelae" stories, Adam serves as mediator of the divine revelation, through whom the Sethites receive knowledge about the earth's future destruction. The *Palaea* does not refer to the Adamic tradition, since Enoch and Noah, unlike the Sethites, have direct revelation from God about the upcoming destruction.[5]

Orlov concludes that the writer of the passage in *Palaea Historica* seems to draw on different, even competing, traditions than Josephus. However, it would be anyone's guess as to whether such alternative traditions explicitly involving Enoch in antediluvian pillar making were current either in Josephus's time or before him. The likelihood, it seems to me, is that such a conflation of narrative elements was bound to be expected in the more than nine hundred years that had passed since Josephus's lifetime to the period of the gathering of the *Palaea Historica*.

## THE EMERALD TABLET

Finally, we are bound to mention the fabled "Smaragdine Tablet of Hermes Trismegistus." Here we have an alternative Hermes-inscription myth, notable in its period for not including any explicit Enochic element. There seems little doubt that this—in our context—late alchemical romance derives ultimately from a musing upon the story attributed to Manetho that Thoth inscribed essential or primal knowledge and that Hermes Trismegistos discovered and transcribed it. Following in Zosimos of Panopolis's spiritual footsteps, so to speak, we see a distinctive alchemical skein taking over the more biblical and apocalyptic scenario of judgment and terrestrial conflagration. The feeling is that any sense of catastrophe has long passed, one that has left secreted signs of knowledge once real to its chosen vessels.

Apparently Arabic in origin—the earliest version was written between the sixth and eighth centuries CE—Hugo of Santalla translated it into Latin in the twelfth century. By the next century it appeared in a version of the Neoplatonic *Secretum secretorum* ("The Secret of Secrets"), pseudonymously attributed to Aristotle, in which form it greatly influenced medieval and late medieval alchemy, inspiring natural philosophers of the distinction of Roger Bacon (1214–1292) and Albertus Magnus (1200–1280). Bacon's writings would transmit the idea that Enoch and Hermes were the same person, though by Bacon's time, the Book of Enoch itself had been long lost, rejected by Jewish and Christian authorities alike, except in Christian Ethiopia, where it was revered within the biblical canon and where it remained hidden to the West until a Scottish Freemason brought it to Europe in 1773 (see page 142).

Bearing the quintessential alchemical mystery, the emerald tablet's discovery is attributed in the text to "Balinas," identified with first-century magus Apollonius of Tyana, who, in a vault below a statue of Hermes in Tyana, discovers a golden throne on which a corpse is seated, still clinging to the Emerald (Smaragdine) Tablet. The text revealed on the tablet relates in poetic, if cryptic, form how the "miracles of one only thing" may be worked, by understanding and directing the universal, single principle that animates the cosmos: an "operation of the sun." Abbot Trithemius (1462–1516) was not alone in taking the riddlelike formula as implying the *anima mundi,* or "soul of the world," a significant insight we shall learn more about in the proper place.

The Smaragdine Tablet has been taken as the preparatory framework for finding the Philosopher's Stone—the secret science of transmutation, the return of the created to the being of the creator. The tablet seems to me an epitome for the idea of *primal knowledge* that we are investigating in this book.

"One thing" can indeed be drawn from this chapter—and it may be a miracle—that is, that according to the most potent myths that have come down to us, science and knowledge of God were once held to be *one:* knowledge so precious that only the greatest could envision transmitting it safely through deluge to a world beyond catastrophe.

# FOUR

# A Sense of Loss Pervades

We've now examined all the available evidence pertinent to the origin of the myth of "Enoch's pillars." What might that myth mean in today's very different world?

The first thing to note is that Josephus's little story represents history's first appearance—albeit condensed—of what has become something of a global industry. I refer of course to that popular enthusiasm for extraordinary knowledge about ancient civilizations: often a heady blend of spiritually frustrated instincts entwined with scientific research, theory, extraterrestrial speculaion, and natural curiosity. Popular interest in ancient historical themes is reflected in myriad flashy, sensationalist TV shows and YouTube uploads ubiquitous to our multifarious screens on anything from "Ancient Aliens" to the "Secrets of Stonehenge" to the "Mayan Prophecies," while the ideological pivot of so much of it—the Bible—is (allegedly) "decoded" by some means or other. Amid a frequently unscholarly and often misleading flood of televisual hyperbole may yet be espied the odd pinnacle poking up from a submerged range of serious documentaries investigating archaeological and ancient historical themes with responsible, forensic thoroughness, though even then, not infrequently chafing at the bit of academic caution in quest of the elusive scoop. Truth is inured to being an unwelcome stranger in human affairs.

One ambitious website, for example, serves as flagship to an attractive, glossy magazine designed to serve this burgeoning interest: *ANCIENT ORIGINS—Reconstructing the Story of Humanity's Past* is regularly packed with a mix of archaeological reports and speculative articles on subjects as diverse as "high-tech" devices used to float the Sphinx up the Nile; a mysterious megalithic monument at Carrowmore ("Unlike Anything Seen in Ireland"); discovery of the oldest Buddhist scrolls; chemical reactions used by humans 5,000 years ago for pigments in the Altai Mountains (Siberia); 8,000-year-old petroglyphs found in a South African crater; sacred sites of the pre-Columbian Diaguita people in Argentina; the moon's ancient origins; a giant Ice Age mammoth tusk found in Mexico; the gods of ancient Carthage; the Vestal Virgins of ancient Rome; ancient Chinese death rituals involving cannabis; Nicaragua's Lost City emerging from the ashes; 5,500-year-old homes found in Scotland beneath a loch; ancient Japanese magical practices; the greatest Macedonian necropolis in Aigai; trophy skulls that help explain the Mayan Empire's collapse; psychic archaeology uncovering lost structures at Glastonbury; a 40,000-year-old Pleistocene-era wolf unearthed in Yakutia, Russia; Mysteries of the ancient Phoenicians; Ma'at, Egyptian goddess of truth and justice; the "Enochian" language used by angels revealed to John Dee and Edward Kelley; "Malta, Shrouded in Megalithic Mystery"; the decomposing bodies of Skull Island, Indonesia; "Ancient Origins of North Americans Settled"; the "Antikythera Mechanism: *who designed the world's oldest Astronomical Computer?*"; "How the Universe Came to Be: The Bible and Science Finally in Accord?"

It makes one wonder how civilization coped before our times on an archaeological diet of the book of Genesis, a few classics, and the odd chronicle of national history. Nevertheless, the fact is that data concerning ancient history gathers at an ever-accelerating rate, and as it does so, emerging questions expand commensurately, leading to a somewhat unreasonable demand for explanations and "answers" (especially when confronted by unexpected or mysterious objects), of which tentative efforts at "solutions" serve to fuel the aforementioned industry. One is reminded of one "explanation" for the Book of Enoch's account of Sethites being corrupted by "angels," a story naturally popular within the industry under discussion; that is, that to explain the overwhelming scale of evils done by men and sustained in the world that seemed insoluble to sensitive minds in late antiquity, it was found necessary to apportion ultimate responsibility to wayward "extraterrestrials" (as we might anachronistically call them)—angels—"descending" to earth for nefarious purposes involving transmission of technical or occult knowledge formerly unknown to a relatively ignorant humanity. Likewise, we find in the gospel that Jesus's principal conflict is with "Satan," for mere men "know not what they do."*

*If it's unknown, it must come from Above,* seems to be the perennial human instinct, for a being poised twixt here and "there" who is often confused as to whence he comes and whither he goes. "Man," according to Genesis, was made of "red earth" (the meaning of *Adam*) yet rendered a living soul by breath of "Elohim" (literally, "gods") breathed into his nostrils; that is, although made of earth, his life, or spirit, came from "above." While man is *in* Nature, according to the Genesis myth, he is not entirely *of* it, so long, that is, as he breathes and lives, which he may continue to do, as Genesis explains with respect to Enoch, as long as he "walks with God." Man has "to do" with God and the world; his business is with imperishable creator and perishable world. "Get right with God," as Aleister Crowley's preacher father used to tell those whom he encountered on the road and had a mind to convert.

While the old understanding of absolute biblical inerrancy used to make "walking with God" a relatively straightforward matter in principle (*subdue lusts*), it is difficult or impossible nowadays for scholarship to take, say, Josephus's account of Sethite pillars as history. One thing

---

*Luke 23:34.

we can assert with confidence today is that the dating of Noah's Flood afforded by literal interpretation of Genesis takes us to a period astonishingly distant, not from us, but from any provisionally scientific date for planetary genesis. It is also the case that any ancient phenomenon that might correspond to a historical flood serving as a basis for the story of Noah's survival would also have occurred at a vast distance in time from the first appearance of our species. Based on biblical accounts alone, Noah's Flood has been dated to approximately 2348 BCE (Bishop Ussher's famous chronology), with the Genesis creation dated by conscientious scholars of yesteryear between approximately 4004 and 3950 BCE. Whereas, the earliest skeletal remains identified as *homo sapiens* discovered *so far* derive from nearly 200,000 BCE (in present-day Africa), with other early skeletal specimens found dating from 100,000 to 40,000 BCE in Asia and Europe. Naturally, given the vast extension of time for human habitation that archaeology reveals, reaching far beyond the generations described in the Bible, the "pillars of Enoch" story is naturally open to dismissal as either historically superfluous or fanciful, or else, on the positive side, as being a valuable symbol of a culturally meaningful myth.

For the purposes of our investigation, Enoch's pillars suggest several things of cultural value, for we have in them a vivid, even stark picture of a depositum of vital knowledge, a product of wisdom and painstaking practice, a body of knowledge so important that it is deemed vital that it survive, even if nothing else should, as a monument to what has been achieved and what is worth passing on, even to unknown hands at some unknown time: something true to outlive Nature's (or the Creator's) predations on established orders of things. It is a powerful, influential image.

Within it we find the idea of knowledge being given definite, lasting form in *writing,* our surest hope of memorable thought, a kind of artificial extension of life in mind. The birth of writing has always been associated with the gods. While the pillars are made at a point in time, their purpose is projected into an unknown future, a form of continuity of memory and experience. This stone-cold writing will keep warm a living knowledge affording the sole means available to rebuild something of what has been lost: to create anew so that past phoenix may rise from present ashes.

We also find within this composite myth the unmistakable note of *loss*. Conflagrations—whether of water or of fire—serve to sever definitively the future from a fast-receding past. The flood becomes the dividing line between two states of humanity, one we call antediluvian— before the cataclysm (the lost); the other, postdiluvian—that which is left afterward, a detritus where humankind has to pick up the pieces. Of course, we nowadays recognize (as did Plato in the *Timaeus*), that there have been many such breaks with the past, and doubtless more to come, and much has been correspondingly lost through deluges wrought on humankind by "outraged nature": loss of knowledge, memory, insight, experience, monuments to vision, ancestral roots, and countless human lives lived well and ill. Pompeii, for example, has become a monument of its own: a collective "pillar," or frozen moment, held immobile by fiercest fire, lava turned cold and dusty, intriguing us with its virtual life turned to death. Pompeii suggests both life and life's absence, its future lost; that is to say, caught in an eternal past by Vesuvius's indifferent ash. The theme of lost knowledge, and its corresponding emotion, *nostalgia,* will become one of the greatest motivators for learning, spiritual awakening, and cultural renaissance in our relatively brief history on this planet.

And then we have the key intrigue of Josephus's story: manifestation. One of the pillars, he tells us, *remains* to this day, in a real place, which, though vaguely determined, stands to testify to the story's truth. What has occurred may occur again: the monument's apparent survival in "Seiriadic land" speaks to a world too pleased with itself. *Your time, too, may come,* it seems to say. Was Josephus saying this subtly to his Roman audience? Prophecies of doom were rife in the Rome he knew; astrologers had been banished from Rome, along with Jews and Egyptians, by emperors Tiberius and Claudius—prediction being too popular and, perhaps, too incendiary of public confidence. This all resonates with us in our very different world, especially given the "realized apocalypse" scenario presented by anxious climatologists, incautious news bulletins, single-issue zealots, and sundry pundits of a world gripped by natural deformations attributed to alleged contemporary "sins" of exploitation, profit seeking, willful ignorance, self-destructiveness, blindness, fanaticism, war—you name it. It's the old judgment scenario, in new, secular form.

So we have in Enoch's pillars a kind of epitome, or template, for a framework still preoccupying many today. And its message runs more or less like this:

*Something has gone wrong.*

We have, it is alleged, lost touch with something our species once knew and understood. There are keys to what this something was. They come from the past, and many still hide in the past: in history, written and unwritten, told and untold, revealed and suppressed, inscribed or mute, in myth and manuscript, magic and legend and mystery.

Evidence exists for forgotten civilizations that indicates ancient genius and the powers of destruction: from nature, from humanity, from ignorance, from overworking of fertile land (Easter Island), to failure to see what was coming—perhaps even from powers above and beyond the milky blue ball of Earth. Guilty men and women have a hand in causing deluges from, it has been alleged, failing to observe spiritual imperatives and ancestral wisdom: punishments for "sin"; that is, getting it wrong with a will, departing from divine knowledge.

And the visible remains of those lost civilizations, are they not taken to suggest superior knowledge and practical skill, ancient science whose precise mechanisms we can only guess at—the stones of Machu Picchu, the pyramids of Giza, the temple of Angkor Wat, the Nazca Lines, Stonehenge, and more to come, under land or sea, still beyond our ken—an as yet silent vista of revelation requiring only spades, bathyscaphes, and "geophiz" to unearth 'em? The world, you could say, is burgeoning with "Enoch's pillars," and anything resembling them is hastily pressed into service of a theosophically stimulated contemporary religion that I am inclined to call "Hancockism" (were it not for its antecedents) on account of that name's ubiquity in the literature of an alleged primal spiritual "Tradition" obscured by time and an ever more remote antiquity. Probabilities may be scarce, but possibilities are end-less. One would be as justified in calling this movement "Old Age" as the journalistic misnomer "New Age."

And, having mentioned the seed of theosophical speculation, we are driven to recognize that *other dimension*. The aforementioned knowl-edge that in its fullness and glory belongs to an unreachable Other Side of a cataclysm, or series of cataclysms, in a lost world. *Whence did this knowledge derive?* What kind of knowledge is it? Is it to be explained as an inevitable product of evolution? What has stimulated such alleged evolution?

Our ancestors were in no doubt. Sciences came from above, ambig-uous gifts of the gods, invisible powers behind perceptible forces. Now, we today may rationalize this ancient and globally widespread belief by saying, aye, indeed: the "above" doubtless denotes the higher mind, that *sapiens* of which mere *Homo* is said to be distinguished from hominid relatives. And who tells us this? Why, *intellectuals,* pre-sumably distinguished by intellectual capacities for innovation and technical prowess like those of the mute ancestor whose works they purport to explain! Well, the modern intellectual undoubtedly finds use for his or her mind, but the Patent Office has not historically been a wing of the Ivy League. Perhaps there is confusion about the meaning of "higher mind." To this question we must surely return in due course, but for now, let us simply make the point that the knowl-edge of which we speak, the one worth saving, worth recording, worth projecting into the future was, in the earliest known myths, the product of men working on earthly materials with insights gifted from worlds apparently higher than immediate natural environments. It has proved naturally logical in our fragmented "space age" to see such higher worlds in terms either of psychology or of distant galaxies, whence have come and whither return aliens (to us, that is) who have, it is said and been believed, descended, or condescended, to unload some superior intelligence into fit human receptacles. This idea was forcibly and memorably presented in Kubrick's *2001: A Space Odyssey* (1968), in which one imagined hirsute hominid in remotest prehistory encounters a pillar (!) that by some inexplicable power, stimulates a leap of, well, *imagination,* in the hominid, who turns a bone into a tool, and, in course of time (identified with evolution), turns a weapon into a space station. Neither Arthur C. Clarke nor Kubrick dared define the nature of the intelligence behind the pillar, only that in quest of it, the new Odysseus—known as "Dave" to his overfamiliar computer—finally experiences something beyond time, space, and his reason, culminating, by visual sleight of lens, in an embryonic being who (in Clarke's original story) will destroy the collective space armory ("star wars") of the apelike mentalities of the world's most violent be-suited protagonists who have used science to destroy, rather than to create. For, according to Genesis, it is a gift to exiled Man to create, and the privilege of God to destroy what he has created. So sayeth Genesis, at least.

## THE FALLEN

It is right at this point that we call into our investigation the idea of the Fall. I refer in principle to the idea of a catastrophic breach twixt man and God, one outflow of which Genesis delineates as the phenomenon of consciousness, or rather, consciousness of being separated, or as we may say, "self-consciousness," as disturbing to the adolescent today as it was to Adam and Eve in Eden: "They knew that they were naked," as the stark biblical phrase has it. They *knew,* and the knowledge was unwelcome. One could easily assert that the entire history of higher religion consists in attempting to overcome this self-consciousness, that is, consciousness of being separate, with inherent, tragic sense of loss: an overwhelming sense of separateness that comes when, for example, one truly realizes a loved one is dead. I well remember the first time this occurred to me, when, aged three, I saw a line written by my late grandfather in a book he had given to my brother, and connecting his handwritten name and message of love to the memory of the man I knew had just died, a mystery darkened my vision. That, I think, was the first time I experienced true loss, and it made me reflective, opening a chamber of melancholy in my soul I never imagined could exist, where love and loss would mingle. Perhaps, in time, it made me an artist—or thinker—wielding the primitive bone of thought.

In Genesis, having eaten of the Tree of Knowledge, Adam and Eve are stung to the core by realization that they are no longer automatically at home in the paradise, or garden, or even at home in their own skins, with their own existence. And, further, they have now come under the "other side," as it were, of their once familiar, friendly creator. They are separated from the living essence of nature, and from God.

This myth of Fallen Man is a deep and mysterious symbol that has exercised the profoundest thoughts of some of the finest human minds for several millennia at least, and it is as valid a subject today for profound rumination as it has ever been.

According to Genesis, before the descendants of Noah were removed from the world that preexisted the Flood, their originators, Adam and Eve, were already exiled from the place of their creation. In terms of visionary artist William Blake, a "flood of time and space" had transformed their vision. A double loss of primal knowledge: but the first fall was not a loss of practical or technical knowledge (as suggested in Josephus's telling of the Sethite pillars story) but rather a loss of a state of being, of *essence:* of being "Man" as he was created to be, with unbroken, reflective intercourse with God, with no tragic self-consciousness, and therefore no fear, untrammeled by knowledge at all, for knowledge is the key to embarrassment.

Now, I am sure I am not the first who has espied here a link between "fallen" humanity and the word in Genesis 6 (*nephilim*) for those born as a result of the sons of God quitting their proper path. In the Book of Enoch, whose "Book of the Watchers" is a kind of "midrash" or explicatory extension of Genesis's account of the nephilim, the idea is eagerly taken up that wicked angels "fell" from their heavenly home, having been entranced by the allure of human females. Desirous of "knowledge" of them—something presumably out of bounds for an angel, however exalted—they "fell to earth," with tragic and miserable results for all who would suffer the appalling consequences of this breach in the divine order.

In the Book of Enoch, these Watchers beget giants who start eating human beings and oppressing the good, while teaching every kind of destructive enchantment: selfish sciences of cosmetics, poisons, weaponry, metallurgy, and according to Zosimos of Panopolis, alchemy, or chemistry, and all that goes with lust for power over others in rebellion against the good. Again, we see a kind of knowledge that comes from a dramatic fall. And, in the Book of Enoch, God instigates the Flood specifically to wipe out the wicked offspring and fatal arts of the nephilim, the fallen ones, and restore a seed willing and able to find the way back to God: of which state, the figure of Enoch is paragon, earning him in the Book of Enoch the liberty of heaven, whence, according to the book, he will come to deliver final judgment upon the wicked Watchers who have contaminated the world with their disobedience and cunning.

## GNOSTICS: RETURN OF THE SETHITES

Within a century of Josephus's writing down the Sethite pillars story, we find individuals in Syria, in Alexandria, in Lyon (France), and in Rome promoting various forms of spiritual philosophy and practice traditionally called "Gnostic," referring to "one with knowledge." What this knowledge, or *gnosis,* consisted of derived in part, I am convinced, from a process of dwelling imaginatively on the text of

Genesis, in conjunction with the Book of Enoch and other apocryphal works, combined with forms of "Christianity" or messianic salvationism that contrasted a condemned world with an eternal Father in heaven.

In gnosis, broadly speaking, we can discern the idea of a "double fall," in which the fallen angel is now, as it were, twofold. First, wicked angels are in radical Gnostic mythology responsible for *fabricating*, not just perverting, the universe, in league with their master, the "demiurge" or creator of the material structure of the cosmos (a notion derived from Platonism), copied deficiently from divine, living *ideas* beyond it. There is a "ruler of this world" (John 12:31) and a Lord beyond it (John 18:36). This explains the corruption of the world, its fatal and sorrowful character for those who become conscious of it, and their existence within it, or under its sway.

Second, "Adam"—or rather the divine *idea* of Man—is now given an *original* heavenly home. Stationed there as the Gnostic *Anthrōpos* (the eternal *idea* of Man), he is a reflection of God, the Father's son, whose original being is Light. And all would have been perfect but for a breach in the harmony of heavenly being: the sensible universe results from the downpouring effects of a primal catastrophe. The image of a spiritually infertile abortion is strong in radical Gnostic texts.

Genesis's account of Eve's sin of surrendering to temptation—that is, eating "fruit of the tree"—is pre-mirrored in some gnostic texts in a drama, or arguably *parable*, of God's Wisdom, the feminine Greek "Sophia" or "heavenly Eve," wanting to "know" God. Desiring to conjoin herself with the transcendent originator of all that exists, she is constrained, for her wisdom is essentially reflective. What she can do, however, due to spiritual fecundity stimulated by reflecting the Father's image, is to generate "seeds" (*spermata*). In several Gnostic myths, the weight of these seeds of *pneuma* (spirit) and her orgasmic state of being (yearning for knowledge of the Father) unbalance her, for in her turmoil, she acts without the Father's will, and being unbalanced, her seeds fall glittering downward into a material dimension ruled by a demiurge's jealous eye.* Seeing the seeds of pneuma (spirit), the demiurge enters a frenzy of sexual excitement. Being a "jealous God," he is dimly aware of a dimension higher than himself but denies it, nor can he understand, or "know" it, his powers restricted to crude, mortal copies of divine ideas; so in some Gnostic schools, the demiurge fashions an animal man out of stuff, the earth, whereupon Sophia pities the poor creature and imparts pneuma—with memory of spiritual origins—into at least some of these creatures. The pneuma, alien to earth, becomes terrified of what spirit is now sunk in: death, decay, and a vengeful "God of the Law" delighting in imprisonment of men, who desires that men stay ignorant, serving wicked angels who manipulate all powers in the material universe. The seed longs to be reunited with the generative home of being, for translation back to a divine marriage in heaven and joy everlasting with the "aeons."†

And what do we find amid these strange developments in the spiritual life of the late Roman Empire? Sometime before 265 CE, a book appears among Gnostics called *The Three Steles of Seth* in which appear *three* steles, or pillars, because, according to Frederik Wisse, translator of the book's extant Coptic version, the text was composed with the Neoplatonic triad of Existence-Life-Mind as a framework,‡ for the knowledge on these steles of Seth vouchsafed to posterity is about awakening to the true seed, the seed of Seth, of eternal life, "another race" whose home is beyond this world, who look to the progenitor, the spiritual being of Seth, identified in some Gnostic systems with "Jesus," called "the Great Seth"—and all true emissaries of Sethian seed.[1]

---

*In some Gnostic myths, the demiurge is created directly out of Sophia's will to know the Father: a tragedy of flawed imitation that produces a spiritually imprisoning universe.
†This seed of pneuma may be compared to the ātman of Hindu Advaita philosophy, one in essence with Brahman, to consciously embrace whom, ātman aspires.
‡This triad may be usefully compared to the "Sat, Chit, Ānanda" of Hindu Vedanta—Existence, Consciousness, Bliss—or satchitānanda, the indivdual's awareness of Brahman, unchanging reality.

The revelation of Dositheos ["gift of God"] about the three steles of Seth, the Father of the living and unshakeable race, which he [Dositheos] saw and understood. And after he had read them, he remembered them. And he gave them to the elect, just as they were inscribed there.[2]

An extraordinary transformation has taken place. Knowledge that predates the Flood, a supposed original knowledge derived from familiarity with God, is no longer astronomical or scientific knowledge, as Josephus related. No, this knowledge is key to Man's secret spiritual identity, accessed within the imagination of the "Knower."

The Sethian Gnostic steles are a call to awakening.

The author of the *Three Steles of Seth* was not the only teacher on the pillars trail. A more traditional-style working of the spiritual awakening theme expressed in terms of the now familiar revelatory stelae—and possibly produced in competition with, and during the same period as, the *Three Steles* (and to whose readers the work would nonetheless have appealed)—is the *Korē Kosmou,* whose survival we owe to John of Stobi, a fifth-century collector of Greek texts in Macedonia. Familiar to scholars as "Stobaeus," John collected many rare extracts from works attributed to Hermes Trismegistos. Without him, these logia would have been lost. Among them is a remarkable work that puts the god Hermes in an unspoiled, blessed setting as teacher to the goddess Isis and to her son, the sun god Horus (Stobaeus, excerpts 23–26).

Its title, *Korē Kosmou,* has been translated as "Virgin of the Cosmos," though a *Korē* is more specifically a Greek statue of a young woman, so a title like "the Cosmic Virgin" (or "Maiden") or even the "Virgin Cosmos" might be closer to the author's intention, for the idea seems to be that the universe, or Nature, is, properly speaking, an object of worship, *once* her divinely spiritual and essentially pure nature is perceived. For the majority of Hermetic philosophical tracts, *gnosis* usually involves perceiving an ineffable, incorporeal energy that sustains the grandeur of the universe; *not* alleged evil in the world, on the otherhand, comes from not recognizing such eternal beneficence. Appreciating such a distinction would turn Egyptian Neoplatonist Plotinus (204–270 CE) "against the Gnostics" in his student philosophy classes for the academic year 264–265. Neither the cosmos nor its creator was evil in Plotinus's philosophy. Deficiencies in the material or sensible world should be traced to distance from the source of the One and not to ill intention in the universe's fashioner. The image Plotinus entertains is one whereby gathering density of matter, on account of remoteness, *naturally* obscures or inhibits the fullness of the "light" of pure spirit projected from the source. Put another way, light diminishes in effulgence as it becomes distant from its source: a natural phenomenon visible universally. Matter to Plotinus is, in a sense, "dark light,"* in that to Plotinus, light is substantial, if highly rarefied and spiritual. Matter is not something evil, just relatively deficient qualitatively, compared to source. The true or enlightened philosopher, however, enjoyed pure mind, in keeping with the true philosopher's aim of reuniting with the One, through raising mind to its source. The whole looks different *once* the "One" is envisioned, its wisdom appropriated through higher, receptive mentation (Plotinus's *nous,* or "king," faculty).

Hear how Isis opens *Korē Kosmou:*

> Give heed, my son Horus; for you shall hear secret doctrine, of which our forefather Kamephis was the first teacher. It so befell that Hermes heard this teaching from Kamephis, the oldest of all our race; I heard it from Hermes the writer of records.[3]

---

*Physics today recognizes that when matter reaches a certain density, light cannot escape from it. This phenomenon—the "black hole"—is natural, analogous to Plotinus's explanation.

Fig. 4.1. The Korē statue made of Parian marble
by Ariston of Paros (550–540 BCE)

Notice how the dialogue of Isis to Horus refers to a "craftsman" (Greek: *technitēs*) who made the universe, but not negatively like radical, cosmoclastic Gnostics.

> And as long as the craftsman who made the universe willed not to be known, all was wrapped in ignorance. But when he determined to reveal himself, he breathed into certain godlike men a passionate desire to know him, and bestowed on their minds a radiance ampler than that which they already had in their breasts, that so they might first will to seek the yet unknown God, and then have the power to find him.[4]

This, Isis explains, would never have happened among mortals, but for one special man whose soul was responsive to the holy powers of heaven; namely, Hermes: "he who won knowledge of all."

> Hermes saw all things, and understood what he saw, and had power to explain to others what he understood . . . for what he had discovered he had inscribed on tablets, and hid securely what he had inscribed, leaving the larger part untold, that all later ages of the world might seek it.[5]

Isis reports Hermes's speech when depositing his books. The "holy books" would be placed in a place absolutely secure from vicissitudes of time and wantonness of men, until an era when heaven made organisms worthy to receive them. After this, Hermes—like Enoch after giving his message to Methuselah—ascended to the stars and was "received into the sanctuary of the everlasting zones."

It should not surprise us then, when we imbibe this message and read it as many men read it before the seventeenth century, that the Hermetic writings, along with the elevated spiritual philosophy of the Neoplatonists, and works such as the similarly late antique "Chaldaean

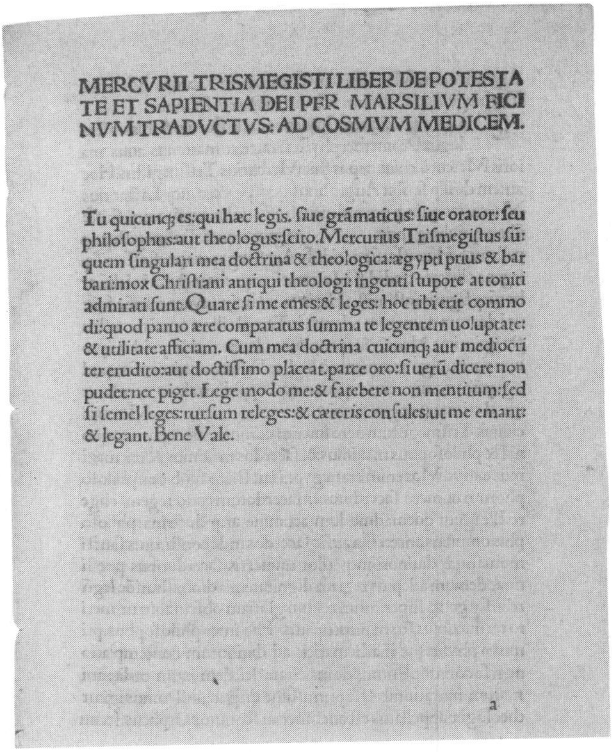

MERCVRII TRISMEGISTI LIBER DE POTESTA
TE ET SAPIENTIA DEI PER MARSILIVM FICI
NVM TRADVCTVS: AD COSMVM MEDICEM.

Tu quicunqʒ es:qui hæc legis. ſiue grāmaticus: ſiue orator: ſeu
philoſophus:aut theologus:ſcito.Mercurius Triſmegiſtus ſu:
quem ſingulari mea doctrina & theologica:ægypti prius & bar
bari:mox Chriſtiani antiqui theologi: ingenti ſtupore attoniti
admirati ſunt.Quare ſi me emes:& leges: hoc tibi erit commo
di:quod paruo ære comparatus ſumma te legentem uoluptate:
& utilitate afficiam. Cum mea doctrina cuicunqʒ aut mediocri
ter erudito:aut doctiſſimo placeat.parce oro:ſi uerū dicere non
pudet:nec piget.Lege modo me:& fatebere non mentitum:ſed
ſi ſemel leges:rurſum releges:& cæteris conſules:ut me emant:
& legant.Bene Vale.

Fig. 4.2. Ficino's
translation of
the *Pimander,*
Treviso, 1471

Oracles," would come to be regarded as constituting a *prisca theologia,* "ancient theology," its purity held to derive from the earliest, golden period of human civilization, when gods and men, so to speak, mingled in mind.*

Such pure "ancient theology" only existed untarnished in an antediluvian, creamy-fresh, unspoiled civilization, successively corrupted over time. The dynamic here is one of return. One desires to return to the remotest past for the key to returning spiritually to the ultimate source. Any progress is in reverse. Ficino, for example, would have

---

*The Latin phrase *prisca theologia* appears in the works of Marsilio Ficino (1433–1499), translator of the most influential Hermetic *libelli.* Ficino was inclined to see even Moses as having inherited Hermes Trismegistos's divine philosophy, or if not inherited, then being contemporaneous with Genesis's supposed author, though Ficino reckoned (following the Manetho legend) that Hermes Trismegistos was not the *first* Hermes.

Fig. 4.3. *Hermes Trismegistus,* "contemporary" of Moses;
floor inlay in Siena Cathedral

disliked the title to Professor Jacob Bronowski's book (and BBC TV
series) *The Ascent of Man* (1974), referring to the idea of human history as being one of gradual, if often painfully interrupted, forward
progress, commensurate with some kind of intellectual and spiritual
evolution and sophistication, reflected chiefly in the development of scientific knowledge, biology, and humane ethics. This optimistic, rather
late-Victorian view was an almost impossible view in Ficino's day, when
most "science" came in translations from the ancients, along with the
laws of righteousness that had sustained a better world.

The wisdom of the ancients, according to prisca theologia under-standing, was that Man was fallen at the start but that a time of grace had revealed truth to godly patriarchs. Any subsequent ascent must be born of the deepest desire to *re*-ascend, to return to lost source through inwardly appropriating, by contemplation, the lost knowledge (involv-ing the notion of a restored state of mind) prevalent in the earliest period, which, through human ignorance or demonic or angelic inter-ference, had fallen from the hands of even the pious, so that the true spiritual teaching was taught amid *shadows* of the real, with the light source beyond the human cave. Such was the esoteric—that is, inner or initiated—spiritual meaning of the doctrine of repentance: to turn again, to travel inward, which is almost to say to turn back again, like the prodigal son of Jesus's famous parable coming back home to his lov-ing father after worldly misadventures and willful, wasteful wanderings inspired by rebellious vanity. Salvation, according to this scheme, is an *apocatastasis;* that is, a return to, or restoration of primal knowledge, involving an ascent to a higher level of being, awareness, and life. That is what has been lost: the point of return and a true means of ascent.

Our contemporary idea of progress, fostered out of the so-called Age of Enlightenment, is dismissed from the prisca theologia point of view as being mere forward movement into the unknown: a void. Such movement constitutes no deep drive, is weak as motive, and represents no true, ardent spiritual desire. We gain nothing by rushing forward into nature. Rather, according to the testimony of the prisci theologi, we make genuine progression toward our deepest goal by looking back-ward, to where the spring of being is most pure: its source.

In point of fact, there could have been no modern scientific revo-lution or "progress" had the Renaissance period not glorified ancient knowledge and begged their and subsequent generations to look to past achievements, exoteric and esoteric. The return of Hermes in transla-tions by Ficino and other men of the time kick-started a movement that encouraged a Leonardo, along with an era whose magian ambi-tions brought forth remarkable men in almost every field of endeavor, people fascinated by what had been inscribed on "the ancient tablets" in purer times, men with the vision to take up the tablets again, to absorb their supposed contents, and then, in due humility, with a deep thirst or desire for experimental or experiential knowledge of the truth, add to them, secure that at last a sure foundation had been recovered from the debris of time. It would lead back to the future.

Science, for such men, was nothing without antiquity. And the essential wisdom of antiquity had been inscribed on the Sethite pillars, where it awaited rediscovery.

FIVE

# How Ancient Is
# the Ancient Theology?

> *Civilization, as we know it today, owes its existence to
> the engineers. These are the men who, down the long
> centuries, have learned to exploit the properties of matter
> and the sources of power for the benefit of mankind. By
> an organized, rational effort to use the material world
> around them, engineers devised the myriad comforts and
> conveniences that mark the difference between our lives
> and those of our forefathers thousands of years ago.*
>
> L. SPRAGUE DE CAMP, *THE ANCIENT ENGINEERS*

My father taught me long ago that the knowledge and wisdom of the
ancient world should never be underestimated. I must say I grasped the
idea firmly and identified with it strongly. It would provide a balancing
fulcrum in my mind through all the tumultuous changes and "progressive modernism" of the 1960s and 1970s when I, among so many others, grew up subjected daily to what the late Christopher Booker called
a culture of "Neophiliacs." Indeed, when, aged eleven, I came to type
up my first "History of the World"—an illustrated survey of ancient
Sumerian, Egyptian, and Greek civilizations—it ended with the pre-
cocious injunction: "Knowledge is the prize we strive to win," with a

warning that all empires fall, usually through losing contact with some aspect of the knowledge that helped them advance to primacy in the first place. There was no question in my young mind as to what kind of knowledge I was talking about. Knowledge was simply that which distinguished the ignorant from the one who knows, who deserved a hearing. It was clear to me such people are rare, while acquisition of a vote, or objects and money, could no more turn an ignorant person into one who "*knew* that he knew" than dressing a wolf in sheep's clothing could provide a mutton chop. The one who knew that he knew was wise, to be followed; the one who knew not, and knew not that he knew not, was a fool to be shunned. He that knew, but knew not that he knew, was asleep and needed awakening.

I cannot recall precisely when Dad and I talked about such matters in simple form, but at this moment as I hold in my hands the very book that inspired my father's thoughts at the time (L. Sprague de Camp's *The Ancient Engineers*), and from which the quotation above is taken, I see, on opening it, the following inscription written in the neat hand of my late mother, Patricia Churton.

Vic,

on our 9th Anniversary 30.10.63.,
with all my love,

Pat.

I was then just three, and I imagine the conversation between my father and myself on what we owe to the ancients, and what has been lost through deluge, inadvertence, and ignorance, probably took place a few years later, in late 1965 or 1966. In my memory, a curious thread links that conversation to the film *The Greatest Story Ever Told* (1965), which tried to re-create the landscape of Jesus's life according to the Gospel of John. I was fascinated by the period—the first century—and disposed to take the movie seriously as history. This is all the more surprising because New Yorker Lyon Sprague de Camp (1907–2000), whose book played a part in inspiring my father's lifelong search for meaning in life, was a materialist. An aeronautical engineer and leading writer of science fiction and fantasy, it was de Camp who coined the now ubiquitous acronym E.T. for "extraterrestrial," a word this remarkable American polymath first gave to the idea of alien life beyond our planet. How interesting the world can be!

My father, also an engineer, respected the technical feats wrought in ancient Egypt, China, Greece, Rome, India, pre-Columbian America, and elsewhere. His time in Hong Kong and Malaysia in the late 1940s and early 1950s also invoked deep sympathy with aspects of Eastern religion and attitudes toward life. I remember he had a copy of the Koran, and some works about Buddhism, Hinduism, and mysticism, as well as an abiding interest in the spiritual meaning of Jesus and the pitfalls of false "self."

My father saw pure, unselfish rationality as being practically identical with divine truth. So when he looked at engineering achievements, he saw them as the work of people who purified thought by following the true nature or laws of the world around them. Natural law was not deceptive, unlike many of the thoughts and words of ordinary men. In Dad's view, the idea of scientifically verifiable law was consistent with truth and law spoken of by time-honored spiritual prophets of humankind, and such truth was universal: things are what they are.

He said the first task of the would-be toolmaker was to create a perfectly flat surface; nothing less would do; it was a prime test of skill. The laws of nature, as he understood them, had an external side, which could be applied to matter, and an inner side that related to disposition of heart and soul: spirit was truth; *being is seeing.* Dad's abiding grief in his soul, I believe, came from living in a society where the practical or scientific aspect was divorced from the inward and spiritual aspect of life. He truly needed both, in unvarnished form, to satisfy his gifts and his inner nature. The postwar world, on the other hand, while providing many opportunities for the engineer, was also increasingly enveloped in a materialist, superficial, acquisitive, and careless atmosphere, intensified further by the fact that large parts of the world were in danger of being overwhelmed by materialist communism, with its perverse, terrifying "crusade" against individual integrity through intimidation, imprisonment, brainwashing, and murder. The spiritually minded person was somewhat "between the Devil and the deep blue sea."

I only wish that he were here and I could ask him what *he* thought was inscribed on the Sethite, or Enoch's, pillars. I rather suspect he would have echoed the view of L. Sprague de Camp above, that the knowledge inscribed on the pillars was likely to have consisted of practical knowledge of how to devise what the deluge had destroyed. I think Dad would also have checked Josephus's text—he gave me my copy of Josephus—and added that astronomy must be included on the pillars because, without it, there was no true reckoning of time, whether for agriculture or anything else, and even life at sea required knowledge of the stars. Besides, in ancient times, knowledge of the stars was indissolubly one with knowledge of the "heavens," the life of eternal, incorporeal beings. He would have said that all this practical knowledge came from observation in the presence of necessity. And I think he would have followed the insight of Isaac Newton that if men closely followed the laws of the universe, they would come to see, unless their hearts were closed, that great intelligence may be discerned throughout creation, whose works bear hints of that which is beyond appearance. Dad would often quote Jesus's "Seek and ye shall find" (Matthew 7:7). If you don't find something, you have either not sought, or you have been looking in the wrong place. As Hermes says in *Korē Kosmou*, the tablets and books he inscribed were not intended to contain *all* knowledge, only enough to be sufficient to lead men and women to seek for themselves. For nothing was gained that was not once lost.

For myself, I find it hard to argue with L. Sprague de Camp's assertion that civilization was indeed the work of ancient engineers who dealt with matter and learned from its ways as well as from their immediate and projected needs by experiment and observation. However, given the dominant materialism of the science I was taught, and which is taught in schools today around the world, I am somewhat disposed to suggest that Enoch's pillar today might have two columns side by side, one column dealing with scientific formulae and the other a spiritual method of reaching and maintaining divine consciousness. However, it is arguable that such a dualist approach to matter and spirit is not just a consequence of living in a modern world, where spirit and matter have effectively been divorced, but that the actual shoots of this tendency emerged painfully in late antiquity *precisely* within contexts where myths of steles of "knowledge"—of Enoch and Hermes—became so vital; that is to say, between the first and fourth centuries CE.

And this must then lead us to a difficult question, a question that I do not think has been put quite in this context before. The question stems from that which serves as title to this chapter; that is: *Just how ancient is the "Ancient Theology"?* That is to say, how do we explain that the bulk of prisca theologia writings in fact appear during more or less the same relatively late period of history and do not appear in anything like the ancient past—be it antediluvian or immediately postdiluvian—the ancient past to which the writings allegedly containing formerly hidden knowledge themselves refer?

To understand the significance of the question we need to grasp something about the history of what is called "Western Esotericism," a discipline that, despite its name, consists mainly of Greco-Egyptian and Eastern sources absorbed into Western philosophical and theological traditions, which were only regarded as specifically esoteric with the growth of new interpretations of occultism and Theosophy in the nineteenth and twentieth centuries.

We have been investigating a little-explored foundation myth of Western Esoteric tradition; namely, the antediluvian pillars of knowledge associated with the names Seth, Enoch, and Hermes. We have observed how the myth appears in its Sethite form toward the end of the first century CE, though it is undoubtedly older, with a related antecedent in an Enochic, apocryphal context from at least the first century BCE, while it is possible, and perhaps likely, that Josephus's Jewish myth is either a version or consequence of, or linked in some manner to, Greco-Egyptian myths of Hermes Trismegistos that possibly date back as far as the late third century BCE, though evidence for the Hermes tablets story is only available to us from the second or third century CE, during the period scholars call "late antiquity," when Gnostic philosophies that found significant uses for myths of antediluvian knowledge appeared and flourished.

We have also explored the possibility that Sethite-Enochic stories were either adapted in competition with Hermes stories or vice versa, generated, that is, from competitive ideological conflict between Jews and Greek-speaking Egyptians for primacy with respect to religious antiquity, and therefore, to spiritual authority, during the first centuries BCE and CE, when many leading Romans were drawn to the mysteries of their Eastern empire, following in the amorous footsteps of Julius Caesar and Mark Antony and of Platonist and Pythagorean legend.

Western Esotericism's principal narrative begins during the heyday of "Gnosis," in late antiquity. It is then that we see distinct, syncretistic strands of tradition appear that will dominate "esoteric" thought in the West. Principal among these strands are Greco-Egyptian Hermetism (normally considered as pagan, though philosophically and liberally henotheist in orientation), Gnosis (predominantly of Christian, though ultimately heterodox orientation), and Jewish Kabbalah, whose origins in late antiquity are still largely obscure, with Kabbalah not attaining fullness as a distinct movement until the Middle Ages (so far as the bulk of surviving literature allows us to believe).

An antediluvian stele myth, it should be noted, ideologically justifies all of these strands, either directly or by implication. In Christian Gnosis we find the emphasis on the line of Seth as being the line wherein was preserved the seed of pneuma, awakening to whose existence constitutes the gnosis or knowledge that appears on, for example, the "Three Steles of Seth." Furthermore, redemptive gnosis constitutes return to the spiritual state of the first Adam, before the Fall and Flood. Gnosis is a knowledge that returns to the origin of Man (who we are; into what we have been thrown; whence we come; whither we go).

The Hermetic tracts of spiritual, cosmic knowledge are plainly represented as derived from antediluvian inscriptions attributed to Thoth-Hermes.

As Gershom Scholem asserted in his *Major Trends in Jewish Mysticism* (1947), the Book of Enoch (and later successor texts II Enoch and III Enoch) are important to understanding the roots of Hebrew Kabbalah. I Enoch may be the critical work that initiates a transition from apocalyptic to mystical Judaism.

*Kabbalah* means a received tradition, a secret tradition derived from revelation obtained through mystical contemplation of God's self-disclosing knowledge, which knowledge was believed vouchsafed to Adam whence it was transmitted by word of mouth and mind to mind, inherited by Moses, fit initiate to divine knowledge. This knowledge manifested exoterically in a system of just law and esoterically in spiritual revelation—regarding which idea of inner understanding of law we can hardly omit the canonical Jesus, whom John 5:46 reports as saying: "For had ye believed Moses, ye would have believed me, for he wrote of me." Saint Paul maintained that Jesus was the "last Adam," in a pre-fallen, immortal state: "And so it is written, The first man Adam was made a living soul; the last Adam [Christ] was made a quickening spirit" (1 Corinthians 15:45). Spirit completes soul.

These aforementioned strands of late-antique spiritual movement proceed in time to bifurcate or disappear, or to reemerge within subsequent centuries, some outliving the collapse into barbarism that followed the end of the western Roman Empire, and others disappearing as distinct movements forever.

While spiritual knowledge-based philosophies may be identified through the Middle Ages in both Christian and Islamic territories, and into the Renaissance and early modern periods—above all in the resurgence of Hermetism and the "ancient theology" in the late Quattrocento and beyond—the conglomeration of self-defined esoteric traditions belongs mainly to the eighteenth and nineteenth centuries. This development came partly as a reaction to materialist scientism. It was spurred on by two organized Western cultural phenomena: symbolic Freemasonry, and the Theosophical Society, founded in 1875.

By the end of the nineteenth century, a central idea of esotericism, encouraged by Theosophy, was established in Martinist circles in Paris, whence it extended about the world in books and esoteric coteries. Owing much to the "theosophy" of Jacob Böhme (1575–1624), Antoine Fabre d'Olivet (1767–1825), and to Louis-Claude de St. Martin (1743–1803)—hence, "Martinism"—the idea is grounded in belief that the first Man was heavenly, close to God, serving to reflect God's pure mind. Falling from concentration on God, this mirror image of God's mind—for Man was made "in the image of God"—fell and shattered, as it were, on contact with base matter. Divided into many fragments, the pristine image, the primal unity of man and God and all knowledge, was lost. These shards of incomplete knowledge have, according to the theory, descended to us in the various religious and spiritual-philosophical traditions, wherein there is truth, but not all-truth. Did we but know how to put all these splintered elements together—which by God's grace and the activation of a pure desire we might yet—we could recompose the image of divine mind and restore the blessed state that preceded the Fall into lower nature; that is to say, religion holds an unfulfilled promise.

According to this model, the strands of esoteric understanding in the different spiritual traditions, be they now called Christian, Jewish, Islamic, Vedantist-Hindu, Buddhist, or pagan, or Gnostic, Hermetic, kabbalistic, Sufic, or Advaitist, Zen-Buddhist, Zoroastrian, Yezidi, and so on share a hidden unity. If the living spiritual essence common to them was grasped in its original state, then we should have the original knowledge of God, reflected in the mirror of restored mind: all things in heaven and on earth would become possible, and we should no longer stumble or sleepwalk through the universe but instead crack it open without breaking it.

In Western Esotericism, this primal knowledge, from which Man has, it is believed, progressively devolved, or been corrupted from, is that which may be inferred from the myth of Enoch's pillars. Finding the lost pillar, symbolically speaking, serves as epitome of the spiritual quest of our kind: a return, or apocatastasis. Thus, we might understand that ancient call from the wilderness: "Return, for the kingdom of heaven is nigh."

Such is the dream.

Now back to the history.

How do we explain that all this "antediluvian" knowledge appears to have been written down so relatively late in history and within such a relatively short period? Was it the case that individuals or coteries had *really* held this spiritual knowledge through the millennia but kept it hidden, as the Hermetic *Korē Kosmou* maintained? It is impossible to disprove entirely such a theory. However, there are better explanations based on evidence afforded by the texts themselves. We can point to significant thoughtforms within these traditions that can be dated quite accurately within intellectual traditions belonging to relatively recent history (such as Greek philosophies of Platonism and Stoicism in the Hermetic tracts). However, the point is whether we *need* to resort to such a task. I should say we do not. What I think we need to do is to ask the question why it was that late antiquity's apparently novel "esoteric" strands *needed* such myths of antediluvian wisdom in the first place.

# SIX

# A Concise
# History of Religion

Unlike our own culture, the world of late antiquity was extremely suspicious of novelty, anything, that is, that made claim to serious attention (unlike fashion in clothes, for example). Every innovation, whether of thought or technique, had to be justified in terms of its fulfilling a promise from the past, which granted authority—the more remote, the greater the authority. Jesus's claim, for example, was that he fulfilled prophetic scripture: his present was justified by the past. Novelty was understood as something childish, whimsical. One aimed to emulate the greatness and heroism of old if one wished for recognition as "new" talent. We have seen this, or caught a glimpse of this, in our brief account of the competition that raged between the claims of Egypt and Israel to hold the keys to the purest cults. Egypt, of course, had the advantage of a highly visible architecture of staggering scope and impressiveness. In this respect, Judaea could only claim its new temple, constructed by order of Herod the Great, an Idumaean Arab who achieved power by the grace of Mark Antony (83–30 BCE). What the Jews did have, of course, was a history and the texts to back it up—and the texts spoke of a glorious, lost temple of old, built by the wisest king in the world, King Solomon, to whom foreign kings and queens paid respect. When Jesus points out the beauties of rural flowers, he asks, "Was Solomon in all his glory arrayed as one of these?" And he takes beauty back to its creative source: God himself. What he—and his followers—had to say about *Herod's* temple, on the other hand, would get him, and them, into much trouble.

In Rome, a man on the rise would make claims for illustrious ancestry. Those who opposed him would say—as was said of Caesar Augustus, for example—that his forebears' hands bore the stain of money changing and manual labor. Julius Caesar could trump most rivals by slipping in the family claim that the goddess Venus was his forebear. If you could win a god to your side, you had a chance to advance. You can't get older than a god.

Now, in such a context, how was any new twist on the profoundest subject of all—divine authority for personal salvation—to be presented? Novelty in religion was particularly disliked. Truth was nothing new; it was something older than time. How best to make the case?

Well, first you make a claim in the name of someone already respected. If you're a Christian, you make a claim that your doctrine came from Jesus, or someone close to him. If you're an Egyptian, it would be wise to have Thoth or Isis on your side. With respect to those individuals and groups whose writings serve as the foundations for Western Esotericism, writings that speak of a saving gnosis or spiritual knowledge of fundamental significance, one had to ask: *Why is this doctrine important now?* The sine qua non of all broadly "gnostic" doctrines was the conviction that common religion had become *corrupt in a corrupted world.* It was not necessarily all wrong, but it had sunk into misinterpretation, distortion, perversion; essential truth had been obscured, and men wallowed in illusion amid the "trees" when they could have been licking nourishment from the sap-filled "wood."

The first Hermetic tractate, known as "Poimandrēs,"* reveals Hermes being granted a vision of the creation itself. It ends with a lament for the sleepers of the world who, loud, arrogant, lost, wander as though drunk, deluded, and as such are dismissed. Hermes has come

---

*Usually dated, in its present form, circa second century CE.

back, as it were, from remotest past to wake people up to a rebirth in sweet sobriety, "right mind," and knowledge of themselves.

It was a staple of myth across the East that the golden age was long past, that its glistening glories had been destroyed by deluges, sometimes divinely sent as punishments for slipping away from proper observance of divine cults. Shorthand, so to speak, for all this severance from the source was the Flood, though in Plato's *Timaeus,* as we have seen, an Egyptian priest informs the Greek Solon that *many* deluges of water or fire have beset humanity, wiping out all memory of great achievements. It is in the course of this speech that the Egyptian describes the great island of Atlantis, just beyond the Pillars of Hercules, that sank into the sea.

In terms of the Hebrew Flood myth, what had existed before it was a world before division, before competing nations, competing cults: confusion of language and of belief. If one could get back before *that* . . . *Why,* what would not be possible? All that purity was, however, long ago, and more distant by the year.

Could it be recovered? And if so, how?

About 40 BCE, around the time Octavian and Mark Antony made plans to rule the empire of the murdered Julius Caesar, Roman poet Virgil wrote his fourth "eclogue": a short poetic, pastoral dialogue. A new golden age was promised. A boy would be born to bring peace to the world; fulfillment was expected imminently. Prophecies encouraging expectations of an overturning of existing conditions flourished even as the empire prospered under Augustus (died 14 CE) and Rome's power in the East solidified. By Josephus's time (37–100 CE), Jewish prophecies of a coming redeemer had already given birth to a new religion, and after 66 CE, an anti-Roman war of liberation, based, Josephus believed, on a colossal misunderstanding: that of a triumphant Jewish messiah. Josephus declared that it was Judaea's conqueror, Vespasian, who was the promised new ruler of the world, and Vespasian became emperor. After Vespasian, son Titus ruled well, followed by younger brother

Domitian. In a cruelly rapacious reign, Domitian revived intense persecution of Christians, and anyone else he suspected might yield him cash and property. When Domitian was assassinated in 96, the "golden age" of Augustus seemed a long-gone thing; nostalgia intensified.

For persons concerned with personal salvation, there seemed little hope in the world as it was. *Was it not time to dream of an antediluvian paradise?* Where could it be found? Did it not exist in ancient *knowledge*? Other than fading inscriptions, the bearer of knowledge was the *book*. A market grew for books of divine knowledge, the desire even in this life for a life beyond it, or at least a way of seeing this world relatively, as though from outside it. The books' message was that wisdom emanated from a world beyond corruption, a world accessible *in the mind*, whence might come a transfigured vision of the world. Such explains the cardinal need for antediluvian authority: a return to lost vision. Hermetism has been called a "religio mentis," a religion of the mind, and its appearance is highly significant in the religious evolution, or arguably, devolution, of humankind. For what was being born in this period was a transformation of the religious universe. The source and aim, and indeed "living space," of religion was *within*. This was a revolutionary situation; "Nature," for proponents of this understanding, had never seemed so distant, so ultimately *unreal*.

To understand the implosive nature of this spiritual change, and why the appearance of Sethite pillars may be regarded as that change's sentinel-like epitome, we need to acquire a broad sense of where humanity had, as far as we can tell, come from—at least where religion was concerned. And as we experience this aerial view, we might usefully have in the back of our minds what, in about 200 CE, anti-Gnostic, Catholic church father Tertullian considered the counterfeit promise of "heretical" *gnosis*. The heretics, said lawyer Tertullian, had the audacity to promise ultimate knowledge: knowledge of where we have come from; who we are; into what we have been thrown; and whither we are heading.

Anthropology seems to suggest to us that before the first civiliza-tions, there was man and nature, or rather, man *in* nature, and in nature was found sustenance, danger, life, and death. There was visible power: water, the earth, fire, and wind rustling the leaves and stirring the waters, humming an old song; and there was an invisible world that ani-mated it all, inflating it with life: gods, spirits, all manner of beings as varied as the creatures of the visible world about them. Below the feet: the earth; above: the sky, clouds, the stars, the sun, the moon. They all mattered; they were all kin, and they all had something to say: in the breeze, in the song and flight of birds, in the earthquake, the thunder, lightning, rain, and rainbow. The voice of gods and goddesses . . . at once content, now angry, here disapproving, there generous, suddenly vengeful, then content again, always . . . unpredictable, apt to caprice. Man was in the universe, and the universe was in him. He could touch the moon with his finger, but the edge of the earth receded from sight.

How long it had been like this, none could say. What was time but another day?

Since we cannot visit those far-off times, we can but speculate about the nature of consciousness enjoyed by our ancestors. They were con-scious, but were they conscious they were conscious? We may think that being so close to nature, there would have been no clear divid-ing line between an inner life of thought and dream, of wish and fear, and an outer world of food gathering, shelter building, and doing what tribe demanded. In such a state, it is hard to imagine much significant individual consciousness, so much mind volume being preoccupied by instinctive action and behavior demanded from without, as though from within. If the individual had a pain in the leg, was it the spirit of the tree that had pricked the flesh for taking her last fruit? The indi-vidual was perhaps immersed in a largely undifferentiated conscious-ness, tuned sharply to signals from other beings, visible and invisible. If the shaman said, "Die!" and everyone believed it—and they surely would—would you be amazed if you carried on living?

Since little had changed, there would be no call to invent. Who would expect it? And there was no writing, so the stories would be memorized and repeated, barely changing over time. The nonindividuated individual, feeling unexamined nature running through and around, might have had some sense of an extraordinary mystery somewhere inside him or her, but this would almost certainly be projected into the unknown dimensions of the world about the tribe, filling any spaces in the known world with entities lent existence by animating soul. He or she was absolutely subject to what was, for such people, overwhelming reality. Perhaps, at night, the subconscious might speak with a different voice . . . who knows?

Archaeology has revealed to us a limited but expanding picture. It may have been in Sumer, lower Mesopotamia, that our notion of "civilization" first appeared around the middle of the fifth millennium BCE. By 3000 BCE the planet hosted writing and a complex of cities, gathered around temples, with priests and liturgies: as apparently remarkable, as it was a relatively speedy development. Civilization would boast written laws and a hierarchy of offices. There were slaves and freer people. And there were walls. Walls were one hell of an invention! With a wall, you could define great spaces, keep out your enemies, and even, to a small but important degree, keep Nature out as well. In the temple, the old marriage of man and nature was exchanged for one of man and god, with nature as an offering from one to the other. Food came into the city from outside like an offering to, and from, the gods. In a city-state, the gods that mattered most were those above, for they had the most obvious advantage. They did not need to mount walls or fly from trees. They could look down and see everything that happened. And man was still confined, as far as his body was concerned, to earth, but it was an earth made more on his, or the priest and king's, terms.

And what can we say in general terms of the religion of the new civilizations that began to appear in the world?

For the civilized, the tribal shaman of the forgotten past had become the priest. The priest had knowledge, and therefore power. He knew, and marked, the times. He read the future, from entrails or constellations. Religion for the masses subsisted in observances organized and run by priests, and the priests were close to power. And the more knowledge they amassed, the more power the priest enjoyed. So we can take it that most people were not close to the priests. The people's presence would be required at some observances but not all. There were mysteries that were not for the sight of "outsiders" to the power elite: there was magic and the need for sacrifices to keep the gods as sweet as the incense consumed before their images. The role of the population was to observe the observances, but not to do very much, except give produce or money, or blood to placate the gods, when demanded. Their task was to provide "victims"—that is, sacrificial animals—for whatever was deemed necessary. Disobedience meant death.

We can say that in general, religion concerned the outer world, and the individual was to the greatest extent cut off from the inner workings of the priesthood, who occupied the place of the nation's collective soul. So much being superintended by the priesthood, the individual had time to think about him- or herself as a phenomenon in the great scheme of things, and if he or she could read and write, reflection on, and comparison with, other's thoughts was possible, so thinking and inner dialogue could be stimulated. There might not be much to say, but remoteness from power allowed a degree of objectification of existence. There was such a being as a thinking individual. However, his or her connection with the world of the gods was somewhat distant. The gods were above. If he or she wanted a more intimate relationship with higher power, the individual could take clay figures into the house. "Household gods" could travel with the family, for the family could travel from civilized place to civilized place.

If, however, the individual wished, or was strangely driven, to experience spiritual interiority, he or she probably knew where to go: not to the city, but to the desert, back to the stream, to the mountain, to the tree, and the dream of old, when man was wild, uncouth, and true. Back in the city, the gods were outside of him, occasionally dwelling in temples, or invoked to attend the summons of the priest. The gods, or their agents, might be encountered in the world. They might offer signs, but generally speaking they looked down on man, and if he looked up to them, he quickly became aware that he was very small, and very mortal, and very vulnerable, and not much more than the dust beneath his sandal. He might, like the psalmist David, sigh and say:

> When I consider thy heavens, the work of thy fingers, the moon and the stars, which thou hast ordained; What is man, that thou art mindful of him? and the son of man, that thou visitest him? (Psalm 8:3–4)

And then something seems to happen, or rather, to accelerate, from the Far East to Greece, during a period that may be dated roughly from the beginning of the sixth century BCE. The voice of individual, questioning, and self-questioning thought begins to be heard. In Greece, pre-Socratic philosophers such as Anaximander (ca. 610–ca. 546 BCE) and Heraclitus (ca. 545–ca. 475 BCE) speculate anew on the origin of the world and the value of life. Pythagoras of Samos (ca. 570–ca. 495 BCE), epoch-marking genius of a symbolic science, founds a secretive school to teach the destiny of the soul and the intelligence of the universe. In China, Lao-tzu formulates Taoist philosophy—the Way of the wise—while in India we observe the development of Vedanta (or "end of the Vedas"): philosophies interpreted from earlier Vedic scriptures (*veda* means "knowledge or wisdom").

Vedantist philosophy locates in human beings an essence or tincture of supreme being, which, applied by discipline of ethics and meditative practice to mortify ordinary "self," may be amplified so individuals might consciously unite with that supreme being, which union constituted enlightened liberation from the world of flux. And in the fifth century, a reaction to Vedantist assumptions, and critical analysis of them, propels into history the teachings of Gautama, the Buddha. He indicates a path beyond "illusory" sense perception, even beyond soul, a radical teaching that does not recognize continuity of essence in human beings in this life or beyond it, but that nonetheless points to enlightenment beyond any thinkable idea of being or individuality. The "self" has become an ambiguous, even nebulous, object.

In Israel, building on wisdom sayings traditional to Egypt and Babylonia, we see the growth of the Hebrew wisdom movement that left masterpieces such as Proverbs, the book of Job, the Wisdom of Solomon, Ecclesiastes, Ecclesiasticus, and numerous time-honored declarations of a faith in God's feminine wisdom that also questions the grounds of faith, endeavoring to justify both faith and the demands of truth.

After Babylonian king Nebuchadnezzar destroys Jerusalem and its temple, with leading Judean families forcibly exiled to Babylonia in 586 BCE, Babylonian thought enters the world of Jewish pundits. While a resigned darkness or pessimism sustains Babylonian thought regarding man's ultimate destiny, Jews resist hopelessness. God's promises must be justified: so sayeth wisdom. We have hints of this struggle I think in the following lines given to Abraham, when he protests against God's determination to slay everyone in Sodom and Gomorrah, righteous or not.

That be far from thee to do after this manner, to slay the righteous with the wicked: and that the righteous should be as the wicked, that be far from thee: Shall not the Judge of all the earth do right? (Genesis 18:25)

That great question, "Shall not the Judge of all the earth do right?" will echo for centuries through the marrow of Jewry. It is the staff with which Job's friends beat him when Job cannot understand how he, a man who did all a man could do to be righteous, still finds himself, without cause or explanation, hideously stricken by every ill fortune. Life too often seemed to deny the very fruit of wisdom teaching; namely, that if one lived aright, observing the wise path, God's blessings would be displayed, a reward for wisdom, as Solomon received glory for choosing wisdom over riches. God had made the world, and the world subsisted on God's laws, and all but man obeyed the law established for creation, but should man obey he would find himself one with the laws of life. This was propounded by the wise as the promise of righteous faith.

Vindication of God's righteousness was expected in real life and time, as Jews believed it had been with the salvation of Noah, and the Exodus to the Promised Land. And, more to the point, the wisdom movement had encouraged the idea that *the individual*—and not only the community—might be justified in faith, and granted the good life. And if Enoch—who "walked with God"—did not suffer the death vouchsafed to fallen Adam, there might be hope in eternity for the righteous.

And those who maintained this vivid faith were surely heartened and could glory in faith vindicated when, in 539 BCE, Cyrus the Great of Persia overthrew the Babylonian empire and permitted Jews to return to their homeland to rebuild the temple of their God. The wise may have said to the exiles returning: "Did we not tell you so? God's wisdom is proven on this royal road to freedom." Has not the judge of all the earth done right?

Alas, far from the glorious prophetic promises that return would lead to a new golden age for those covenanted to Jahveh, the land of their fathers remained largely unrestored, ruled by Persian satraps, with political independence denied as delay upon delay frustrated completion of Zion's temple. The nation did not recover its former stature and, not surprisingly, while wisdom was respected, a clamor for political and religious liberation was heard for a return of the Davidic line of kingship under God. Ample prophetic tradition existed to justify such a hope: "Shall not the judge of all the earth do right?"

In 332 BCE, Persian dominance fell to Alexander the Great's forces, and Judea fell to Ptolemy I, and then the Seleucids—descendants of Alexander's generals. In 167 BCE, Seleucid king Antiochus IV, having determined to crush the Jews, desecrated Jerusalem's temple, an abomi-

Fig. 6.1. Cyrus the Great from a relief at his residence, Pasagardae. The crown and four wings depict a tutelary deity.

nation avenged by campaigning Hasmonean leader Judas Maccabaeus (the "Hammer"). By the time of Judas's death in battle in 160 BCE, his comrades had embarked on an era of fighting with Seleucid kings and generals anxious to subdue the Jewish homeland, led now by Hasmonean high priests, frequently as opposed to one another as to Greek-speaking, Syrian forces.

"Shall not the judge of all the earth do right?" *Whose side was God on*—those favoring the Greeks, or those longing for complete renewal of traditional piety? In 63 BCE, Judah became a Roman Protectorate, and in 40 BCE, in gratitude for the king of Idumea's assistance in the civil war that followed Julius Caesar's assassination, Octavian and Mark Antony made an Idumaean king over the Jews. What a scandal! A king of the Jews installed by pagan Gentiles! Determined to stay, Herod married into the Hasmoneans, murdered them, and began rebuilding the temple to show what a godly king he was. When, in 6 CE, Herod's son Archelaus failed to govern as Rome desired, provoking a bloody massacre in the temple, Judea fell under a Roman procurator's direct rule, with Galilee and Perea to the north ruled by Herodians.

And still, apparently, *no messiah,* no anointed king sent by God and acceptable to the pious. There were two desperate hopes: one, the example of Judas Maccabaeus, righteous warrior; and two, prophecy.

After the seemingly endless catalogue of letdowns that followed return from exile, a new class of Hebrew literature emerged. It built on any hint found in older prophecies (Isaiah, Ezekiel, Jeremiah, Amos, Hosea, Joel) that justified the historical process to which Jews were subjected in the light of a plan to vindicate God's righteousness before the peoples of the world. It was understood by apocalyptists that the delay of enacting the "Day of the Lord" was due to persistent sin. Apocalypticism went with a call to holiness. "Waiting on the Lord" could become, as in the case of Luke's Simeon waiting in the temple, a way of life.

## SEVEN

# From Apocalyptic to Gnosis—and Back to Religion

*Apocalyptic* means "to bring out of hiding," or "to reveal a secret," and the secret that apocalyptic texts were believed to reveal concerned the wisdom of the "times," times set by God in his heavens, through his angels, that governed all things on earth. If one could read the *signs* of the times, one could garner fresh hope and faith in a future that, rather than appearing all black, as it so often did, in fact promised a glorious coming-to-be of the Lord's presence, a purification of all creation, a fiery flood of Holy Spirit. There was everything to hope for, and to fight for.

The Book of Daniel chapters 7 and 12 well express the apocalyptic mind-set, which undoubtedly influenced Christian interpretation of Jesus's first-century operation. Apocalyptic themes are explicit in Matthew 24, Mark 13, 2 Thessalonians 2, and the book of Revelation. There have also survived a host of noncanonical apocalypses, Jewish, Christian, and Jewish Christian, pseudepigraphically attributed to Moses, Adam, Baruch, Abraham, and other patriarchs. The Book of Enoch contains powerful apocalyptic elements that may have greatly shaped the operation of Jesus and his closest entourage.*

---

*See my books *The Mysteries of John the Baptist* and *The Missing Family of Jesus,* which detail links between Enoch and Jesus and John the Baptist's activities, explaining much that has hitherto been mysterious to historians and believers.

The Book of Enoch carries a highly original explanation of how Jews found themselves in such a depressing cycle of historical miseries. The book's cure is effected by Enoch's assisting in the condemnation of the Watchers. Having spent his existence in the corridors of heavenly power, following assumption from earth, Enoch is privy to God's secret designs and willing, if ordered by the "Lord of spirits," to reveal them to those who needed to know. Like Elijah, who was also "taken up" to the heavens, Enoch was a herald figure. Had he been Greek he would have been Hermes, because in the Book of Enoch he delivers God's proclamation against the Watchers to their leader, Azazel, accused of polluting the world with evil spirits.

We tend to think of apocalyptic scenarios as being fearful as well as extreme, but to Jews desperate to be free of all they considered polluting of their faith, apocalyptic expressed hope. The judge of all the earth would be shown to do right (you could view it in advance). There were, of course, those for whom optimism alone was inadequate, preferring to revel in memories of Judas "the Hammer" socking it to the Greeks, and winning. If they could get the holy will of Judas in tune with the times arranged by the prophetic scriptures, then, would not the holy angels themselves lead them against the foe and restore purity to the land of promise? Such hopes are plain from New Covenanter material discovered at Qumran and brought to our attention again in this age.

Those favoring Judas Maccabaeus's methods were called "zealots" for their zeal for the Lord, dubbed "bandits" by Josephus: dangerous, misguided fools whose untrammeled taste for conflict and self-sacrifice would invite even greater disasters than those already visited upon Jewish people. Events proved Josephus correct. The destruction of the temple in 70 CE, the defeat of Bar Kokhba's revolt of 135 CE, and subsequent enforced dispersion of Jews from Jerusalem mark the end of the apocalyptic-zealot resistance. Imminent apocalyptic would be transformed into immanent gnosis: such is my argument in simple terms.

It would be surprising if the coincidence of these tumultuous historic events with the appearance of gnostic-type movements in Syria and Alexandria and elsewhere could not in some measure be accounted for by the collective blow to the idea that God supported the zealot expectation of armed deliverance within time. The collapse of Zealot Messianism as an external historical pressure, after it found itself—whether in its Christian or non-Christian Jewish forms—in direct conflict with the Roman Empire, left a vacuum, and I should contend that that vacuum was filled by, among other responses, a perhaps embittered imperative to *interiority:* otherworldly mysticism, drawing on existing traditions of mystical initiation and individual spiritual training. Such reactions to a crisis of faith *in the world* would amalgamate and bifurcate into many fractious forms during the next three centuries, one form involving a move to solitariness, as interiority's physical correlative. It is no surprise that our earliest copies of Hermetic tractates come from a cache of Coptic codices buried in Upper Egypt close to one of the earliest known Christian monasteries, Chenoboskion, near Nag Hammadi.

In all the movements to which we have drawn attention in this and the previous chapter, we have followed a scheme suggesting that the presence of God has been historically "re-sited." At first God is in nature, and experienced there, where humankind is. Subsequently, with cities and civilization, God—whether singular or plural—is found in the cult, *in religion,* organized in temple, law, and religious observance. God is effectively *over* humankind, outside of the individual, who has barely a claim to significance. God is a being, or beings, to be dutifully propitiated by offerings. There is *distance*—humanity subjected, God objectified—and with the distance goes a particular range of fears, separation anxieties, if you like, that can be manipulated by priests who command the relationship between humanity and God.

We then observed an awakening of individual mind, a pan-cultural wisdom movement, sophistication in philosophy, and the search for a reality of God observable in the realm of individual human conduct: something like a "science" of right action guaranteeing right result, where "the beginning of wisdom" is the "fear of the Lord"

(Proverbs 9:10). In the Jewish context, this development of individual relationship with a personal God will lead to a corresponding hope and expectation that God's essential justice and wisdom would be found as true in the outer world as in the thinking mind, as real in human politics as in the natural order.

By the middle of the second century CE, utter failure of terrestrial apocalyptic hope and effort may have caused, and perhaps inevitably, the siting of God beyond the cosmos altogether . . . a path to which begins in the *soul,* yet goes beyond that link with the world, to the vital spark that, according to gnostic coteries, is the seed of pneuma, or spirit, akin, or even identical to the ātman of the Vedantists (Vedantists, like Jesus's parable,* also compared the divine rule-in-man to the mustard seed), though Christian Gnostics tended to think of the spirit in Pauline terms of "holy spirit" and as something opposed to "the world."

One can discern here an *internalization* of the apocalyptic hope, arguably prefigured in the teaching of the historical Jesus. In the Christian Gnostic scheme, the world is destroyed, and the kingdom is restored, when identification with the holy pneuma occurs. Thus, the individual is reunited with the heavenly source, in what Gnostics called the "plerōma," or fullness, the spiritual site of realized resurrection: from a relative siting of God in the soul to an *absolute* siting or reunion in the divine fullness, or plerōma. In mystical contemplation, the gnostic could be in heaven, for did not Jesus say the "kingdom of heaven" is within?†

Astute readers will have realized that the mystical siting of God within the individual soul may also be seen as fulfillment of a return to primal knowledge available to Adam and his Sethite seed, before that seed was again overwhelmed by the gods of nature. In the Sethian Gnostic scheme (Gnostics who revered Seth), the pillars become spiritualized

---

*Matthew 13:31–32.
†Luke 17:21.

and internalized, safe from conflagration of water or fire by baptism of the Holy Spirit.

Internalization of the apocalyptic hope, and of its spiritualization, becomes arguably visible when we compare the account of the world's corruption at the hands of the Watchers in the Book of Enoch—written in the heyday of apocalyptic—and the account of Man's fall into nature in the first tractate of the Hermetic philosophical writings (*Corpus Hermeticum*).

It will be remembered that in the Book of Enoch's account, the plight of humankind is perverted by the Watchers in heaven who have gazed down at the beauty of the daughters of men and descended to earth to sate their lust, with disastrous miscegenation for the human race. In the first libellus of the philosophical *Hermetica,* called "Poimandrēs," descent to earthly existence is dramatized to show a dichotomy within human nature. The drama combines the fallen angel idea with, apparently, a prevalent Greek myth of Narcissus and Echo (found in Ovid's *Metamorphoses,* circa 8 CE), where, in revenge for Narcissus's rejection of Echo's love, Nemesis has Narcissus captured by water nymphs as he gazes into a pool and falls in love with his own image. This idea is cleverly utiliized in "Poimandrēs" to explain how primal Man fell. Made in the image of God, that image, reflected in water, properly fascinated the heavenly Man, but mistaking his reflection in nature for reality, he becomes alienated from spiritual reality.

> Having all authority over the cosmos of mortals and animals without reason [*logos*], the man broke through the vault [of heaven] and stopped to look through the cosmic framework, thus displaying to lower nature [Greek *stoicheia* = elemental substance of material cosmos] the fair form of god. Nature smiled for love when she saw him whose fairness brings no surfeit [and] who holds himself all the energy of the governors and the form of god, for in the water she saw the shape of the man's fairest form and upon the earth its shadow. When the man saw in the water the form like himself as it was in

nature, he loved it and wished to inhabit it; wish and action came in the same moment, and he inhabited the unreasoning form. Nature took hold of her beloved, hugged him all about, and embraced him, for they were lovers.

Because of this, unlike any other living thing on earth, mankind is twofold—in the body mortal but immortal in the essential man. Even though he is immortal and has authority over all things, mankind is affected by mortality because he is subject to fate; thus, although man is above the cosmic framework, he became a slave within it.[1]

In the Hermetic myth, angelic lust is translated from heaven to the weakness of nature, which, however—should humans attend to their "immortal" part—can be transcended with gnosis. Thus, it is cardinal Hermetic doctrine that man's greatest pitfall, or sin, is "love of the body"; that is, confusing image with essence. He should look within to find the eternal world to which he properly belongs, whence his authority over nature derives.*

A considerably darker myth of how divine pneuma came to be embroiled in human existence may be found in church father Irenaeus's account of the doctrines of Gnostic heresiarch Saturninus. Saturninus, we are told, came from Antioch ad Daphne on the Orontes in Syria. He was allegedly a pupil of Menander, follower, Irenaeus believed, of Jesus and Paul's contemporary, the Samaritan Simon Magus. Written in about 180 CE, Irenaeus's hostile account of Saturninus insists that he influenced Alexandrian Gnostic teachers Basilides and Valentinus a couple of decades earlier.

The first notable thing in this account is what could be a kind of remarkable precursor to the Darwinian account of the evolution of

---

*The account's author was possibly familiar with Greek travel writer Pausanias's reworking of the Narcissus story, in which Narcissus falls in love with his twin sister, since predominant Hermetic doctrines allow for kinship, even harmonic correspondence between divine and natural worlds.

*Homo sapiens,* that yet, with originality, attributes the definitive "evolutionary" step beyond the purely natural order, to the arrival of pneuma, a position comparable to the appearance of the resonant pillar before the hirsute hominid at the beginning of *2001: A Space Odyssey.*

> Saturninus, like Menander, set forth one father unknown to all, who made angels, archangels, powers and potentates. The world, again, and all things therein, were made by a certain company of seven angels. Man, too, was the workmanship of angels, a shining image bursting forth below from the presence of the supreme power; and when they could not, he says, keep hold of this, because it immediately darted upward again, they exhorted each other, saying, "Let us make man after our image and likeness" [Genesis 1:26]. He was accordingly formed, yet was unable to stand erect, through the inability of the angels to convey to him that power, but wriggled [on the ground] like a worm. Then the power above taking pity on him, since he was made after his likeness, sent forth a spark of life, which gave man an erect posture, compacted his joints, and made him live. He declares, therefore, that this spark of life, after the death of a man, returns to those things which are of the same nature with itself, and the rest of the body is decomposed into its original elements.[2]

One presumes that, according to our general idea of human evolution, man would have wriggled in an unevolved, vulnerable state considerably longer, but for the "spark of life" from above. Earthly man is then made in the image of a heavenly original, and depends for his elevation from earth on a higher, nonearthly power. While the conclusion is close to that of Hermes Trismegistos's Narcissus-like fall, the mechanics are considerably less harmonious, or some might say more realistic, in its portrayal of the deficiencies of the natural world, which have clearly evoked a sense of disgust and horror among those devoted to an eternal world sited within.

⚭⚭

The world weariness evident in late antiquity, where something like mysticism begins to flower in doctrines akin to the *jñāna* ("knowledge") yoga that would flourish in the Advaitist schools of India, and which may be contemporary in origin to Syrian and Alexandrian movements, may have much to do with distressing periods of gross political instability following emperor Marcus Aurelius's death in 180, which threatened the Roman Empire during the late second and third centuries, and which doubtless encouraged some people to surrender any but the barest hopes in life in this world. The "elemental powers" that sustained the empire seemed to be weakening, and the future looked bleak. Spiritual philosophy was one way to keep the flame of hope aborning. Christian Gnostics looked to the "living Jesus" within and above, while Catholics looked both beyond the grave and to the terrestrial return of Jesus in judgment. Hermetists and Neoplatonists looked to the "One" beyond all manifestation.

However, if the aforementioned resiting of God's presence *in the soul* of man, or some men at any rate, makes anyone imagine this as a spiritual *evolutionary* step from external religion that was somehow inevitable or progressive, they will be disappointed. Indeed, history shows that it was largely through combat with Gnostic doctrines that Catholic doctrines hardened as bishops assumed more authority in deliberating what was and was not "right belief," hence the word *orthodox,* meaning "straight teaching." As the empire under Constantine the Great (272–337) found cause to seek an understanding with the Christian Church, it insisted that the church conform to a consistent, legally attestable doctrine. Thus, in the fourth and fifth centuries, conflict ensued over the content of the church's creeds, in efforts to alienate "heretics." As we all know, the end of the western Roman Empire saw the launch of the Roman Catholic Church as inheritor of the classical religious settlement, which would dictate much of the Western political settlement as well in times to come. In short, we see the overarching dominance of religion once more, in the sense of a relationship with

God supervised by priests and external observances. Minority mysticism was either reserved for monks who accepted the creeds and eschewed the flesh or severely repressed as capital heresy.

Of course, the "God within" schools did not die out completely. From the tenth century, we have the appearance of Sufism in Islam, Bogomilism in Bulgaria, the roots of Western "Catharism," the Mandaeans in Mesopotamia, possibly the Yezidis in Kurdish Mesopotamia in some form, while in the Far East we have the continuity of Advaitist schools of "union," Buddhism and its Zen offshoot, survivors of the Manichaean Church, and Taoist contemplatives.

One problem with the religious "settlement" of the Roman Empire in late antiquity was that it did not settle some of the more fundamental problems of religion, and historically, the failure shows: the relation of Man to Nature being an outstanding problem. And it wasn't only a problem for the church. Even within the Hermetic corpus, for example, contrary doctrines occupy intellectual and spiritual space. In some texts, Nature is infused with divinity, and properly regarded, espoused as something to be worshipped: glorious, and in its essence somehow eternal; the sun is hailed as the visible god. In other texts, the great sin is love of the body, and that means anything "merely" material; that is, natural. Flesh's corruption reveals it as something not to be attached to. In other texts, the idea of continual and wondrous regeneration in the natural order is stressed (with spiritual analogies).

In the Christian Gnostic material also, there exists a salient problem involved with what it means for humanity to be involved with the created order. For some, Nature is a vicious prison into which Man has been cruelly cast—plaything of a malevolent demiurge and vicious, jealous angels, from whose predations hope lies only in their ignorance of the higher world, and the spirit's knowledge of it. In the more "Valentinian" texts, however, procreation in this world is redeemed by a spiritualized sex practice, with emphasis that one is guiding the seed of pneuma to the light beyond this world. It is not a long step from there to the Catholic idea of purgatory, except that the life of the spirit in this world is the purging, before return to Pleroma in its purest state.

And it is plain the Catholic Church took into itself a number of Gnostic ideas and "catholicized" them, especially where negativity to the sexual act and procreation were concerned. It is unclear whence "Encratism" (hatred of the flesh, sex, and marriage) really derived. Isaac Newton considered it a Gnostic doctrine, even *the* Gnostic doctrine, but it is arguable that it was as much a virus in the Gnostic schools as it would prove to be in the Catholic Church. Sex is a fearful sin, that's the essence of it, and we still struggle with this issue. Why? Because sex "brings us down to earth" and binds us by challenging free will, with "nature" on its side, so to speak. In Catholic terms sex cannot be free of sin because of the literal interpretation of the first Adam's sin, for whom procreation followed expulsion from paradise.

One might ask then, was it sinful of Enoch's parents to have had sex, even though their son "walked with God" and was perfectly acceptable to God? This challenge is still with us.

It probably would not be such an issue for our times were it not for the "Religion" party's reaction to science. As far as I know, science means knowledge of Nature, on the basis that Nature is all we can have verifiable, measurable knowledge of. It is then arguable why people expect science to answer questions beyond this fairly extensive remit! However, we must here recall the premise of the pillars of Enoch: *that there was a time when knowledge of God and knowledge of science, or Nature, was one.* Thanks to conflict between religion and science, we now find ourselves with an either/or choice on many issues. For example, when we say a thing is "natural," we are inclined to conclude that it is therefore right. And that puts us straight back in the doubt that existed at the end of the Roman Empire regarding Man's position with regard to Nature.

Is our species entirely natural, or something else? Whence derives humanity's essence?

The Religion party's historic problem with Nature may be seen to go back to the myth within the Book of Enoch; that is, that knowledge of sciences additional to those known to Sethites came to earth through sinful angels, and this knowledge created havoc. From its inception, the church has had the problem of declaring what was licit and what was illicit knowledge. By the Middle Ages, the church's general approach was that the only knowledge human beings needed existed already and it was probably impiety to want more. Technology does nothing to ameliorate the sins of men, who are, in orthodox thinking, lazy beasts anyway, always looking for a trick to outwit hard work and self-mortification.

Still, against an overwhelming prejudice against science (until knowledge started returning from the East in Latin translations) a number of thinking Catholics took the view that God revealed his secrets to the pure of heart and that Jesus did not forbid people seeking truth wherever they might find it. So long as the lid could be kept on this sort of thing via monastic discipline and the law of the land, leeway was possible. But when the search for truth led to ideas that questioned established doctrine, that was another matter, as Copernicus, Galileo, Giordano Bruno, and many others would painfully discover.

It is clear historically that hostility to science, subtle or outright, has probably hastened decline in respect for church doctrine in the Western civilized world, while hostility to religion has undermined the allegedly scientific character of communist states in the twentieth century. Since the nineteenth century, some decline of external religion and the ascendancy of science has, as is well known, stimulated a recrudescence of the "God within" understanding, visible in revived Rosicrucianism, symbolic Freemasonry, Thelema, pagan mysticism, Martinism, popular mysticism, and neo-Gnosticism, together with adoption of Eastern spiritual traditions in the Western world and the persistence of Blavatsky's Theosophy. While shunned by a conformist "science party" media, these developments are living facts signifying more than some imagined "regression" to superstitious modes of thought or vain hankering for a pre-technoscopic or pre-scientific past. In the thinking culture at large, knowledge of God and knowledge of science seem to ache for reconciliation, a kind of return to the Lost Pillars of Enoch and their hypothetical knowledge.

This search seems vital, in my thinking, to our own era, and eminently worth undertaking. We are not, however, the first people to consider such an idea. The next section of this book is devoted to those movements of thought that have taken the "antediluvian pillars" idea of a unification of knowledge and run with it. And this is no mere investigation for the sake of it. What is at stake here is "Man"; that is, the phenomenon, however it may appear in gender terms. The emblematic *type* of restored Man is Enoch, and tradition informs us that he will appear again when knowledge is again fully divine.

# PART TWO

# HERMETIC PHILOSOPHY
*Seeking Concordance,
or Reuniting the Fragments*

## EIGHT

# The Unitive Vision

*We cannot, therefore, expect the physiognomy of Jewish mysticism to be the same as that of Catholic mysticism, Anabaptism or Moslem Sufism. The Passion of Christ, the relation with the Savior &c. are foreign to Jewish mysticism.*

GERSHOM G. SCHOLEM,
*MAJOR TRENDS IN JEWISH MYSTICISM*[1]

## KABBALAH

It is right that we begin this chapter with the warning above, expressed back in 1941 by pioneering scholar of Jewish Kabbalah, Professor Scholem (1897–1982). Aware that the *Sefer Yetzirah* ("Book of Formation")—the first document of Jewish speculative mysticism vital to "Kabbalah"—is usually dated to the second or third centuries CE (that is to say, to the heyday of Neoplatonism, Hermetism, and Christian Gnosis), Scholem insisted that Hebrew Kabbalah cannot be reduced into a synthetic amalgam of gnostic philosophy, as though the faith orientation of its mysticism was but a coating. Kabbalah, Scholem believed, is absolutely committed to the doctrine of one God creating the universe in its entirety, as revealed in the Pentateuch (or Torah, the first five books of the Bible). While *kabbalah,* or "tradition received," is doubly secret—in that it concerns fundamental secrets of life, vouchsafed to a few who constitute a discreet elite—its secrets violate no established Mosaic doctrine and are intended to illuminate perception of the living God whose spirit is manifested in revelation, creation, and redemption.

Scholem asserted that Jewish Kabbalah's appearance belongs to that historical phase of spiritual practice in which the site of man's relationship with God has moved from external cult to inward soul. Since Scholem dates the *Sefer Yetzirah* approximately to the period of Mishnah formation by the "Tannaim" who followed late first-century Jewish spiritual hero Johannan ben Zakkai (died circa 90 CE),* he glimpses a parallel interest between both the preservation of Pharisaic oral traditions by the Tannaim after the loss of Jerusalem's Temple and the kabbalist emphasis on direct relationship between individuals and God, where the great events of exodus and redemption may be internalized and eternally repeated as types for renewed spiritual life.

In the wake of the Temple's loss in 70 CE and disintegration of the Sadducaean party, rabbis of Pharisaic background were faced with honoring Israel's covenant with God in the absence of priestly sacrifices. They advocated a new emphasis on prayer as the primary form of devotion and sacrifice. One could say that the proto-kabbalist or mystic took this inward tendency much further, employing a special attitude to the written revelation of Hebrew tradition, one that saw language itself as revelatory, the cosmos having been created and constructed by "word" of God (Genesis 1:3, "God *said* . . ."). Divine scripture becomes the new temple, supported by the pillars of God's name and qualities, and with a Holy of Holies, or direct presence, and a place of mysteries for an illuminated few. For the kabbalist mystic, the spirit of God breathed within the very letters of the divine text. The letters were outward forms of God's inward breath. Thus there was outward meaning (the letter) and inward essence (the spirit). The mystic could ascend in spirit,

---

*The Mishnah ("repeated study") was collected from the late first century CE and edited in the early third century by Judah ha-Nasi.

a trajectory analogous to the smoke that once rose heavenward from the Temple's Holy of Holies when the chosen priest made a sacrifice on the people's behalf. This analogy perhaps explains why kabbalist practices were always preceded by ascetic preparation to mortify the ordinary self. Interestingly, we already see the internalization of the temple in the writings of Paul, who tells his converts that they should know that their bodies are the temple of God and must be pure unto the Lord, so Holy Spirit might dwell within them. Paul famously claimed experience of an inner ascent to the "third heaven," offering witness to things not to be uttered to ordinary believers (2 Corinthians 12:2).

Preferred material for mystical speculation was found in existing visionary themes that had emerged with apocalyptic. Prime topics included the Genesis creation story, Ezekiel's vision of the wheels and divine throne, and any tradition (such as the Book of Enoch) connected with the Lord's throne-chariot and sacred beings in divine attendance with access to the "many mansions"—or *hekhaloth*—of heaven (John 14:2).

You could say that in the absence of actual Sethite pillars of knowledge in Genesis, a written revelation was sought that referred back to Adam's inner, spiritual understanding of Seth's patriarchal progeny. God was leading his chosen to the spirit of the word that survived cataclysm: the creative word itself. Following the tradition of Jeremiah, Johannan ben Zakkai believed the loss of external temple was God's judgment. Going a step further than prayer, the kabbalist's restoration of faith's living sap required inner ascent and enlightenment, to the level enjoyed before Adam fell from divine will and mind into the willed and created.

Recognizing the temptation to criticize or suspect elite knowledge revealed to the chosen, Scholem draws attention to the belief that this knowledge, wisdom, or gnosis was believed to have once been shared in antediluvian times by Adam's Sethite progeny: "the purer and more nearly perfect it is to the original stock of knowledge common to mankind . . . that Adam, the father of mankind, possessed is therefore also the property of the mystic."[2] The view was that the mystics had transmitted Adam's secret divine revelation down through the ages, though Scholem considers it unlikely that the mystics themselves took the claim literally but reverenced the tradition nonetheless.

This perhaps helps us further to date the first stirrings of a "kabbalah," for it was in the second century that belief in hyperprivileged access to esoteric knowledge by master beings was at its height, with Jesus, Simon Magus, Apollonius of Tyana, and Hermes Trismegistos presented as masters of secret understanding of the ways of God and the nature of the world. Primal knowledge came from above, and figures with access to the above were the ones to listen to.

Whether or not Kabbalah received key structural dynamics from Gnostic or Neoplatonic sources is still uncertain. Gnostic emanations, or *aeons,* from an ultimately unknowable divinity appear very close to the *sephiroth* (meaning "numbers") that feature in the kabbalist text *Sefer Bahir,* dating from at least the eighth century. Since Kabbalah posits a privileged gnosis, questions have long persisted as to whether Jewish mystics of the proto-kabbalist period owed formative principles to the philosophical mysticism of Gnostic circles. Did they develop in parallel or from common roots? I recall the late Jewish philosopher and master of Gnostic studies Hans Jonas (1903–1993) relating to me in 1986 how he experienced an angry exchange with Gershom Scholem in Jerusalem over this issue. Jonas was inclined to wonder whether at least some of the early radical Gnostics were Jews, for who else would be so concerned with excavating hidden meanings in Genesis and with trying to explain why a transcendent God might have limited influence on earthly events? (It could have been Greco-Egyptian "Christians" hostile to Judaism or Jewish Christianity.) As for Scholem, he held it an article of faith that no Jew could ever possibly entertain the idea that the personal God of Jewish revelation was not also the creator of the universe or that there could ever be a "two gods" hypothesis acceptable to Jews (with reference to the radical Gnostic idea of "Ialdabaoth," jealous demiurge or craftsman of the material cosmos). I believe Jonas was inclined to consider the possibility of what so outraged Scholem because Jonas took into account the trauma endured by Jews during the second-century diaspora. An existential crisis could have stimulated psychological and spiritual effects exacerbated by increased familiarity with pagan and Platonist speculation, especially in Alexandria, where, as we have seen, Jews had long found themselves competing with Greco-Egyptian religious culture.

Jonas was a science-minded philosopher, not a theologian or defender of the faith, nor did he have specific interest in making Kabbalah more respectable, which Scholem was concerned with, given Kabbalah's generally poor reputation among Jewish scholars influenced by the Jewish enlightenment (Haskalah) before the publication of Scholem's sea-changing book, *Major Trends in Jewish Mysticism,* in 1941. Jonas's concern with Scholem's work was logical, since Scholem understood Kabbalah as enshrining spiritual knowledge, for which he used the Greek term *gnosis,* the very subject of Jonas's important studies of the 1930s, subsequently condensed into *Gnosis und spätantiker geist,* begun at Marburg during the end of the Weimar Republic, when Jonas studied under existentialist philosopher Martin Heidegger (1889–1976). Heidegger's philosophy greatly influenced Jonas's view of the Gnostics' significance; that is, Jonas saw the Gnostics as proto-existentialists, individuals who, *for the first time in history,* underwent radical alienation from the natural, created world and felt thrown back into themselves by the weight of negating forces dominating a value-free world. In these conditions, the only redemptive path was to re-envision and experience the material world as counterfeit or ultimately insubstantial.*

The *Sefer Yetzirah* is a proto-kabbalist text concerned with the universe's fundamental structure. Accepting the universe, the text posits

---

*See the UK TV series *Gnostics* (made by Border TV for channel 4, 1987) for interviews between myself and Hans Jonas, conducted in New York and Hamburg in 1986, further elements of which appeared in my books *The Gnostics* (1987) and *Gnostic Philosophy* (2005).

a doctrine of its creation by three meanings of the Hebrew consonants *s, f, r* and "thirty-two wondrous ways of wisdom"—ten calibrations of empty space, plus the twenty-two letters of the Hebrew alphabet divided into categories of three. The consonants *s, f,* and *r* comprise the Hebrew word for *book* (the "written"), and the universe is conceived as an expression of language and, simultaneously, of number or reckoning. An appendix to the work ascribed its wisdom to Abraham, who, we are told, received it directly from God, but kabbalist documents also attribute reception of God's interpretative secrets to Moses, Noah, and, of course, to Adam. Thus we have a claim to a single system of revelatory knowledge of supposed antediluvian origin, before the corruption that precipitated the Flood. The surprise perhaps is that Enoch is not named in the *Sefer Yetzirah* as its source, and this may be due to the fact that leading rabbis of the period regarded the Book of Enoch as uncanonical, insofar as it presumed to be a holy text anterior to Moses's Torah, only from which a trustworthy account of Enoch might properly be sought.

As for Josephus's Sethite pillars story, since it did not appear in scripture at all, the kabbalist was unlikely to build on that specific image, though the mystic certainly dealt with the essential *idea* of a special knowledge preserved through the cataclysms of time.* Nevertheless, deviating from the rabbinic schools, Jewish speculative mysticism could hardly avoid serious interest in Enoch, as is evident from the composition of II Enoch and the later III Enoch, which would appear by the seventh or eighth centuries, where Enoch's activities were stimulated by scriptural inferences, massively elaborated and increasingly liberally interpreted, so that in III Enoch, Enoch is actually transfigured by fire into the archangel "Metatron," who has a governing role in the universe, practically inseparable from Jahveh, having assumed the divine nature and become integral to the universe's governance.

---

*One might speculate as to whether the famous twin pillars of the sephiroth ("numbers") in Kabbalah may owe as much to the myth of Sethite pillars as repositories of divine wisdom as to the more obvious images of the Solomonic temple pillars of Jachin and Boaz, or of the Tree of Life's dualism of severity and mercy.

◌◌◌

While this is not the place to explore further the fascinating key ideas of Kabbalah, it is important to recognize at this point that we shall find that in all subsequent attempts to seek a unitive vision of knowledge from supposed antediluvian times, whether it be as *prisca theologia* (ancient theology), *prisca sapientia* (ancient wisdom), or that ancient knowledge dear to Isaac Newton that had once been both science *and* religion, we shall find Kabbalah playing a role—hardly surprising in the light of its claims (a) to be an inheritance from primal revelation, and (b) to be unequivocally monotheist; that is to say, a unitive knowledge system backdated to earliest times, based on fundamental principles governing natural and spiritual realities, with nature the expression of inward spirit.

## RAMON LLULL (1232–CA. 1316)

Explicit questing for a unified science of divine and human knowledge found its champion in the Middle Ages in the person of Catalan mystic Ramon Llull. Llull operated in Majorca at the time kabbalist speculation reached its zenith with the appearance of the mammoth *Zohar, or Book of Splendor,* attributed to Jewish mystic Moses de León (1230–1305) in Spain, circa 1275.

Fig. 8.1. Ramon Llull
(1232–ca. 1316)

In 1274, the Franciscan Llull experienced a vision on Mount Randa, Majorca. Envisioning two primary figures of what would come to be called the Lullian Art, the revelation established in Llull a principle of integrating ideas pictorially and systematically. It is not surprising that Florentine Renaissance genius Pico della Mirandola (1463–1494) would consider Lullism "a Cabalist method,"[3] for the Lullian Art analyzes and synthesizes the universe in terms of principles integrated in numerical sequences. These are discernible through diagrams of interacting wheels. Knowledge would be enhanced through pursuing the almost mechanical logic of Llull's diagrams, based on the notion of a limited number of essential ideas underlying knowledge. When combined logically with others, these ideas could expand knowledge. Llull had found a kind of "unified field system" of divine expression and cognition.

A notable pictorial allegory illustrating Llull's ideas shows us four men. Each sits beneath a tree: a Gentile, a Jew, a Saracen, and a Christian, with the Gentile—presumably a pagan—finding the other three men all doing the Lullian Art. While of different faiths, the three have perceived a unity they share, and this unity is characteristic of the "fountain of life or mystical truth."[4] In other words, before the truth of God was divided by competing or hostile religions after the Flood, its essence constituted what was essentially true and universal in Judaism, Christianity, and Islam, even though each claimed an authoritative revelation of one God. Llull was emphatic that only Christianity had fully recovered this unity, but for purposes of irenic persuasion of Jews and Muslims that this was so, it was important to establish primal principles of knowledge: that foundation on which they could all agree. Looking to traditional science to establish first points of concord, Llull observed that the wise of each faith all agreed on the theory of the elements. Four elements formed a harmony: earth, air, fire, and water. In Llull's *Tractatus de astronomia* (1297) he advocated an astral medicine formulated from grading the elemental qualities in seven planets and twelve zodiacal signs.

Having established a scientific basis, or agreed knowledge, for con-

cord, Llull addressed the theological principles held in common that
superintend the elemental universe. As the bases for concord, Llull
focused on God's names or attributes. He pointed to nine "dignities"
of God: Bonitas (goodness), Magnitudo (greatness), Eternitas (eternity),
Potestas (power), Sapientia (wisdom), Voluntas (will), Virtus (strength),
Veritas (Truth), and Gloria (glory)—the nine derived from what Llull
called the "nameless A." While we might find the nameless A in the
Revelation of Saint John the Divine (1:8: "I am the Alpha and the
Omega, the beginning and the end"), Llull seems to have borrowed his
dignities from the kabbalist text *Sefer Bahir.*

Published in Provence in about 1174, with some components going
back to tenth-century Babylonia, and possibly much further, the *Bahir*
took the ten numbers (sephiroth, or sefirot) of the *Sefer Yetzirah* and
transformed them into ten attributes familiar to Kabbalah today, deriving from Kether (or Keter = Crown), Elyon (God Most High), and
downward from Binah and Hokmah to Geburah, Hesed, Tiphereth,
Hod, Yesod, Netzach, and Malkuth.

The nameless A seems to correspond to the kabbalist's *En Sof,* or
Nothing/Eternity,* while Gloria seems to correspond to Hod (majesty,
splendor, glory), Bonitas with Chesed (merciful kindness), Sapientia
with Hokmah (wisdom), Virtus with Netzach (strength), Veritas with
Binah (understanding or intelligence).

Llull further combined his union of scientific elements and divine
attributes with a Platonist treatment of three principal geometric figures. The triangle represented the divine trinity, the circle the heavens
(having neither beginning nor end), and the square (being fourfold), the
elements, a scheme in tune with the Christian Platonism of a contemporary text, *De divisione naturae* by Christian philosopher Duns Scotus
Erigena (1266–1308), whom Llull met in 1297.

It is arguable that despite Llull's system having derived in the first

---

*—and to the second-century Gnostic *Bythos,* or unknowable "depth" from which the
Gnostic divine emanations are projected as a Pleroma, or "Fullness."

Fig. 8.2. Lull's
Tree of Science from
a 1505 edition of
Llull's work

place from revelation, not deduction, we see in it a step toward scientific method with his increasingly sophisticated diagrammatic applications of formulae demonstrable to contemporary assumptions, while drawing on what he considered incontestable principles elemental to knowledge.

Similar concerns are deducible from remarkable works produced by Llull's fellow Franciscan contemporary, Oxford scholar-genius Roger Bacon (ca. 1219/20–ca. 1292). Bacon attempted a reform of his university's curriculum to harmonize, where possible, the findings of science, or "natural philosophy," and theology, with an emphasis on collecting facts before deducing truths. For both Llull and Bacon, knowledge was something that had to be *recovered* and integrated with other knowledge. In Bacon's assessment of the *Secretum secretorum et notulis,* mistakenly attributed to Aristotle, Bacon reported that some identified

Enoch with "the great Hermogenes (Hermes Trismegistus), whom the Greeks much commend and laud." Bacon believed Enoch possessed "all secret and celestial science" and, as Hermogenes, enjoyed access to knowledge exceeding that of his own time and that it was a sacred duty for men of learning to bring to light: a scientific call to action for the sake of a religious vision.

While Llull gave his life to a mission to convert Muslims, he believed that only through prayer, not force, would Muslims be brought to what he believed to be the logical conclusion that Christ the Word was God. He died not long after being stoned by an angry Muslim mob in Tunis, while tragically, and to no useful purpose, violence and force would prevail in Catholic Spain's dealings with God's Jews and God's Muslims.

## THE ALEMBIC OF FLORENCE: HERMETIC PHILOSOPHY REBORN

*What we now call the Christian religion existed amongst the ancients, and was from the beginning of the human race, until Christ Himself came in the flesh; from which time the already existing true religion began to be styled Christian.*

SAINT AUGUSTINE,
*RETRACTIONES* 1.13.3; 427 CE

A remarkable set of circumstances combined to turn late fifteenth-century Florence into an engine for disseminating the idea of an antediluvian knowledge underlying all subsequently divided knowledge systems. What made this leap possible?

First, there was money, and with money came power. Banker and statesman Cosimo de' Medici (1389–1464) and son Lorenzo de' Medici (1449–1492), given the sobriquet "the Magnificent," ruled Florence through that extraordinary period dubbed with hindsight the

Fig. 8.3. Cosimo de' Medici
(1389–1464)

Fig. 8.4. Lorenzo de' Medici
(1449–1492)

"Renaissance," or rebirth. The seed of rebirth lay in the attention given by the Medici rulers to brilliant, daring thinkers and artists. Everyone has heard of Michelangelo and Botticelli, but it was Cosimo's Platonic Academy that put high-octane fuel into the intellectual and spiritual sphere, launching a movement whose ramifications extend to our own times. What they hoped to see reborn was the positive, visible culture of antique Greece and Rome, integrated with the spiritual essence of Egypt, Persia, and Judaea, and in which rebirth the primal knowledge of Adam would be recovered for the renovation of a fallen world.

The kick-start occurred when Cosimo persuaded the pope to move his ecumenical council of 1438–1439 from Ferrara to Florence. The Ferrara council intended to establish better relations with, and, where possible, theological union of, the Greek Orthodox Church of the Byzantine Empire, based at Constantinople—at the time threatened with extinction by Muslim Turks—and the Roman Catholic Church, which wanted its pontiff accepted as head of the universal church, notion Serbian and Russian Orthodox authorities rejected outright. In the course of frustrating events, Cosimo encountered brilliant Greek scholar Georgius Gemistus Pletho ("Plethon"; ca. 1355/1360–ca. 1452/1454), who introduced Cosimo and Florence's concerned intellectuals to Plato's works and those of his followers in late antiquity, unknown in their entirety in the West since the fall of the Roman Empire, after which, the more earthbound works of Aristotle dominated Christian scholarship.

Plato's philosophy of an intelligible, spiritual world of formative, primal ideas was regarded as closer in spirit to the Christian revelation of heaven and the creative Word, while Neoplatonists such as Porphyry, Plotinus, and Iamblichus had given Plato's philosophy a decidedly esoteric, theurgic character, allegedly revealing ancient mysteries derived

Fig. 8.5. Gemistus Pletho from a fresco by Benozzo Gozzoli, *The Procession of the Three Magi* (1355–1452)

from ancient sources, transmitted in symbols, riddles, and mysteries. In this worldview, neither Athens nor Jerusalem was the source of inspiration; *Egypt was*. And who had given Egypt her writing, her philosophy? The name Hermes Trismegistus hovered above the most ancient mysteries. Plato and Pythagoras had, it was believed, derived the seed of dynamic inspiration from Egypt.

But first . . . Plato.

Pletho believed the Greek inheritance of Platonic philosophy was central to opening Christianity's inner soul, opening it to spiritual energy, illumination, and mental expansion. All of this Cosimo liked. A vision emerged of a new age where Man might recover his ancient, lost dignity or divine character: hidden powers awaiting rebirth. To honor the revelation, Cosimo founded a "Platonic Academy" at his Villa Carreggi, overlooking Florence's outskirts. Brilliant men gathered at Fiesole to study reverently "the divine Plato." Cosimo commissioned scholar, physician, and priest Marsilio Ficino (1433–1499) to translate Plato's complete works from imported original Greek-language versions: an enormous, but eminently worthwhile task. Ficino's Latin translations would infuse religious thought in the West. But there was more to come!

Fig. 8.6. Marsilio Ficino from the fresco *Angel Appearing to Zacharias* (1490) by Domenico Ghirlandaio, Santa Maria Novella, Florence, Italy

In 1453, Europe received a shock when a Turkish army and fleet seized Constantinople, last bastion of the Byzantine Christian empire. Monasteries, home to precious Greek manuscripts, were endangered. Manuscripts headed west to a ready market.

In 1460, monk Leonardo da Pistoia returned from Greece with a special package for his client, the aged Cosimo. Cosimo laid his startled eyes upon complete versions of the works of Hermes Trismegistus: fourteen libelli, handwritten in Greek, lost to Catholic Christendom for a thousand years. Hermes had knowledge before Plato; indeed, Plato implied that the most profound philosophy derived from Egypt. Here was authentic "ancient theology."

While quotations attributed to Hermes were familiar to medieval scholars, with one complete text known in a Latin version—the *Asclepius*—this was nonetheless a staggering moment, for those earlier texts had but whetted the appetite. As a collector par excellence, Cosimo understood it; Hermes's revelation preceded Moses, giver of the law, for had Moses not been raised in Egypt? Although not a view universally held among churchmen, the supposition of an antediluvian Hermes was taken seriously. Identification with Enoch thrust Hermes practically back into the lifetime of the first man, Adam! Furthermore, Christian church father Lactantius in the seventh book of his *Divine Institutions,* written circa 400 CE, had declared Hermes an ancient witness to Christian truth, which made Hermes a Christian-approved prophet, even though apparently a pagan. But then, had not Saint Augustine written that the thing called Christianity had *always existed* before it appeared under that name with the incarnation of God in the man Jesus?

Cosimo had the keys to the most ancient theology in his hands . . .

Was this not pristine thought at its purest: springwater of the soul, luminous cascade of life-giving insight coruscating about the secret corridors of Florence's Medici sanctuary? What providence was this? Cosimo requested that Villa Careggi houseguest Ficino leave aside his vital work on Plato and switch to translating Hermes, that Cosimo might imbibe the divine wisdom before quitting earth, which time Cosimo felt was imminent.

Ficino produced the first extant Latin translation of the fourteen tracts in 1464. The collection became known as the "Pimander" because the first tract concerned the revelation to Hermes of a figure named (in Greek) *Poimandrēs.**

In 1471, Ficino's idiosyncratic translation appeared in print (Treviso, December 18, 1471). While regarded as momentous by aficionados, the publication has recently been exposed as an appallingly bad version, the work of Flemish humanist Geraert van der Leye and possible

---

*This name seems to be a compound of the Greek for "guide" or "shepherd" (*poimēn*) and "man" (*andros*); that is, it meant "shepherd (or guide) of men" or "of man." It of course resonates in Christian culture with the title Jesus gives himself in John 10:11: "I am the good shepherd." Scholar Peter Kingsley has, however, drawn attention to the ungrammatical character of the compound *Poimandrēs*. "Poimandros," Kingsley believes, would have been more correct. *Poimandrēs,* Kingsley argues, should be considered a Greek transliteration of an Egyptian phrase: *P-eime nte-rē,* meaning "the knowledge of Re," or "the understanding of Re," closely conforming to the figure's Greek self-designation as the *nous tēs authentias,* or "intelligence of the supreme authority."[5] As Thoth was child of sun god Re, and sometimes called Re's "heart" (or seat of intelligence), this etymology would secure the growing tendency in Hermetic studies since Jean-Pierre Mahé's *Hermès en Haute-Égypte* (vols. I–II, 1978) to ascribe composition of the Hermetic tracts to a genuine tradition of infra-Egyptian thought, albeit mediated through a syncretic Greco-Egyptian lens for the benefit of Greek-speaking seekers after truth. Certainty, however, is impossible, since we know so little about the ultimate provenance of the Hermetic philosophical tracts, except to say that it now seems likely—since the discovery of several Hermetic tracts in the Coptic Nag Hammadi library of Gnostic codices—that they were composed originally not in Greek but in Coptic. It is worth noting, however, that in the Egyptian alchemist Zosimos of Panopolis's sole reference to this revelatory figure, he employs the name *Poimenandra* (possibly meaning "shepherd" or "guide" of men), perhaps punning the Greek name, but certainly taking him as worthy of Zosimos's alchemical correspondent, the lady Theosebeia's, respect, recommending she "hurry back" to her "spiritual kind" exemplified by this figure.[6] If Zosimos had seen Kingsley's Coptic phrase behind the word, we might rather have expected something respecting Re perhaps. It is of course possible that the name we have in our versions as *Poimandrēs* (Latinized as "Pimander") was in late antiquity known in variant versions, as translators and copyists found the name as delivered to them difficult or confusing. We have no early Greek or Coptic version of the tract concerned to make comparison. We can only assert that the name was given to "mind of the supreme authority."

provider of the manuscript, Italian Francesco Rolandello. That a disaster seems to have occurred during transmission of manuscript to metal type attracted little remark in the period, and that suggests that people did not necessarily trouble themselves to read very much of what they might have paid good money for. One thinks of Stephen Hawking's *Brief History of Time,* which sold like hot cakes because it was a work people felt they *ought* to have, but it does not seem to have been read very much.* From this somewhat mixed-up beginning, Hermes would nonetheless re-enter the thought-world of the sixteenth and seventeenth centuries, a handy source, name, and literary encouragement to those seeking an ancient philosophy behind all philosophies, a primal revelation of quintessential knowledge.

Campanelli's detailed analysis of the fate of the Hermetic corpus in the fifteenth and sixteenth centuries shows that even with improved translations (in terms of intelligibility), there was no authentic mirroring of the Greek text within the printed realm for nearly a century after Cosimo received his first copy, and it was not strictly a "Hermetic Tradition" that was in vogue but rather more a discourse about Hermes. Furthermore, the editions that did appear were not commercially successful, so perhaps one should be careful about using words like *revolutionary* with regard to the influence *on the ground* of the rediscovered Hermes. However, it is clear that the interest in the work was less in

---

*The real state of the first printed version of the "Pimander," from which version the largest number of sixteenth-century versions followed throughout Europe, was discovered painfully by Latin scholar Maurizio Campanelli after a meeting of Ficino enthusiasts at the home of Professor Sebastiano Gentile in 2002, detailed in Campanelli's "Premessa" (Preface) and "Introduzione" to his reconstructed Ficino translation of *Mercurii Trismegisti Pimander sive De Potestate et Sapientia Dei* ("On the Power and Wisdom of God"—note the use of Llullian divine attributes!), nino aragno, Torino, 2011, a translation effort by Ficino that was in its unmaimed form rarely literal with attempts to smooth the language into more graceful form and seen through the interpretive eyes of Ficino's adopted Neoplatonism. While various editions that followed the 1471 Treviso publication corrected some errors, or employed an alternative, correct Ficino manuscript (these versions enjoyed little success according to Campanelli), the *Greek* original did not appear until Adrien Turnèbe's edition, published in Paris in 1554.

terms of what the tracts were *saying,* even where that was clear, than in what they *represented:* a kind of confirmation of a hoped-for dream of the past, as being more pure and inspirational, as well as more mysterious, than the present; indeed, Ficino had produced not perhaps a philosophy, but a romance.

By the end of the sixteenth century, this idea of a package of knowledge issuing from earliest antiquity would be joined again to the image of the pillars of Seth, or pillars of Enoch.

# NINE

# Restoring Harmony

## *From the Sun to Infinity*

It was in 1484 when Ficino and Cosimo's son Lorenzo de' Medici were introduced to the brilliant "Conte di Concordia," Giovanni Pico della Mirandola (1463–1494), a young, long-haired genius of exceptional mnemonic talents who since boyhood had undertaken to learn *everything*. Dissatisfied by formal education, Pico was inspired by the idea that in the obscurer traditions of religion, philosophy, and history, fragments of a greater revelation were secreted. Ancient knowledge had been corrupted by the human tendency to sink into a darkness of mind through failure of spiritual ambition. Pico was ambitious. His title, Count of Concord, comes from *Concordia*, meaning "harmony"; literally, "with one heart." That unity epitomizes Pico's soul. He ardently desired to reconcile and harmonize all the philosophies and religious traditions of the world.

To achieve this harmony, Pico believed it necessary to penetrate the surface of any inherited statement, doctrine, or belief. He desired to access the core of the idea, its symbol-heart. The secreted idea was expressed through symbol, and in that symbol lay an idea's dynamic universality, its spiritual essence. Divinity was diffused throughout the universe. The visible universe was symbolic of a higher order of being. A raised consciousness could be granted vision of coherent patterns, a matrix of wondrous correspondences linking every level of reality: a kind of proto-quantum universe.

Pico practiced deep contemplation,* striving to pass *through* appearance, or rather pass upward, with a heart fed on love and yearning for the highest, an aspiration the angels would permit, should Man turn from lower nature and seek divinity. Of the reality behind this aspiration Pico was absolutely convinced. Learning was cultivation. If you cultivated the right seeds in your self, they would fructify consciousness, giving access to all levels of being. Knowledge was a vast tree with many branches, but the sap was in essence *one,* from God, being the expression of his ineffable love and limitless creativity. Man the Magus had theoretically unlimited knowledge open to inquiry.

Pico received the idea of the One permeating all outer manifestations and differentiation from not only close mystical reading of the Bible and Ramon Llull, but especially from Neoplatonists whom he studied in depth. Being himself something of a *neo*-Neoplatonist, with that syncretistic temper of late antiquity, Pico also drew on the wisdom of Hermes, and as much again, if not more, he learned from the Kabbalah taught to him by Jews such as Flavius Mithridates, who, fleeing increasing persecution in Spain, sought refuge in Florence.†

Pico began his famous "Oration on the Dignity of Man" of 1486 with a quotation from the Hermetic *Asclepius,*‡ *Magnum miraculum homo est:* "A great miracle is Man." Well, Pico was himself one such miracle, if we confine our idea of miracle to the unexpected possibility rather than the impossible expectation. But Pico surely saw the Llullian and kabbalist potential of that word *dignity.*

Llull used the word *dignity* for a divine attribute. Pico believed that Man was *in potentia* a dignity of God, God's reflection in the world, but

---

*Ever the priest, Ficino's translation of the Greek "gnosis" was *contemplatio dei:* contemplation of God, or "divine contemplation." The essential idea is close to the proper meaning of *yoga;* that is, "union."

†In 1492, Ferdinand and Isabella of Spain expelled all Jews who would not convert to Christianity. By the end of the next century, even the Muslims who *had* converted—the Moriscos—were driven out, starved, or killed. Many Jews came to tolerant parts of Italy.

‡A work Ficino had not included in his "Pimander" for Cosimo, as he had no Greek version to translate.

more than this, that Man could rise on the Tree of Life, if he so willed, and willed in the holiest way with sacred love and desire. This dangerous idea of Pico's suggests that Man is potentially, if not already in fact, a *co-creator* with God, a role reserved in III Enoch for *Enoch-as-Metatron,* utterly transfigured, divinized man who "walked with God." The highest aspiration was to desire, *really* desire, God, and nothing else, and that surely implies ultimate identification with God. When the aspirant has succeeded in his desire, then the cosmos will be his to move in at will, for he will operate in one expression of his essential nature, for as the Hermetic axiom has it: *mundus imago dei,* "the world is the image of God," and man is made *in* the image of God. Here lies the paradox of the microcosm/macrocosm that would so enchant pioneer physician Paracelsus (1493/4–1541). The transfigured Man has overcome the Fall. Not surprisingly then, Pico believed strongly in "Magia," holy magic, the art of the magi (true science), based on divine knowledge of the natural world, and turned to a great upward, returning movement of apocatastasis: restoration.

Magic, for Pico, consisted in the wedding of lower things to the powers and virtues of higher things ("as a farmer weds his elms to vines" as Pico expresses it in his *Oratio*), to—as the Smaragdine Tablet expresses it—"work the miracle of the one thing." Mind could engage matter, and through purified mind render matter fit for service, by transcending its low status: a holy alchemy. Man could breathe life into low elements and make them chariots of the heavens, as God had breathed soul into Man. As we know, a diamond is only carbon worked on by natural forces. If only we could generate a "diamond footprint"! Potentially, everything possible lies within the grasp of reborn, spiritualized Man, free to roam in spirit and thus rule matter.

And in what was Man reborn? The fourth tractate of the "Pimander" reveals, Pico recognized, that to be *reborn* was to be "baptized" in what Hermes called the *kratēr,* or "bowl," of *nous,* of divine intelligence, higher mind, receptive to spiritual thought, forsaking mere earth and the clamor of ubiquitous fools who scoff at the true builder; it was to join the cosmic ark, built in many ages in many forms after the flood that perennially washes away the filth of time. It is spiritual truth that survives flood of water and fire, even of air and earth.

The miracle of man, Hermes taught, was that while of mortal nature, he shared also in the divine nature from which he came, but such powers lay unrealized until man surrendered lust for earthly things and embraced the highest. Initiated knowledge (gnosis) was only for those who knew how to respond to the miracle of human being. For those who did: an exceptional freedom, liberty to move up or down the great chain of being, to understand and see what is low, and to rise to what is greatest, to go "all the way"—with that achieved within reflected in all achieved without. The stars would not be too high for the miracle-man to grasp. Already, through amazing, limitless *imagination,* the great divine gift of creative thought and will, man can share in life from the depths of oceans to the heights of birds, from the revolutions of planets to the essence of the sun. His mind may hold all in its grasp. In less than a second, the mind may jump in time or move mountains. Nothing in nature will withstand the heavenly man once he fully realizes his dignity. As Pico declared in his *Oratio,* "We shall fly up like earthly Mercuries!"—a soaring ambition and unconscious prophecy of the Mercury rocket missions undertaken by NASA in the early 1960s, though Pico says that like earthly Mercuries, with winged feet, our flight's destination is to the "embraces of our blessed Mother," by which he almost certainly means Lady Wisdom, divine Sophia who calls the soul from the mud of earth and upward to the light. Embrace this Lady Wisdom, and nothing can impede Man's penetrating vision if he so wills it. And *Will* is key to Pico because he knows from Llull and any number of other sources that Will is one of the chief attributes or dignities of God above. "Thy will be done." If we do God's will, then, if we do so willingly, we are doing our own *true will,* and therefore, and thereby, man is transformed from object into subject. He may *will,* and he is free to obtain what he wills. His destiny is in his own hands. He may, if he chooses, sink lower than the beasts; he may rise to near-angelic heights (Enoch is waiting), and perhaps beyond, and achieve what appear to the ignorant as miracles. He will know himself as he is: actualized potential, divine power.

Pico has, as it were, split the atom of Man's hidden or occulted nature. Man will be as God because he wills to join himself to God, and God is to be all in all, and Man is made in his image and therefore has a destiny to fulfill, if only he will. The precursor of this potential freedom from false ego is Christ, and that is why Pico will boldly declare that Jesus used true magic for his miracles—a view that would get this exciting young man into perilously deep water with church authority.

Having heard this exposition of some of what Pico understood as "Hermetic philosophy," it sometimes surprises, as I see it, that Hermetic philosophy has not infrequently been denigrated as a mere weaving of elements from Stoicism and middle Platonism, with superficial smatterings of Egyptian lore. While there *is* plenty of variation, and arguably contradiction, in Hermetic tracts regarding the precise status of nature and how best to regard it, and while there is little systematic, logical philosophy as students today know it, there is nonetheless, and despite the corpus's obviously disparate authorship, a discernible *operative* magical philosophy, though it may at one moment seem optimistic, while at other times pessimistic. Nevertheless, the balance of the whole may reflect the duality of human experience and the risks involved in willing anything without assiduous prior understanding and purgation of the soul. But perhaps I may be accused of applying Pico's harmonizing tendency! Anyhow, the Hermetic tracts contain spiritual knowledge, directed to accommodating the breadth and depth of the world and *actively* ascending to its power source, in thought and, by extension, in deed. Philosophy provides the thought, science the deed—religion the Will.

As Edgar Wind demonstrated eloquently in his book *Pagan Mysteries in the Renaissance* (1958), "Renaissance" culture delighted in complexity, esotericism, concordance of classical and Christian philosophy and symbolism, allusion, riddle, ambiguity, and paradox, while at the heart of Renaissance thought may be discerned the idea that, as Catholic scholar Désirée Hirst put it, "an all embracing truth might be discovered in the depths of antiquity, which was restated by the Christian faith, but had always existed."[1] This quest was derived from a spiritual impulse that flourished in late antiquity.

Pico sought this hidden truth as something that had been received by what were known as "Brachmans" and "Gymnosophists" (Hindu mystics), by the Persian mage Zoroaster (Pletho wrote a book on Zoroaster*), by the Egyptian sage Hermes, by Pythagoras's disciples, by the Sibyls, by the Druids, by Jesus, and by kabbalists. All these sources held portions of the kernel of original philosophy or primal knowledge; such was secreted in their mysteries, regarded by mystical humanists as a proper garden to explore. Ancient truth was also believed to be secreted in classical mythology and myths of many peoples.

Scholars and artists of the European Renaissance embraced classical imagery in a search for primary spiritual principles. According to Ms. Hirst: "Above all, beneath the laudable curiosity about earlier religions and Eastern beliefs can be discerned a serious attempt to find the element of truth basic to all creeds, in fact a genuine syncretism."[2] For example, Pico rejected Ficino's genial interpretation of the classical Three Graces as denoting Beauty, Love, and Joy for his own *trinitas* of Beauty, Intellect, and Will, where Beauty comes from the heavenly world and Intellect and Will turn toward her, whereafter, in the ultimate ecstasy, the three become *one*.

We have mentioned Pico's *Oratio de Dignitatis Homini*—described famously by Renaissance scholar Ernesto Garin as the "manifesto of the Renaissance"—a wonderful text intended as an opener to a great debate in which Pico called for savants to debate his "900 Conclusions," published in Rome. This was, as Ms. Hirst puts it in her unduly neglected text *Hidden Riches* (1964), "to work out a common doctrine within the

---

*Zoroaster's oracles were published for the first time with commentaries by Gemistus Pletho under the title *Magika logiatōn apo tou Zōroastrou Magōn* ("The Magical Oracles of Zoroaster the Magus") by Tiletanus, Paris, 1538. Interestingly, Désirée Hirst believed that Ficino's line of initiated descent—Zoroaster-Hermes-Orpheus-Pythagoras-Philolaus,—came to him from the mind of Pletho.

deepest and most mystical teachings of Christianity, Judaism and Islam."[3] This was clearly challenging, to say the least, to de facto Catholic authority, which was based on the idea that there was no salvation outside of the church, with other religions being irrelevant or hostile to Christianity, asserted as the one true, self-sufficient revelation of God to humanity.

One of Pico's more famous conclusions was that nothing furnishes such a clear demonstration of Christ's divinity than does Kabbalah: a contention that could be twisted to imply that the doctrine of Jesus's messiahship required Jewish support.* At this point Pico hit a confrontation between "religion" as the site of God's presence and the "inward soul" or mystical, sometimes gnostic, experience: a distinction we examined in chapter 4.

Unnerved by the potentially revolutionary nature of many of Pico's *Conclusiones,* the pope requested a commission to investigate them. Six conclusions were condemned as heretical, seven bordered on heresy. Pico was forbidden to deliver them, and when Innocent VIII read Pico's rushed *Apology,* or defense and arguable submission, the pope condemned all nine hundred conclusions. Pico escaped to France, but French authorities

---

*Pico is regarded as a pioneer of "Christian Cabala"—note the English spelling *Cabala* to distinguish it from Kabbalah in the service of Judaism. German scholar and Catholic linguist Johannes Reuchlin (1455–1522) would publish the most, to many, remarkable "clear demonstration" of Jesus's divinity afforded by Kabbalah in the very year Pico died. *De verbo mirifico* ("On the Exalted Word") appeared in 1494 with a centerpiece argument that Jesus's Hebrew name, Yeshua (a late form of "Yehoshua"), may be produced by simply inserting the Hebrew letter shin into the middle of the four letters of the tetragrammaton, the four letters constituting God's name (yod, hé, vau, hé). Shin, which letter looks like a trinity of flames (ש), was considered to represent the Holy Spirit. In the *Sefer Yetzirah,* the letter shin is said to represent the king over fire. It has also been taken as a glyph for the heart as well as the letter denoting "shabat," the seventh day of peace and rest after creation. When *sh* is permitted descent into the Name, the *unutterable* Name of God becomes audible; that is to say, the word is, as it were, made flesh or real to the senses and "dwells," or is now heard, manifest in the world: God identifies himself with man, his "Son," and the Son with the Father, by means of the Holy Spirit. The Name, then, is said to represent the incarnation of God in Jesus, the miraculous fulfillment of prophecy, held as a secret within God until the time was fulfilled. This argument did in fact convert some kabbalist Jews to an acceptance of the Hebrew name of "Jesus" as the messiah.

were instructed by the pope to detain him. Briefly imprisoned, he was back in Fiesole as Lorenzo's houseguest by summer 1488. Innocent VIII died in 1492. His successor, Pope Alexander VI—remembered for scandalous debaucheries—pardoned Pico for his earlier work in 1493, while the publicly chastened Count of Mirandola and Concordia devoted himself to deep studies at Florence's Dominican convent of San Marco. There he found inspiration in its prior, Savonarola (burned at the stake for heresy in 1498). Pico withdrew from material attachments while his brother managed the family estates. Pico died on November 17, 1494—poisoning was suspected—just as Florence fell to the army of Charles VIII of France, which disaster ended the glorious period of relative liberty of mind instituted by banker Cosimo and son Lorenzo, patrons of the new magus and of a profound tremor in Europe's soul.

## FRANCESCO GIORGI: COSMIC HARMONY

Born in Venice in 1466, Franciscan friar Francesco Giorgi (or "Zorzi"), unlike "Phoenix of the wits" Pico, lived to make old bones, dying in 1540. In 1525, his book *De Harmonia Mundi* ("On the Harmony of the World")

Fig. 9.1. Francesco Giorgi,
*De Harmonia Mundi,*
published in 1525

FRANCISCI GEORGII

VENETI

MINORITANAE FAMILIAE

DE HARMONIA

MVNDI TOTIVS

CANTICA

T    R    I    A

Talia probariae, (ſ iritus quibus ſpirat.

was published, dutifully dedicated to Pope Clement VII. It is a comprehensive working-out of a pristine knowledge theory: divine harmony. When God made the universe, his nature infused everything in it with the perfection of his almighty being, a sign of which was *harmony*.

Differences, even opposites, existed at all levels, but all resolved themselves ultimately in harmony. God separated the light from the darkness, the land from the sea. He gave two lights, sun and moon, sway over night and day, and all the orbs of heaven respected one another's position. Clearly there had been harmony at the start: harmonies of heaven and earth, harmony twixt Man and God.

*So what had gone wrong?*

Man had become progressively blind to divine harmony, his sights had sunk below the level first granted to him in his innocence when he lived harmoniously in the "garden" with beasts of earth and fowl of air, when all things responded to his powerful word. The cure for the loss was restoration of what was lost: harmony. There should be harmony in music, harmony in design, harmony of speech and dress, harmony of Catholic or universal doctrine, harmony in political and social relations, harmony within and without the body: a binding of man on earth to the harmonies and music of harmonious spheres beyond.

Needless to say, scholars have discerned echoes of Francesco Giorgi's vision in act 5, scene 1 of Shakespeare's *Merchant of Venice* (Giorgi's home territory) when Jessica is enjoined to sit down and ponder.

> *How sweet the moonlight sleeps upon this bank!*
> *Here will we sit and let the sounds of music*
> *Creep in our ears. Soft stillness and the night*
> *Become the touches of sweet harmony.*
> *Sit, Jessica. Look how the floor of heaven*
> *Is thick inlaid with patens of bright gold.*
> *There's not the smallest orb which thou behold'st*
> *But in his motion like an angel sings,*
> *Still choiring to the young-eyed cherubins.*

*Such harmony is in immortal souls,*
*But whilst this muddy vesture of decay*
*Doth grossly close it in, we cannot hear it.*

Do we hear in Shakespeare the whole choir of Hermes and Neoplatonism? 'Tis "love of the body" that inhibits hearing this sweet harmony and seeing how all the parts work with the One beyond the shattered vision of the earthling.

Giorgi carefully wove a Christian cabala out of Plato, Zoroaster, Hermes Trismegistus, Origen, and Neoplatonists such as Proclus, linking this happy, harmonious band to the plow of revealing a lost harmony of the universe that only wanted seeing for it to be real again. Man must look back to look forward.

On the one hand, the Friar of Venice's thesis derives its spring from the Pythagorean discovery (or rediscovery) that the pitch of notes depends on the length of the string, that the intervals in the scale are governed by numerical ratios of 2:1 for the octave, 3:2 the fifth, and 4:3 the fourth: all audible analogs of a transcendent harmony. On the otherhand, Giorgi borrows what he can from kabbalist sources that suit his theme, such as the figure transliterated into English as "Metatron," whom Christian cabalists of the period could identify with the archangel Michael.

Figuring strongly in III Enoch and works inspired by it, as the elevated Enoch's apotheosis, Giorgi himself sees Metatron as the soul of the messiah, as a cosmic idea, linked to the proportion and judgment of the universe. There is much play on the medieval picture of God as "Great Architect" of the universe (its inner mind), a picture permeating the lore of organized Masonic fraternities. Metatron is instrumental, and inherent, to harmonic construction and maintenance of the universe, a kind of "King's Master Mason," on the visible creative level, but more, a real metaphysical power, identified with the *anima mundi,* or "soul of the world," a "second God" (as Hermes calls the cosmos in *Asclepius* X): that which animates and sustains existence, an idea Christian cabalists saw in the orthodox person of the Holy Spirit, and the breath that was first breathed into Adam that raised him a living soul from red earth.

The depth of Giorgi's knowledge of Hebrew and Aramaic is particularly evident in his *In Scripturam Sacram, et Philosophus, tria millia Problemata* (Venice, 1536), a question-and-answer text of medieval scholastic type, which shows throughout its commentary on the Old and New Testaments Giorgi's commitment to two traditions of law—one written, one oral—that he considered it his generation's duty to bring forth and harmonize as universal knowledge. The papacy, however, was less impressed, sniffing the vapors of ungovernable *change* in the air. Giorgi's book on Holy Scripture was put on a list of censored works, forbidden to Catholics "until corrected."

There is little doubt that the relatively small number of persons affected by this movement of integrating divers traditions of ancient knowledge came to an enlarged understanding of the meaning of Christianity, and an illuminating interpretation of the word *Christ,* and further, expanded vision of the possible scope of science. The movement undoubtedly contributed to the fermenting of a genuinely liberal culture, and by *liberal* I mean the word in its authentic sense, that is, a *generous* culture, one confident in its liberty and disposed to offering bounty, enlightenment and forebearance, given to fairness, to listening to the other person's point of view with a view to learning from it, not simply opposing it because it appears at first sight inimical to the familiar. It is a culture that allows for exchange, change, growth, and above all, is one that in seeking concord based on common interest, benefits all. The prisca sapientia idea called and calls people to seek commonality and fraternity in an ideal of ancient, universal knowledge, uncorrupted by violent differentiation and the wounds of time. It is a cultural prize that needs to be understood and projected if it is to be a treasured possession of individuals everywhere, as the concerns of human welfare may suggest to the thoughtful.

We have in this chapter really only skipped over the surface of the vast and varied continent populated and cultivated by those in the fifteenth and sixteenth centuries enchanted by the "unitive vision" and inspired by a primal antediluvian knowledge-experience. I have written elsewhere on the effect of Hermetic philosophy (or philosophies) on Western culture generally, whether as inspirer of operative science or devotion to alchemy, and numerous scholarly books are nowadays available that examine these fascinating developments in enriching detail and that contain much I must forebear from repeating here, lest we lose sight of our main thesis.

However, before we explore one extant example of an organizational ideal that has fostered both the genuinely liberal culture I refer to and the ideal of a Giorgian *harmonia* of celestial and worldly knowledge based on an antediluvian original, we must attend to two figures for whom the prisca sapientia was not simply a gateway to a personal mysticism, but something that inspired a shiftt from medieval to modern science.

## COPERNICUS

A German from Royal Prussia in the kingdom of Poland, Nicolaus Copernicus (1473–1543), like Pico, studied canon law at Bologna in Italy (1496–1501), having moved there after undergraduate work at Kraków—but again, like Pico, Copernicus found himself drawn beyond the bounds of law. Attending to the humanities, he soon acquired rare mastery in traditional astronomy. Returning to Warmia, Poland, in 1503, Copernicus made astronomical observations by 1514 that pointed him to a theory of heliocentricity. Contrary to more than 1,300 years of Ptolemaic philosophy, contrary to theology, and contrary to common sense (can we not see the sun moving across our sky?), Copernicus was satisfied that some largely forgotten antique theories of Pythagoras's pupil Philolaus and of Aristarchos of Samos (ca. 310–ca. 230 BCE) accorded in principle with his refined observations.

While Copernicus's theory occasioned some controversy, the astronomer chose to continue quietly embellishing his study. Knowing

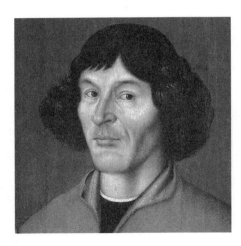

Fig. 9.2. Nikolaus Copernicus
(1473–1543)

the ruckus his theory would raise, he held back publication of his fin-
ished work until the year he died. While his *De revolutionibus orbium
coelestium* ("On the revolutions of the celestial spheres") of 1543 exhibited the kind of magisterial astronomical knowledge tradition ascribed
to Enoch and Hermes, the book, though widely read and debated (and
condemned by Florentine Dominican Tolosani in 1546), was still something of a time bomb. It did not "blow up" fully until the church decided
to clip Galileo's wings seventy years later, when "Copernicanism" was
treated more as a heresy than an astronomical theory. In 1616, the Curia
put Copernicus's work out of bounds for Catholics, "until corrected."

It would seem that the church (or "religion" opposed to inner experience) had again reached its limits where antique sources were concerned, and, in the process, cut the most ancient traditions from under
its own feet. For on the very page where Copernicus presented the new
universe as a series of cycles about Solis (the sun), consisting of Mercury,
Venus, the Earth (moving on its orbit with the moon going round it),
Mars, Jupiter, Saturn, and finally, at the rim, the sphere of the immobile
stars existing farther away than the radius of the sun to the outermost
planets, we find the words *Trismegistus visibilem Deum* (shorthand for
"as Trismegistus said, the sun is the visible God"). Copernicus claimed
textual support from Hermes Trismegistus, who seemed to have known

what he, Copernicus, had recovered from obscurity. Including this quotation projected a very important idea. It was not simply a nice piece of scholastic, literary rhetoric to smooth passage of the theory before classically read and patristic-minded papal inquisitors.

What Hermes meant, implied Copernicus, was that the sun is the most apt symbol for God, not only as omniradiant source of light and life but also, more particularly as regards astronomy, if the sun be *like God,* then it follows that *the sun does not move.* Now, the church had long accepted Thomas Aquinas's identification of Christianity's God with Aristotle's "unmoved mover." So, if the *sun* (the visible God) did not move, then the earth simply had to! It wasn't just a question of mathematics and fallible human observation. The key to the theory lay already secreted—and that by divine providence—in ancient lore. *And why, anyway, should the Christian church automatically favor pagan Ptolemy over inspired Hermes, prophet of Christianity?*

Trismegistus's tractates were widely understood to have been either in tune with the antediluvian wisdom of the most ancient patriarchs (Enoch in particular) or to have been composed around the time Moses received God's law, so Copernicus is saying, subtly as he can, "You may choose to argue with Trismegistus, if you wish," but if you do, kindly ask this question: Did not church father Lactantius declare Trismegistus a prophet of Christianity, an example of what Saint Augustine had exalted as "the thing now called Christianity" *before the church,* and certainly before Ptolemy and Aristotle? In Adam's time, religion and natural philosophy (what we now call "science") were *one,* of absolute truth and always in agreement, like a radius drawn from a sphere's center in any direction. And how could this not be, for as everyone knew, the universe was made by the *Word.*

Without realizing it perhaps, Copernicus had deposited a deeply discomfiting question at the Vatican's portal, one of enormous import for future relations between church and science, one that would leave *knowledge* in the ultimately impossible situation of accommodating a rift between material and spiritual knowledge, with the one maimed

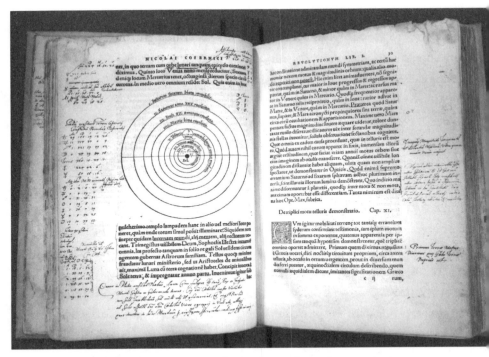

Fig. 9.3. *Copernicus de revolutionibus orbium celestium;*
quotation from Hermes Trismegistus

limb doubting the existence of the other. Copernicus's work raised a
most awkward dilemma: *Is it in the church's interest to sunder the fabric
of knowledge?* As we know from what happened to Galileo, the church
would see the question entirely reversed. *Was it for mathematics and
human observation to rip a gash in the garment of faith?* And these are
pertinent, living questions for us today—and I write this book in an
attempt to answer them.

In Copernicus's day, the Big Questions were not those we like to project
back upon former times. We regularly skew our sense of the reality of
what has passed, by seeing past events as but steps in a development of
things that have become apparent or important *to us.* Thus our historians of science like to see Copernicus as a "hero of modern experimental

science," his ideas initiating a "revolution" and suchlike. Now that may be quite valid, with the benefit of prejudging hindsight of what is now considered significant: valid for us anyway, and doubtless with reason. However, that was not the lens through which Copernicus and the intellectual world in which he lived actually operated.

A few years ago, I was asked to review a fascinating tome by Professor Robert S. Westman.* *The Copernican Question: Prognostication, Scepticism and Celestial Order* (2011) traced precisely how—and how slowly—Copernicus's heliocentric science merged into European intellectual currency. Westman found the triumphalist view of a "Copernican revolution" ushering in modern science a romantic conceit of science history.

By an ironic twist, it transpires that Copernicus was probably motivated to focus on planetary order for the benefit of a more credible *astrology*. By the time Isaac Newton finally proved heliocentricity, more than a century and a half later however, astrology's grip on natural philosophers' concerns—the word *scientist* was not employed until the 1830s—was failing. Credibility accorded astrology's ancient spouse—theoretical and mathematical astronomy—left her exposed to the "normalization" of the cosmos. In the process, the cosmos lost meaning, and it is arguable that Copernicus's original intentions were defeated by what was mistakenly called, for the first time in 1855, "Copernicanism."

Somewhat surprisingly, the inadvertent hero of Westman's narrative is not Copernicus, but Pico della Mirandola. As Pico's *Oratio* had put Man at creation's center, Pico could not allow mere stars to frustrate the limitless potentialities of Man's free will. Pico's objections to judicial astrology were marshalled in his highly influential *Disputationes* (1496), which he was working on at the time of his death in 1494. Pico criticized judicial astrology for its frequently wild sense of mathematical and

---

*My review was published as "Superstition and Magic in Early Modern Europe: A Reader/*The Copernican Question: Prognostication, Scepticism and Celestial Order*," in the *International Journal for the Study of the Christian Church* 15, no. 2 (2015): 155–58, edited by the late Geoffrey Rowell.

Fig. 9.4. Pico della Mirandola
(1463–1494)

observational discipline. As Westman puts it in chapter 3 of his work
(p. 86): "No trust in the numbers, no trust in the prediction of effects."

Pico's ridicule of what he regarded as prognosticators' pretense
to prophecy also promoted skepticism toward "theorical" astronomy,
meaning astronomy's value-neutral observational and mathematical side,
which was Copernicus's forte. But note the coincidence of dates: publication of Pico's posthumous *Disputationes* coincided with Copernicus's
arrival in Bologna to live with, and assist, Domenico Maria Novara
(1454–1504), leading prognosticator and *mathematicus*.

The second part of Westman's book shows that since Copernicus
was limited to contemporary intellectual categories, we should resist
thinking of "modern science" passing through a time of otherwise dark
ignorance in the guise of a revolutionary genius. Copernicus was a man
of his time; the debates went to the limits of knowledge of highly intelligent men. Those recognizing Copernicus's value to prognostication supported him. What *they* wanted was a "modern science," so to speak—of
*astrology*. Copernicus's pupil Rheticus showed how Copernicus's science linked the earth's "eccentric" to the destiny of earthly kingdoms,
a divinatory usage supported by leading Lutheran theologian Philip

Melanchthon (1497–1560). Melanchthon opposed heliocentricity on "common-sense" and biblical grounds. For him, as for many others, the leap to heliocentricity was just too wild, too dangerous, too dizzying.

Thirty years after publication of *De Revolutionibus* (1543), there was still no "Copernican Revolution" but there was plenty of opposition to astrology, much of it coming from Rome. Westman examined new generation "Copernicans" such as German Michael Mästlin (1550–1631) and Englishman Thomas Digges (1546–96); both men preferred planetary models to astrology. Tübingen's significance is rightly emphasized. Tübingen mathematician and astronomer Mästlin tutored not only Johannes Kepler (1571–1630)—one of the few determined heliocentrists at the start of the seventeenth century—but also Johann Valentin Andreae (1568–1654), creator of the Rosicrucian *Fama Fraternitatis,* an unlikely spin-off from astronomical debates that followed unanticipated *novae* in 1572 and 1604. Mästlin also influenced Galileo.

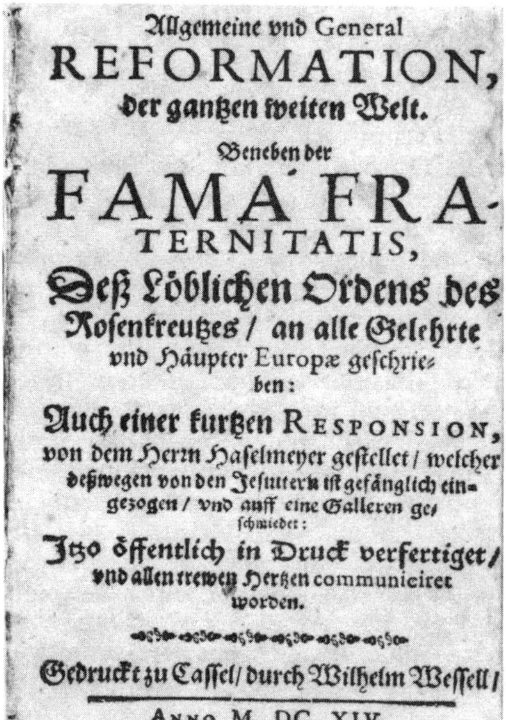

Fig. 9.5.
*Fama Fraternitatis,* 1614

Allgemeine vnd General
REFORMATION,
der gantzen weiten Welt.

Beneben der

FAMA FRA-
TERNITATIS,

Deß Löblichen Ordens des
Rosenkreutzes / an alle Gelehrte
vnd Häupter Europæ geschrieben:

Auch einer kurtzen RESPONSION,
von dem Herrn Haselmeyer gestellet / welcher
deßwegen von den Jesuitern ist gefänglich ein-
gezogen / vnd auff eine Galleren ge-
schmiedet:

Itzo öffentlich in Druck verfertiget /
vnd allen trewen Hertzen communiciret
worden.

Gedruckt zu Cassel / durch Wilhelm Wessell /
ANNo M. DC. XIV.

Fig. 9.6. Johann Valentin Andreae
(1568–1654)

Kepler's conclusion to his *De Stella Nova* (1606) may be compared to
the opening to Andreae's *Fama Fraternitatis:* "I believe," wrote Kepler,
"that at last the world is alive, indeed, seething, and that the stimuli
of these remarkable [planetary] conjunctions did not act in vain." The
foundation document of what would become known as Rosicrucianism
(the *Fama,* ca. 1610) declares the signs of the times and a hidden fraternity's determination to reap and distribute the benefits.

> For Europe is with child and will bring forth a strong child, who
> shall stand in need of a great godfather's gift.
>
> . . . Howbeit we know there will now be a general reformation,
> both of divine and human things, according to our desire, and the
> expectation of others; for it is fitting, that before the rising of the
> sun there should appear and break forth Aurora, or some clearness,
> or divine light in the sky.

A new era had opened in what Novara called the "science of the stars";
it included prognostication.

Three years later, the game changer arrived. Kepler borrowed one of Galileo's telescopes from the Elector of Cologne and observed Jupiter's satellites. The cosmos became "normal," with new eyes coming from new lenses. While the possibility still remained for a "Reformed Astrological Theoric"—Kepler continued to make modest prognostications—astrology increasingly went one way, astronomy another.

Copernicus had made people ask questions, rather than just settle with authority, and *that is how beliefs change.* And I think it remarkable that at the very time the Catholic Church pulled away from the revelations of astronomers, we find Mästlin's mathematics pupil Andreae calling on the figure of Enoch, harking back to antediluvian knowledge-experience before all division, whose pillar still "stood" as an example that knowledge was knowledge and that theology and natural philosophy (science) belong together, being one at the start of Man's journey.

> Our Philosophia is nothing new,* but is the same which Adam received after his fall and which Moses and Solomon applied. Also she ought not much to be doubted of, or contradicted by other opinions, or meanings; but seeing the truth is peaceable, brief, and always like herself in all things, and especially accorded by with Jesus in omni parte and all members. And as he is the true Image of the Father, so is she his Image; Thus it should not be said: "This is true according to philosophy but false according to theology," for everything which Plato, Aristotle, Pythagoras, and others recognized

---

*"Our Philosophy" is that of the Brethren of R.C., a fraternity the document says was founded by "Frater C. R.," who had departed the bigotry of Western monastic life in the fourteenth century and gone to "Damcar" (a misreading of "Damar") in Arabia, where he found that Damar's savants shared their knowledge in an open-hearted manner, which knowledge Frater C. R. brought back to Europe. Finding it unwelcome, Frater C. R. maintained it in a discreet society that met regularly in a "House of the Holy Spirit," which, while in plain sight, was passed unseen by the world. Andreae's narrative is a powerfully sustained polemical and satirical allegory. See my book *The Invisible History of the Rosicrucians* (Inner Traditions, 2009) for a detailed account of the genesis and development of Rosicrucianism.

as true, and which was decisive for Enoch, Abraham, Moses, and Solomon and which above all is consistent with that wonderful book the Bible, comes together, forming a sphere or ball in which all the parts are equidistant from the center, as hereof more at large and more plain shall be spoken of in Christianly Conference.[4]

Alas! The interests of organized, external "religion" were decided in this era of "reformation" to be more important to the experience of individuals, however honest and truthful they might be. The effect was to split the body of knowledge, and the body of the church ever wider. And by-products of that fissure were persecution and war.

In theory, of course, it could all have been avoided. Andreae's work was dedicated to what he believed was vital: a *second* reformation of Europe, a reformation of the heart, a reformation of knowledge supported by a liberal culture of love and brotherhood and spiritual idealism; of tolerance, knowledge-sharing, and honest debate; of unpretentiousness; and of care for the poor and the needy.

## GIORDANO BRUNO (1548–1600)

Living in faraway Tübingen in Württemberg, southern Germany, Johann Valentin Andreae was only thirteen when Dominican friar Giordano Bruno was condemned as an "impenitent heretic" and burned at the stake in Rome's Campo de' Fiori. It may not have been brought to Andreae's immediate attention at that age, but we know the event cast a shadow over expectations among Andreae's friends as they grew up in a great university town. At stake was the future of liberty in Italy, and the threatened Venetian Republic in particular, and the implications for knowledge and truth across Europe, sundered between Protestant and Catholic camps, with constant interference to scholars exhibited on both sides of the divide, while only the Church of England groped for a *via media* between religious extremes.

Bruno may be compared to Copernicus only in this perhaps: that

Fig. 9.7. Statue of Giordano Bruno (1548–1600) in the Campo de' Fiori, Rome

he was another genius arguably purloined by the interests of the history of science in the nineteenth century as one of science's "martyrs." This arguably misleading simplification came about because in the course of writing his many books on what we might call today "consciousness expansion" through application of magical memory systems and Hermetic philosophy, Bruno vehemently championed Copernican heliocentricity, asserting his prescient belief that the universe consisted of an infinite number of worlds. Only an *infinite* universe, he believed, was consonant with an *eternal* God, of whom the cosmos was a living reflection (*mundus imago dei*).

In point of fact, while these beliefs—as philosophical theories—were objectionable to Rome's inquisitors into whose hands Bruno was eventually betrayed, the charges that carried the most weight were those asserting that he had frequented homes of the upper echelons of hostile Protestant countries (England and Protestant German states in particular) and had founded a heretical sect of "Giordanisti" to subvert (that is, reform) the Roman see. Following Pico's intellectual lead, Bruno was outspoken about church government and held questionable or condemned theological points of view, such as a belief that Jesus worked miracles by magic, performed as a magus—which miracles might be repeated by those with knowledge of the art.

While Bruno had certainly written stimulating books on cosmology while living at the French ambassador's residence in Protestant London in 1584 (*On the Infinite Universe and Worlds, The Ash Wednesday Supper,* and *On the Cause, Principle and the One*), Bruno's chief sin as far as his inquisitors were concerned seems to have been that he was a theological privateer, a freethinking reformist who had broken the bonds of his order and made himself useful to Rome's enemies, employing illicit magic while advocating doctrines designed to undermine the existing polity of the Roman see; that is to say, Bruno was fundamentally a *religious* martyr, suspected of politico-religious subversion rather than, strictly speaking, a martyr to "science" who died for the truth of his research. There were many keen and brilliant natural philosophers accepting of the Roman Curia's authority to decide matters of faith and doctrine. Bruno consented to argue about such matters, trusting in his own effervescent inspiration, as against Rome's authority to decide about the virgin birth, transubstantiation of wine into blood, Jesus's divinity, and the nature of God's relationship to his creation, among other things to which his inquisitors were sensitive. Furthermore, Bruno practically identified God with the cosmos, a conception tantamount to pantheism.

Frances Yates's influential book *Giordano Bruno and the Hermetic Tradition* (1964) not only introduced the world to an unseen power in the history of ideas dubbed "the Hermetic Tradition" but also challenged historians of science by asserting Bruno's was essentially a religious vision, and by that we mean a vision informed by occult, Neoplatonic ideas, powerfully infused with what he considered authentic divine revelation evinced in the works of Hermes Trismegistus and others of the ancient tradition that Ficino and, more outspokenly, Pico had recommended. Bruno had picked up Pico's fallen standard and added a whole new set of colorful pennants of his own.

And in this context lies Bruno's interest to our story: that in employing to an extraordinary degree the prisca theologia idea, Bruno linked the reformation of the entire Catholic Church, and by extension, the reformation of the world, to the rediscovery of what he believed was the original science and original religion; that is, the primal knowledge of Man in his purest origins as inhabitant and potential master of an infinite universe.

For Bruno, heliocentricity was nothing less than a divine revelation. Its principle was universal: fire, light, centrality, source, with the One diffused in multiplicity throughout a living and eternal universe. The sun stood as a "monas," one point from which creation in two to three dimensions may extend. If Man so chose, he could live consciously in God's mind, for the cosmos was God's mind manifest, permeated with spiritual life. This meant that Pico's revaluation of the magus and the art of the magi stood as centerpiece for a reformed religion whose "Catholicity" or universality was—to Bruno's vision—at last rejoined to ancient Egyptian principle (where religion and science were one). The universe was a living temple of infinite divinity "whose center is everywhere, circumference nowhere," to use a dictum popular among scholars drawn to Hermetism. Bruno advocated cosmic consciousness, and in equally boundless enthusiasm, or as he himself called it, "heroic furor"—a spiritually enflamed state of untrammeled desire akin to ecstatic prayer—came to believe along with other spiritual reformers of his time that an era was imminent when the church would realize that its future lay in seizing upon fresh revelation and bring itself home to the source of all being.

The method to achieve this harmonious denouement lay in what Frances Yates called Bruno's "Hermetic Egyptianism." Having read paeans in praise of the sun's spiritual power in the books of Hermes, Bruno had taken them to heart. The new cross on the Catholic altar would be the symbol of the ankh, its progenitor, as Bruno believed; the priests would be magi, armed with the knowledge of the temples of Egypt. Like priests described in the Hermetic *Asclepius,* they would rediscover means for infusing their statues with divine life, with spirit, through magical evocation and invocation—a most controversial element of the Hermetic writings, believed by conservative scholars to be tantamount to idolatrous magic. What was divine music, asked Bruno, but magical incantation? A temple should be a powerhouse of divine spirit tending to harmonious animation of the whole world, an extension of divine light consonant with spiritual unfolding of the secrets of the human mind, until life became a great dance of light and life and love. The sun symbolized union of divinity and creation.

Yes, Bruno was undoubtedly a Utopian (a "nowhere man") because he believed the Fall of Man was a fall from something resembling an ideal *topos;* that is, a loss of knowledge of what the true *Eu*topia (good place) consisted of. He believed that knowledge was now streaming back into consciousness, and that Copernicus's exercise in planetary realignment (theorical astronomy) appeared as a manifest sign of spiritual change, while the philosophy of Ficino and the prisca sapientia were alike harbingers of the true wisdom of the ancients recovered. And Bruno really seems to have believed that he could, once circumstances fell providentially into place, reveal the glory of his vision to the pope, and the church would see that this was the way to transcend mere "doctrinal" differences that separated the Body of Christ in the church, a magnet of love that would attract adherents of hostile confessions and reinstate pure divinity of incarnate deity in an enlightened new world, one promised by Jesus as the age of Holy Spirit, and the wholly spiritual universe would be both one, within and without the soul of a transfigured humanity.

*They couldn't let this man live, could they?*
They didn't.

The Catholic Church's intellectual leaders were perhaps beginning to wonder what was more dangerous to the religious body: new theories of "natural philosophy," or the appeal to Hermes and the prisca theologia amplified in Florence and magnified about Europe? The problem with the Hermetic influence was that through its tolerance of an idea of magic, it insinuated itself deeply into spiritual questions—the church's claimed prime territory—whereas, one could always get the "theoretical" astronomers and mathematicians—the Catholics among them, at any rate—to admit theirs were but *theories,* little touching on the lives of the faithful and offering no spiritual instruction, carrying no absolute authority, with questionable degrees of certainty. In some respects, the choice was understood as one between Plato and Aristotle, and the firm logic of the scholastic, down-to-earth Aristotle took the lead, under the intellectual impetus of men such as Jesuit-educated Marin Mersenne (1588–1648) and priest, philosopher, and astronomer Pierre Gassendi (1592–1655)—men unafraid of looking into Galileo's discoveries while debating technical matters with relatively open minds, but protective of Catholic doctrine at the same time.

As it was, it was Calvinist-raised Isaac Casaubon (1559–1614), famed as one of the most brilliant men in Europe, a man who sought a middle way between Protestantism and Catholicism, who gave the most powerful ammunition to the anti-Hermetic cause. In the year of his death (1614) his philological analysis of the Hermetic "Pimander" appeared. He concluded that not only could it not have come from antediluvian times, nor even Mosaic times, but was, on linguistic and philosophical grounds, the work of men who dwelled in late antiquity. Once this hatchet was seen clearly—and such did not happen overnight—it would be impossible to justify the kind of reformation that filled a Giordano Bruno with such overoptimistic fervor.

It does seem odd, then, that in the same year Casaubon's work

Fig. 9.8. Isaac Casaubon
(1559–1614)

appeared, Andreae's *Fama* was, without his consent, first published in Kassel, Germany, and with it an extract from Italian satirist
Traiano Boccalini's *News from Parnassus* (Venice, 1612) titled "On the
Reformation of the Whole Wide World." Perhaps its accompanying the
*Fama*—which promised imminent revelation of a hidden fraternity holding all Nature's vital secrets while desirous of sharing them with the honest savants of Europe—was intended to alert readers of the latter to see
its contents, too, as a *literary play* rather than a historic revelation. We
know that this inference was barely recognized, and the *Fama* came to
many sympathetic scholars across Europe as a momentous revelation and
impetus to join the imaginary, or conceptual, community of wisdom.

Boccalini's "Reformation of the Whole Wide World," on the other
hand, told of a satirical debate called by Apollo on Mount Parnassus
as to the best method of righting the world's wrongs and perfecting its
governance and society. It was a satire on the Council of Trent, which
had been intended to shore up the Catholic Church's doctrine against
perceived threats of Protestantism by measures of reform. In Boccalini's
satire, the populus gather at the foot of Parnassus, anxious to hear the
conclusions arrived at from "on high" as to what reforms might be

anticipated. In the end, however, as none of the participants can bring themselves to accept the convictions of the other delegates, the waiting crowd is to be mollified by a final announcement of a lowering of the price of vegetables, and—yes, this stunning news succeeds in eliciting widespread rejoicing! Such is the sad nature of man and the disappointment of politics! A colder realism, a harsher cynicism had entered the soul of Europe in the seventeenth century, the true harbinger, one might say, of the "modern world" and its scientific revolution.

But new things have strange beginnings. In January 1824, English essayist Thomas de Quincey (1785–1859) argued in the *London Magazine* that "Accepted Freemasonry" received its formative impetus from the arrival in London, after 1614, of the message of the brethren of the Rose-Cross (Rosicrucians) as told in the *Fama* ("The Fame of the Fraternity"), and that the key figure in transforming London's trade guild of freemasons (architects and craftsmen in "freestone") into a society of mysteries was Dr. Robert Fludd (1574–1637), learned Paracelsian doctor and early defender of the Rosicrucians in print.

Fig. 9.9. Dr. Robert Fludd
(1574–1637)

Fludd fought a "paper war" with Marin Mersenne over prisca theologia themes first advocated in Florence by Ficino, Pico, and subsequently denied the authority of many of Fludd's cherished sources. Mersenne took particular exception to Fludd's interpretation of tradition, such as Fludd's identification of Christ with "Metatron" and the anima mundi (soul of the world).

And this little coda may give us pause before considering why it was that in the first-ever printed document emanating from London's "Accepted Free-Masons" (the *Constitutions,* 1723), the figure of Enoch receives a prominent place, along with his pillars, while those same *Constitutions* claim that it was *Masons* who transmitted through the ages the antediluvian arts vouchsafed to Adam, Seth, and his progeny. Freemasons treasured the wisdom of the lost pillars of Enoch!

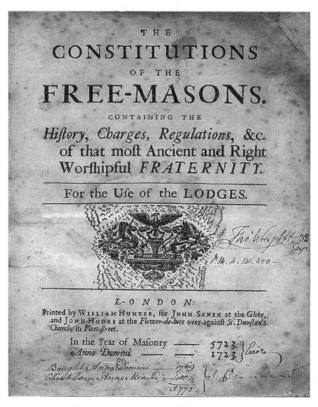

Fig. 9.10. *The Constitutions of the Free-Masons,* 1723

# TEN

# The Lost Pillars of Freemasonry

At the heart of Freemasonry lies a search for something lost. If we want to discover what that something might have been, and what caused it to be lost, I think a search for Enoch's pillars would make an interesting start. However, tracing Enoch's role in the formation of Masonic mythology is no easy task, for until the printing in London of the *Constitutions* of "Accepted Free-Masons" in 1723, such "Freemasonry" as did exist in the British Isles functioned chiefly by oral tradition in secret, with limited records kept.

It will help readers unfamiliar with Masonic history if they first understand that until relatively recently the word *freemason* meant a stonemason who worked in "freestone." Freestone was stone whose grain favored fine carving, like sandstone. The term "freestone mason" first appears in thirteenth-century records. Over time, "freestone mason" was shortened to "freemason." It didn't necessarily indicate participation in a lodge or mason's haven on a construction site. We don't know precisely when lodges of craftsmen appeared separately from work sites. Assemblies, chapters, or congregations of masons are recorded from the fourteenth century, with written records of meetings among Scottish masons extant from the late sixteenth century, though Scottish lodge members called themselves "masons," not "freemasons."

It appears that in the seventeenth and eighteenth centuries, the word *free* in "freemason" was sometimes taken to suggest civic status; that is, that a man had received the freedom of a particular municipality to practice business, being recognized as independent, no longer bound as apprentice to a master and willingly subject to and supportive of municipal regulations. Such a conflation may be implied by the seventeenth-century appearance of the hyphenated expression "Free-Mason" or "Free-mason," especially linked to meetings where gentlemen who were not practicing freemasons had joined a lodge.

By the late seventeenth century, there existed English lodges with members who were gentlemen and nonmasons, but with the presence of at least one member of the trade, as demanded by a London Masons Company regulation of 1663.

In 1773, Scottish Freemason James Bruce returned to Europe from Africa with the "lost" Ethiopic Book of Enoch—too late, it transpired, to affect a restoration of Enoch to Masonic significance then occurring in America, where Enoch featured in a "Rite of the Royal Secret" of 25 degrees. Promoted by Freemasons Estienne Morin and Deputy Henry Andrew Francken, some time between Francken's establishment of an "Ineffable Lodge of Perfection" in Albany, New York, in 1767, and Morin's death in 1771, "Morin's Rite" was the seed from which eventually sprang the Ancient & Accepted (Scottish) Rite whose 13th degree is known in Great Britain as "The Royal Arch of Enoch" and in the United States as the "Royal Arch of Solomon" or "Master of the Ninth Arch." Enoch appears in the degree legend as a visionary builder. The legend's elements derive from "Royal Arch" Masonic ritual, biblical accounts of Solomon's Temple, the Sethite and Cainite Enochs of Genesis, Josephus's Sethite pillars, and Samuel Lee's account of excavations on Jerusalem's Temple Mount in the reign of Julian the Apostate (*Orbis Miraculum,* 1659).

The idea of "restoring" Enoch to Masonic significance can be traced to an idea planted in the 1723 and 1738 *Constitutions.* There we learn that "the old masons" revered Enoch's pillars. However, Enoch's signifi-

Fig. 10.1. Reverend James Anderson

cance dimmed subsequently in Masonic life, and some brethren considered this a deficit. It is then rather curious that the only *written* evidence for *Masonic* interest in Enoch before the 25-degree rite derives from *after* the Grand Lodge of England's establishment in London between 1716 and 1718. Reverend James Anderson's Free-masons' *Constitutions* (1723) included a footnoted account of Enoch's pillars in line with the tradition first recorded in the *Palaea Historica* (late ninth–early tenth century) that Enoch inscribed all known science on marble and brick to survive the Flood. Enoch's role is not supported by *pre*-Grand Lodge *written* evidence, which rather indicates that late medieval Masons attributed civilization's partial re-constitution not to Enoch but to Hermes, discoverer of a pillar made by *Jabal* before the Flood, knowledge from which was, they believed, preserved via Pythagoras, Euclid, and a continuum of lodges.

So where did Anderson get his ideas about Enoch and Masonry?

## LATE MEDIEVAL EVIDENCE
## FOR ANTEDILUVIAN PILLARS

Pre–Grand Lodge English sources are catechetical, regulatory, and where "historical," craft-centered and sometimes confused. Orally transmitted "Old Charges" probably originated as rights-asserting texts compiled when masons' assemblies suffered rare state interference. While

Scottish evidence for lodge minutes, membership regulation, and craft history is copious from the end of the sixteenth century, Enoch's pillars are unknown as such in Scottish craft legends, Jabal being named as antediluvian pillar maker (see David Stevenson's *The Origins of Freemasonry*, 19–20).

The British Museum's Cooke MS (Additional MS 23, 198), named after Matthew Cooke, editor of the first printed version of 1861, is dated circa 1450, making it the second-oldest Masonic manuscript after the "Regius Poem" (ca. 1390–1430), wherein "noe" (Noah) is the poem's sole reference to an antediluvian patriarch.[1]

The Cooke MS declares that the building of "Enock" by Cain's master mason Jabal ("Jobell") marked the first practice of "the science of Geometry, and masonry." For Masonry and geometry's importance, the manuscript cites as authorities Herodotus, Bede, Honorius of Autun's *de Imagine Mundi*, the *Apocalypse of Pseudo-Methodius* (attributed to bishop and martyr Methodius), the *Etymologiae* of Isidore of Seville,

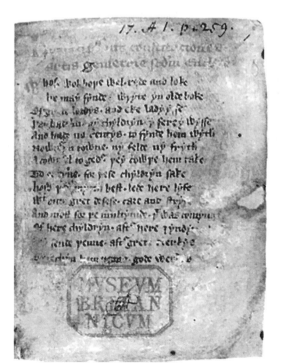

Fig. 10.2. The first page of the "Regius Poem"

and Ranulf Higden's *Polychronicon*. It is uncertain which version of Higden's *Polychronicon* was consulted for the Cooke MS, for there were three translations known to the fifteenth century: one by Lord Berkeley's chaplain John of Trevisa from 1387, a second by an anonymous writer (ca. 1432–1450), and another version of Trevisa's translation, with an eighth book, printed by William Caxton in 1480.

The Cooke MS states that "Jobell" (Jabal) shared brother Jubal and half brother Tubal Cain's knowledge that God intended to punish sin by vengeance of fire or water and that they entreated Jabal to make two stone pillars, one of marble (proof against burning), the other of "lacerus" (that "would not sink in water").* On the pillars, "some men say" the "seven sciences" (liberal arts) were inscribed, together with the rest of the brothers' craft knowledge, including music. Both pillars survived Noah's Flood, and "as the polychronicon seyth," one was found after "many years" by "putogoras" (Pythagoras) and the other by "hermes the philosopher" (Hermes Trismegistus), who expounded the science found on the pillar. While "Cam" (Ham) began the "tower of Babylon," his son "nembrothe" (Nimrod) is described as a "mighty man upon the erthe," a "stronge man like a Gyant and he was a grete kynge." The benign reference to being like a giant is redolent of the familiar "giants" born of the corrupted daughters of men in Genesis 6, otherwise a story discarded by the Old Charges.

James Anderson consulted the Cooke MS, but while drawing on the "Charges" section for his *Constitutions*, discounted most of the manuscript's patriarchal narrative, despite practically identical narratives about Jabal making the pillars and of Hermes's discovering one of them being attested in all pre-1723 copies of Charges containing patriarchal history—while all add to the Cooke MS the detail that Hermes (variously spelled) was son of Cush, son of Noah's son Shem (despite Genesis holding Cush to be Ham's son), with only three variants, as

---

*Unlike Josephus's pillars of brick and stone, where the latter would survive should water dissolve brick (*Antiquities of the Jews*, bk. 1, ch. 2). "Lacerus" should be Latin *lateres*, or "burnt brick or tiles."

indicated in the following list: Dowland's MS (transcript thought to represent a manuscript of ca. 1500); the Lansdowne MS (ca. 1560); the Grand Lodge No. 1 MS (1583); York MS, No. 1 (ca. 1600); Grand Lodge MS (ca. 1632); Sloane MS, No. 3848 (1646); Harleian MS, No. 1942 (ca. 1660; Cush's father is named as "Lucium" son of Shem); Lodge of Hope MS (ca. 1680; unique in following Genesis in naming Cush as Ham's son); the Antiquity MS (1686); the Alnwick MS (1701); and the Papworth MS (ca. 1714; where Cush is son of Noah).[2]

That Hermes is shown as Cush's son renders it problematic to assume late medieval and early modern Masonry habitually *identified* Hermes with Enoch, as Arab geographer Ibn Battūta (ca. 1304–ca. 1377) maintained, along with Persian Abu Ma'shar (died 886 CE), Harranian Sabian tradition, and Roger Bacon's thirteenth-century reflections on pseudo-Aristotle's *Secretum secretorum*.[3] Hermes's kinship with Cush perhaps preserves knowledge of the civilization of the Upper Nile. Noah's curse on Ham's son Canaan is removed by substitution of a Shemite Cush (and Hermes) who thereby receives Noah's blessing (Genesis 9:26). Early Masonic tradition sidesteps biblical curses on both Cain and Ham's progeny, suggesting a Masonic prejudice for universality among all Adam's progeny gifted with liberal arts, and a preference for science and art over doctrine, evinced in praise for the biblically condemned "Rebel" Nimrod's construction of Babylonia, with its idolizing of graven images.

Before considering why Anderson deviated from manuscript tradition in asserting "Enoch's pillars," and why Anderson avoided reference to "father of wise men" Hermes Trismegistus, we must establish whether the Cooke MS's cited authorities could have informed a Masonic understanding of Enoch.

While the Cooke MS is keen to cite Ranulf Higden's *Polychronicon*, there's no encouragement there for elevating Jabal, rather than Enoch, as patriarch of science. Drawing on Isidore of Seville and Josephus, the *Polychronicon* informs us that "Enoch founded letters, and wrote some books, so says Saint Judas in his epistle," and that this son of "Iareth" held "God almighty always his way, and was translated and brought in Paradise." Being descended through Seth and seventh from Adam, he was "best," unlike Lamech, seventh from Cain, who was "worst." Seth's sons, busying themselves with geometry and astronomy were good to the seventh generation, but then "God's sons" (Seth's lineage) took daughters of Cain's lineage and begat giants.[4] ("The children of God going to the daughters of men, which is to say, the sons of Seth going to the daughters of Cain.") We then learn that "men in that time" shared Adam's knowledge of God's punishment and made two great pillars containing what they had learned through great travail, one of marble against water and one of "brend [baked] tyle" against fire.

According to Harleian MS 2261 (an anonymous fifteenth-century translation), the pillars were still in Syria, as Latin translations of Josephus indicated. According to John Trevisa's translation, the learning was written in books and put inside the pillars, the one of "stoon" (stone) extant in Syria. A similar story occurs in the *Polychronicon* in chapter 9, where Nemproth's grandson Ninus—the name allegedly originating Nineveh—son of Belus,* having overcome Ham and King Zoroastes [*sic*] of Bactria, burns the books of the seven liberal arts Zoroastes had secreted in *seven* pillars of brass, and seven of tilestones (one pillar for each art, presumably), in hope of avoiding divine conflagrations.[†]

Hermes only turns up in the *Polychronicon* as "lord Mercurius" in chapter 14, son of Maia, daughter of Atlas (the Latin has *Atlantis,* or the island of Atlas), and "wise in many arts" (Trevisa has "cunning in many crafts") on which account he was called a god after his death (Trevisa has "as it were, a god").[5] The *Polychronicon* knows nothing of Hermes dis-

*Anderson has "Belus"—understood as "Lord"—as the familiar name Nimrod was called by his "friends."
†The "seven pillars" may derive from Proverbs 9:1: "Wisdom hath builded her house, she hath hewn out her seven pillars: She hath killed her beasts; she hath mingled her wine; she hath also furnished her table." The seven pillars themselves may refer to the planets, possibly related to the seven "days" (or perhaps originally angels) of creation in Genesis.

covering a pillar, nor does it add Isidore of Seville's note in *Etymologiae,* book 5, chapter 1 ("The originators of laws") that "Mercury (that is Hermes) Trismegistus first gave laws to the Egyptians."[6]

It is interesting to compare these accounts of Hermes by Isidore (560–636) and Ranulf Higden (ca. 1280–1364) with those used by Ficino in his "Argumentum" for Lorenzo de' Medici that opened his translation of the "Pimander." Ficino's account draws on Cicero's *De natura deorum,* which refers to *five* Mercuries, the fifth of whom (according to Ovid's *Metamorphoses*) on Jupiter's orders killed Argus Panoptes (a mythological giant with one hundred eyes and a favorite of the goddess Hera) before fleeing to Egypt, where he "gave the Egyptians their laws and letters," taking the name Theuth or Thoth. Saint Augustine condemned the occult nature of Hermes's writings (quoting *Asclepius* 23, 24, 37) to condemn the controversial "idol-making" passage where spirit is infused into statues (*De Civitate Dei,* bk. 8, xxiii–xxvi). Nevertheless, Augustine did consider Hermes older than the Greeks (*De Civitate Dei,* bk. 18, xxix) with some good points: "For as for morality, it stirred not in Egypt until Trismegistus's time, which was indeed long before the sages and philosophers of Greece, but after Abraham, Isaac, Jacob, Joseph, yea and Moses also; for at the time when Moses was born, Atlas, Prometheus's brother, a great astronomer, living, and he was grandfather by the mother's side to the elder Mercury, who begat the father of this Trismegistus."

Augustine confirmed that Hermes had known the belief of one God and his Son, which preceded Plato. Ficino's *Argumentum* slightly garbled Augustine's account to give the best spin theologically possible for Hermes, doubtless to please patron Cosimo de' Medici. Ficino wrote in 1463:

He [Hermes] is called the first author of theology: he was succeeded by Orpheus, who came second among ancient theologians: Aglaophemus, who had been initiated into the ancient teaching of Orpheus, was succeeded in theology by Pythagoras, whose disciple was Philolaus, the teacher of our Divine Plato. Hence there is one ancient theology [prisca theologia] . . . taking its origin in Mercurius and culminating in the Divine Plato.

Given the variant traditions, it is not surprising that the earliest versions of Masons' Charges add their own blend, on account of their own interest, which interest was *not* spiritual philosophy.

We may conclude that the Cooke MS displays scant respect for cited authorities. Two facts may be adduced from this. First, if "old Masons" ever were—as Anderson would maintain in his *Constitutions* of 1738—emphatic in revering Enoch's pillars, such reverence did not derive from the Old Charges alone, if at all. Second, the Old Charges give more attention to Josephus's antediluvian pillars than to the biblical pillars of Solomon's Temple (Jachin and Boaz), which would dominate Masonic pillar symbolism after London's Grand Lodge extended itself throughout England.

Why did Anderson discard the Old Charges pillar narrative? First, he may have consulted the *Polychronicon* and suspected its authority had been abused in the Old Charges. Second, wishing to demonstrate his own academic authority, Anderson's familiarity with Josephus's narrative would have alerted him to the contradiction between Josephus's Sethite pillars and the Cainite lineage supported by the Old Charges. The theologian in Anderson favored Josephus as the authority.

Third, while the Old Charges' crediting Hermes for discovering one of the pillars would have lent authority to their account in the fifteenth and sixteenth centuries, such authority was now diminished. French Huguenot scholar Isaac Casaubon's *De rebus sacris et ecclesiasticis exercitationes* XVI (1614) had redated the *Corpus Hermeticum* on philological grounds to the third or fourth century CE, undermining Hermes Trismegistus's prisca theologia status. Concerned to modernize Masonic history on rational grounds, Anderson probably favored the substance of Casaubon's critique. If Anderson was aware of the medieval identification of Hermes with Enoch, then he may have considered that his elevating Enoch over Jabal accorded Enoch sufficient recognition. Suspicion of Free-masons' histories was further supported by Oxford professor of "chymistry," Dr. Robert Plot's *Natural History of Staffordshire* (1686), which included the "Free-masons'" historical scheme from a manuscript scroll of Charges, perusal of which led Plot to conclude that nothing could be found more historically "false and incoherent."*

It is thus ironic that the most fulsome written linkage of Enoch's name to Freemasonry appears in Anderson's *Constitutions* (1723, 1738); ironic because controversial, outspoken Anderson—former student of the Protestant Marischal College, Aberdeen—was central to the radically novel phase of craft development initiated by London's Grand Lodge after 1716. Judging by the *Constitutions,* the Grand Lodge was critical of preexisting Masonry and disposed to innovate, not least by operating altogether independently of the freemasons' trade, advancing a new social ideal founded on what it considered enlightened principles suitable for a new Hanoverian and Newtonian age, dominated politically by Whigs.

---

*The passages that most concerned Plot doubtless included (a) the story of one "Nymus Grecus" being at the construction of Solomon's Temple before bringing Masonry to Charles Martel (ruled Francia 718–741 CE) and (b) attributing Masonry in England to Saint Alban and "St Amphibal" with regulations confirmed subsequently by the Anglo-Saxon king Athelstan (ruled 924–939 CE) and "son Edwyn" (Athelstan had a brother, not a son, called Edwyn). The main cause of "incoherence" has been satisfactorily solved by Dr. Stanley Aston in AQC (Transactions of the Lodge Quatuor Coronati 2076, premier research Lodge of the United Grand Lodge of England) 99, 102–3, and in AQC vol. 103 (1990), and by Geoffrey Markham (AQC 98, 66 ff.). See Cryer, *York Mysteries Revealed,* 15, 28 ff. References to "Nymus Grecus" follow a mistranslation of "Carmen XXVI" by Alcuin (or "Albinus," born ca. 732–804), co-architect of York's new minster, conscious promoter, through enhancing York Minster's library, of the seven liberal arts, and the man responsible for establishing the liberal arts at Aachen as trusted servant and teacher of Emperor Charlemagne, advising him on Aachen's cathedral, following the pattern of wise Solomon. Numerous versions of Old Charges apparently confuse Charlemagne with Solomon and Charles Martell (his grandfather), and "Carolus Secundus," while Alcuin's name "Albinus" was probably confused, deliberately or accidentally, with Alban, producing the incoherent historical sequences that so annoyed Dr. Plot.

Masonic enlightenment was considered ideally as originating in Adam's heart, created by the universe's "Great Architect" whose knowledge of liberal arts was passed subsequently through lodges of practical geometers, albeit frequently interrupted by calamities, such as Gothic invasions and the collapse of the Roman Empire and its "Augustan Stile," now recovered, Anderson asserted, from Gothick "Impropriety" (the 1723 *Constitutions,* 38–39) and revealed by enlightened science inspired by classicism.

Having degraded the glories of medieval masons, Anderson presented the "Grand Lodge" as the next "revival" of authentic Masonry after that of "Mason King" James I, though still rooted in antediluvian paradise. Page 2 of the 1723 *Constitutions* elevates Cain's son Enoch as inheritor of Adam's primal knowledge of geometry (synonymous with "Masonry"), his name "Enoch" given to the world's first city, interpreted as "Consecrated" or "Dedicated." This Enoch is all but conflated in significance with his Sethite namesake.

> Nor can we suppose that SETH was less instructed, who being the Prince of the other Half of Mankind, and also the prime Cultivator of Astronomy, would take equal Care to teach Geometry and Masonry to his Offspring, who had also the mighty Advantage of Adam's living among them.*

A footnote on page 3 expands on the virtues of Sethite lineage.

> For by some Vestiges of Antiquity we find one of 'em, godly ENOCH, (who dy'd not, but was translated alive to Heaven) prophecying of the final Conflagration at the Day of Judgment (as Saint Jude tells us) and likewise of the General Deluge for the Punishment of the World Upon which he erected his two large Pillars, (tho' some ascribe them to Seth) the one of Stone, and the other of Brick,

---

*Reverend James Anderson, *The Constitutions of the Free-Masons,* 2.

whereon were engraven the Liberal Sciences, &c. And that the Stone Pillar remain'd in Syria until the Days of Vespasian the Emperor.

The direct linkage of the two biblical Enochs into one Masonic lesson is noticeable in the words of the "Master's Song" appended to the same 1723 *Constitutions*.

> CAIN a City fair and strong
> First built, and call'd it Consecrate,
> From ENOCH'S Name, his eldest Son,
> Which all his Race did imitate:
> But godly ENOCH, of Seth's loins,
> Two Columns rais'd with mighty Skill:
> And all his Family enjoins
> True Colonading to fulfill.*

Anderson's "columns" story derives in part of course from Josephus's account of Sethite pillars. In the second, revised book of *Constitutions* (1738, 4), Anderson perhaps attempts to reconcile discrepancies with an interesting admission.

> ADAM was succeeded in the Grand Direction of the Craft by SETH, ENOSH, KAINAN, MAHALALEEL and JARED, whose Son, Godly ENOCH died not, but was translated alive, Soul and Body, into Heaven, aged 365 Years. A.M. ["Year of Masonry"] 987. He was expert and bright both in the Science and the Art, and being a Prophet, He foretold the Destruction of the Earth for Sin, first by Water, and afterwards by Fire: therefore ENOCH erected Two large PILLARS,* the one of Stone and the other of Brick, whereon he engraved the Abridgement of the Arts and Sciences, particularly Geometry and Masonry.

---

*Anderson, *Constitutions*, 75, v. 2.

Anderson's asterisk refers to an important side note:

*Some call them SETH'S Pillars, but the old Masons always call'd them ENOCH's Pillars, and firmly believ'd this Tradition: nay Josephus (Lib i, cap. II) affirms the Stone-Pillar still remain'd in Syria to his Time.

Bearing in mind that Anderson's caveat concerning "the old Masons" may reflect tremors between the new "Grand Lodge" regime and pre-existing lodges, we must ask why Anderson allows *Enoch* mastery of the pillars *at all,* having already discounted the "Old Charges" reservation of the role for *Jabal,* son of Adah and Lamech, at variance with Josephus's ascription of the pillars to Seth's, not Enoch son of Cain's, lineage. Whether the "old Masons" who—according to Anderson—"always" referred to "Enoch's Pillars," intended Cain's son, or Seth's descendant (or a conflation of both) remains an open question. Certainly, Anderson identifies the pillar-building Enoch with the prophet of the world's judgment (Jude 14), raised to heaven directly while alive (Genesis 5:24).

It is possible that Anderson drew not on English "Free-mason" traditions regarding Enoch but on *Scottish* oral tradition. Aspects of Scottish and English Masons' traditions were at this time distinct. According to David Stevenson, Anderson's father, James, was a leading member of the Lodge of Aberdeen, serving as master in the 1690s and as "keymaster" in 1719, and his son may have been initiated there, too, so Anderson might have got his idea of "old Masons" and "Enoch's pillars" primarily from Scotland.[7] *Hermes's* role as pillar finder and transmitter is, however, explicit in the Old Charges, and since Hermes had long been identified with Enoch, that fact might arguably have stimulated a tradition concerning Enoch's pillars.

As for Anderson's competing ascription "Seth's Pillars," he could cite "Mason King" James VI of Scotland's *His Maiesties Poeticall Exercises at vacant houres* (1591): translations from Guillaume de Salluste Du Bartas's two epic poems *Semaines* ("Weeks") dealing with the

Fig. 10.3. *Du Bartas,* 1641 edition

creation of the world and subsequent biblical history. Joshua Sylvester undertook the English translation, and *Du Bartas his deuine weekes and workes translated and dedicated to the Kings most excellent Maiestie by Iosuah Syluester* was printed in London by Humfrey Lownes in 1613, soon becoming a literary staple.

A chapter headed "The Columnes," from the "Second Week," describes "Seth's Pillars." Discovered by Heber, Shem's great-grandson, Heber instructs son Phalec how to use them. Opening a jasper-and-marble pillar, statues of "four Lovely Dames" (the liberal science *quadrivium* of arithmetic, astronomy, music, and geometry) are revealed. "Old Seth" is described as "Adam's scholar" who taught his children the nature of the stars and their courses, and "by Tradition Cabalistick" his progeny knew God would twice bring this world "to nought, By Flood and Flame" (p. 360). They who called Seth their "Grand-sire" (forefather) thus built the stately pillars with a "hundred learned Mysteries therein." This designation could easily accommodate Enoch, most distinguished of Seth's progeny.

Within the marble spire Heber and Phalec marvel at "a pure Lamp burning with immortal light."*

The light reveals in statuesque allegories principles of Astronomy, Music, Arithmetic, and Geometry.

> Heer's nothing here, but Rules, Squires, Compasses,
> Waights, Measures, Plummets, Figures, Balances.
> Lo, where the Workman with a steddy hand
> Ingeniously a level Line hath drawn,
> War-like Triangles, building-fit Quadrangles,
> And hundred kindes of Forms of Manie-Angles.
>
>         . . .
>
> The compleat Circle; from whose every-place
> The Centre stands an equi-distant space.
> See heer the Solids, Cubes, Cylinders, Cones,
> Pyramides, Prismas, Dodecahedrons:
> And there the Sphear, which (Worlds Type) comprehends
> In't-selfit-self; having nor midst nor ends:
> Arts excellence, praise of his peers, a wonder.[8]

*Compare with the ever-burning lamp found in the tomb of Father C.R.C. in the *Fama Fraternitatis* (in the 1614 printing from Kassel, Germany, and in MS form as early as 1610).

Heber then prophesies to Phalec all of the ways in future times that these arts inscribed by "learned Elders" will transform and bring to order, harmony, symmetry, and beauty the whole world, along with the heavens, their "Starrie Arches of the stately Temple" depicted on a sphere (p. 359). Du Bartas's eulogy of the liberal arts reads like a golden tribute to that "Masonry" envisaged by Anderson: craft and learning combined in an apotheosis of divine creativity, even perhaps suggesting the furniture of a "lodge," with its pillars and spheres and workman's tools linking the divine spirit to the creation, on the Hermetic principle "as above, so below".

> Yea, even our Crowns, Darts, Lances, Skeyns, and Scales
> Are all but Copies of Heav'ns Principals;
> And sacred patterns, which to serve all Ages,
> Th'Almighty printed on Heav'ns ample stages.[9]

Du Bartas's French contemporaries, such as Guillaume Postel (1510–1581), were familiar with Enoch's "Cabalistick" links. Postel's *De Etruriae regionis* (Florence, 1551) insisted the Book of Enoch's prophecies were canonical in Ethiopia, and having collected cited fragments of text, Postel asserted in *De Originibus* (Basel, 1553) that an Ethiopian priest had confided to him the lost book's meaning. Postel's Enoch research inspired mathematician John Dee (1527–1608). In the early 1580s, Dee prayed that God show *him* what God had shown in heaven to Enoch. The prayer appears in Méric Casaubon's 1659 edited collection of Dee's angelical conferences, *A True & Faithful Relation of What Passed for Many Years between Dr. John Dee and Some Spirits* (London, 231): "I have often read in thy [God's] books & records, how Enoch injoyed thy favour and conversation; with Moses thou was familiar; And also that to Abraham, Isaack and Jacob, Joshua, Gideon, Esdras, Daniel, Tobias & sundry others thy good angels were sent by thy disposition, to Instruct them." This point is also made in Dee's famous "Mathematicall Preface" to Henry Billingsley's translation of Euclid's *Elements,* published in 1570. Since man is made in the image and similitude of God, he may potentially enjoy intercourse with spirits and angels. When Dee was instructed, through the mediumship of scryer Edward Kelley, to obtain a language to communicate with angels, that language came to be called (but not by Dee) "Enochian," presuming Enoch's familiarity with the language of heaven.

By Anderson's time, so much scholarly work had been expended on Enoch's lost and fragmentary prophecies that it had become acceptable in literary circles to interchange ascription of the pillars to Enoch or Seth. Thus Dr. Thomas Browne's 1642 bestseller, *Religio Medici* ("A Doctor's Religion"), dealing judiciously with obscure ancient writings the doctor might wish to preserve, opines: "I would not omit a copy of Enoch's pillars, had they many nearer authors than Josephus, or did not relish too much of the fable"; that is, the account sounded legendary and historically unreliable. A footnote adds: "For this, the story is, that Enoch, or his father Seth, having been informed by Adam" of the coming conflagration, decides to preserve the sciences with two pillars.*

So, while Anderson had precedence to accept the term "Enoch's pillars," he was careful not to ascribe extraordinary value or meaning to them. That they meant something to "the old Masons" did not dispose him to explore why. It may be the case that Enoch represented a problematic figure for the new Grand Lodge, because the antediluvian pillar legend could confuse attempts by the new order to emphasize the pillars Jachin and Boaz at Solomon's Temple: features that would eventually become essential lodge furniture for Freemasons worldwide. It is notable in this regard that according to Masonic historian Neville Barker Cryer, a "Grand Lodge of All England" based at York existed "from or before 1725 to 1744 and from 1761 to 1792."[10] After 1720, London's Grand Lodge began offering charters to new lodges in areas where York's

---

*Sir Thomas Browne's Works*, vol. 2, *Including His Life and Correspondence: Religio Medici-Pseudodoxia Epidemica Part One*, ed. Simon Wilkin (London: William Pickering, 1835), 35. Sir Thomas Browne (1605–1682) also knew John Dee's son Arthur in Norwich. Browne was a correspondent of accepted Free-mason (1646) and Dee-enthusiast Elias Ashmole (1617–1692).

Grand Lodge of All England had an interest. This move caused ructions. Cryer suggests one point at issue may have been York Masons' attachment to "antediluvian Masonry." Was something missing in the new regime's conception of "Free and Accepted Masonry"? Could it have been knowledge preserved by Noah, lost to the flooded world of wicked humanity?

## ANTEDILUVIAN MASONRY

Anderson's 1723 *Constitutions* does offer antediluvian credentials for the craft: "NOAH and his three Sons, JAPHET, SHEM, and HAM, all Masons true, brought with them over the Flood the Traditions and Arts of the Ante-diluvians, and amply communicated them to their growing Offspring" (*Constitutions,* 3). While Anderson's new edition of 1738 mentions that "the old Masons" firmly believed in Enoch's pillars, he also asserts that postdiluvian preservers of the Arts and Sciences enjoyed a distinct identity. When Noah and sons "journeyed from the east [the Plains of Mount Ararat, where the ark rested] toward the west, they found a Plain in the Land of SHINAR and dwelt there together, as NOACHIDAE,* or Sons of Noah."

This "Noachida" identity was supported by additions to the "First Charge" (printed in the second edition of the 1738 printing) that "a Mason is oblig'd by his Tenure, to obey the Moral Law as a true Noachida," and later in that Charge, "For they all agree in the 3 great Articles of Noah, enough to preserve the cement of the Lodge."[11]

These additions may reflect an effort on London's part to ameliorate sore points of difference with York or other resisters, without giving anything substantial away. However, the 1738 *Constitutions* are also notable for excising celebration of the two Enochs from the *Master's Song* (p. 200). Anderson's perhaps disingenuous explanation for cutting the first two verses was because it was now deemed "too long." The result,

---

*The asterisked side note tells us: "*The first Name of Masons, according to some old Traditions" (1738 *Constitutions,* 4).

however, is immediate elevation to centrality of Solomon and "master mason" "Hiram Abif," now the central mythic figure of the craft's "3rd degree" (known since 1725). It was not, however, in the Grand Lodge's interest to deter persons disposed to link "Free and Accepted Masonry" with a supposed union of science and religion in antediluvian antiquity, for this supposition attracted learned men to the craft. Such a one was antiquarian William Stukeley (1687–1765), who joined a lodge in London in 1721 (pre-*Constitutions*). Indeed, it was while researching *William Stukeley: Science, Religion and Archaeology in Eighteenth-Century England* (2002) that David Boyd Haycock discovered a rare manuscript by Stukeley in the Wellcome Institute: *Palaeographia Sacra, or Discourses on Monuments of Antiquity that relate to sacred History Number 11 A Dissertation on the Mysterys of the Antients in an explication of that famous piece of antiquity, the tables of Isis* (1735). It reveals in his own hand Stukeley's holding to the prisca theologia theory: an uncorrupted revelation before Moses, which Moses, then Christ, tried to reinstitute. There is a distinctly Enochic ring to this. According to Haycock: "The function of this theory was to clear away constantly the debris of ignorance—brought about by mankind's perpetual tendency to corruption—by holding forth a vision of the original and true."[*]

Stukeley sought an original, patriarchal religion linked in Newton and follower Dr. Desaguliers' minds with mathematics. Thus, Stukeley believed Druids constructed Stonehenge as a branch of Masonry: patriarchal science brought from the East. In an account of his life published in 1753, Stukeley explained how his curiosity led to initiation into the "Mysterys of Masonry, suspecting it to be the remains of the mysterys of the antients," which gave its adherents a more "sublime" conception of religion[†]

---

[*]Haycock, "William Stukeley: In Search of Ancient Mysteries" in *Freemasonry Today,* issue 6 (1999), 22; see also Churton, *Freemasonry: The Reality,* 328–30.
[†]Churton, *Freemasonry,* 327. For more on Stukeley, see page 230. As events transpired, London's Grand Lodge lost this distinguished member. Stukeley organized his own lodge at Grantham, Lincolnshire.

A few years later, York's foremost promoter of Masonic independence, Jacobite sympathizer Francis Drake, addressed York's Grand Lodge of All Englishmen (*Totius Angliae*) at the Merchants' Hall in the city on Saint John's Day, December 27, 1726. Two London printers would print the address in London in 1734.[12] Drake urged brethren to make proper acquisition of the Arts and Sciences befitting the craft, as had been observed in London with lectures at meetings. Amicably congratulating Anderson on his new history, Drake insisted that a Mason should value knowledge and understanding of Noah, Nimrod, Moses, Babylon, Josiah, and Zerubbabel, as well as Solomon.

> THUS far our Author [Anderson]; and I am persuaded you have not thought me tedious in giving you so much of the Works of that Great Man instead of my own. From what he has said, the great Antiquity of the Art of Building or Masonry may be easily deduc'd. For without running up to Seth's Pillars or the Tower of Babel for Proofs, the Temple of Belus alone, or the Walls of Babilon, of both which the learned Dr. Predeaux has given ample Accounts, which were built 4000 Years ago, and above 1000 before the Building of Solomon's Temple, are sufficient Testimonies, or at least give great Reason to conjecture, that three Parts in four of the whole Earth might then be divided into E-P-F-C & M-M [Entered Apprentice; Fellow Craft, and Master Mason].[13]

An "advertisement" found in Grand Lodge archives, detached from its source and bearing the same date as Drake's speech (1726), appeared (presumably in London) to announce an almost certainly fictitious meeting of "Antediluvian Masonry" to be held at the Ship Tavern, Bishopsgate Street, on the Feast of John the Baptist. A satirical swipe at the idea of Masons being made in the "antediluvian manner" it at least evinces the idea's currency, arguably treated as a pretentious novelty: "several lectures on Ancient Masonry, particularly on the signification of the letter G, and how and after what Manner the Antediluvian

Masons form'd their Lodges, showing what innovations have lately been introduced by the Doctor [John Theophilus Desaguliers, Fellow of the Royal Society (1683–1744); grand master 1719] and some other of the Moderns. . . . There will likewise be a Lecture . . . shewing that the two Pillars of the Porch were not cast in the Vale of Jehosophat but elsewhere; and that neither the Honorary, Appolonian, or Free and Accepted masons know anything of the matter; with the whole history of the Widow's son [Hiram Abif?] killed by the Blow of a Beetle."[14]

While such ructions may help to account for subsequent developments of a Noachite theme in an emerging Masonic Royal Ark Mariner degree in the late eighteenth and nineteenth centuries,[15] they tell us little of what Enoch meant to the genesis of a purely symbolic Freemasonry or that which preceded it, other than, arguably, linking the Flood to the Sethite knowledge pillar constructed to survive it. While the antediluvian Masonry issue is suggestive, no evidence survives to link it definitively to "the old Masons'" veneration for Enoch's pillars.

Nevertheless, frustrated brethren in due course suspected something *was* missing from the new regime's conception of "Free and Accepted Masonry." Evidence supporting the existence of "another" privileged form of symbolic Masonry indicates at least a hypothetical Enochic content: content based on III Enoch's identification of the archangel Metatron with Enoch. Pursuing this inquiry will lead us to the threshold of a lost Freemasonry.

# ELEVEN

# Esoteric Masonry and the Mystery of the "Acception"

Shortly after Anderson gained approval for his first draft of the 1723 *Constitutions,* translator and Royal Society fellow, Robert Samber ("Philalethes Junior," 1682–1745) attended a feast to celebrate Tory Jacobite the Duke of Wharton's grand mastership, an appointment embarrassing to the Grand Lodge's ruling clique of anti-Jacobite Whigs. Reported as one dismayed by proceedings, Samber asked how demolishing a mountain of venison pastry could contribute to building the "spiritual house": plainly referring to Saint Paul's analogy of the new spiritual temple surpassing the old (2 Corinthians 5:1), and an analogy used by Dr. Robert Fludd in his second published defense of the Rose-Cross Brotherhood (1617).[1]

Samber's esoteric conception of Masonry is revealed in a prefatory letter to his translation of De Longeville Harcouet's *Long Livers* (which includes a recipe for the "Universal Medicine" by the alchemist Arnold of Villanova, 1722). Samber's epistle addresses the Grand Master, Masters, Wardens, and Brethren of Freemasons of Britain and Ireland as "a chosen Generation, a royal Priesthood," suggesting the lineage of Seth (Seth appears on page xxxv, and is compared to "FALSE BROTHER" Cain on page xviii), and especially those who have passed through "the veil" whose "greater Light" reveals the "celestial cube" of the celestial Jerusalem (page v) as the source of harmony. For Samber,

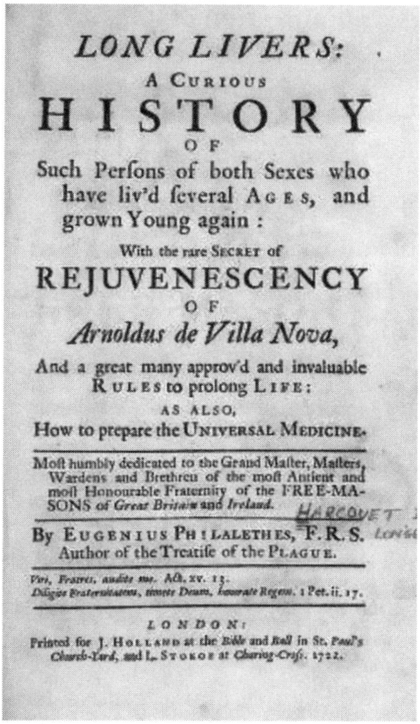

**LONG LIVERS:**
A CURIOUS
# HISTORY
OF
Such Perfons of both Sexes who
have liv'd feveral AGES, and
grown Young again :
With the rare SECRET of
## REJUVENESCENCY
OF
*Arnoldus de Villa Nova,*
And a great many approv'd and invaluable
RULES to prolong LIFE :
AS ALSO,
How to prepare the UNIVERSAL MEDICINE.

Moft humbly dedicated to the Grand Mafter, Mafters,
Wardens and Brethren of the moft Antient and
moft Honourable Fraternity of the FREE-MA-
SONS of *Great Britain* and *Ireland.*

By EUGENIUS PHILALETHES, F.R.S.
Author of the Treatife of the PLAGUE.

*Viri, Fratres, audite me. Act. xv. 13.*
*Diligite Fraternitatem, timete Deum, honorate Regem. 1 Pet. ii. 17.*

LONDON:
Printed for J. HOLLAND at the *Bible* and *Ball* in St. *Paul's*
*Church-Yard,* and L. STOKOE at *Charing-Cross.* 1722.

Fig. 11.1. Samber's
*Long Livers*

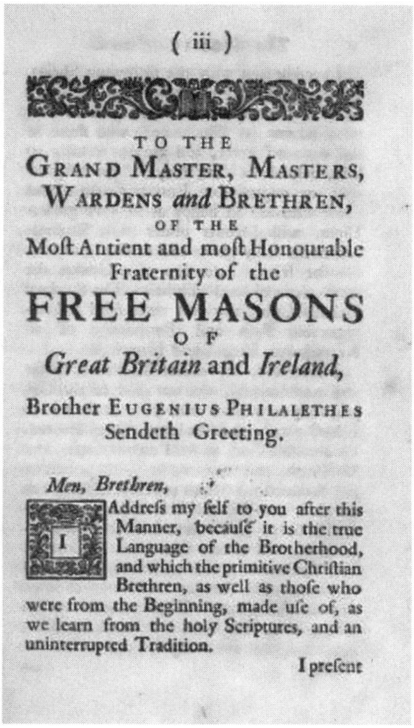

---

( iii )

TO THE
GRAND MASTER, MASTERS,
WARDENS *and* BRETHREN,
OF THE
Moft Antient and moft Honourable
Fraternity of the
# FREE MASONS
OF
*Great Britain* and *Ireland,*

Brother EUGENIUS PHILALETHES
Sendeth Greeting.

*Men, Brethren,*

 Addrefs my felf to you after this
Manner, becaufe it is the true
Language of the Brotherhood,
and which the primitive Chriftian
Brethren, as well as thofe who
were from the Beginning, made ufe of, as
we learn from the holy Scriptures, and an
uninterrupted Tradition.

I prefent

Fig. 11.2. Symbolic Freemasonry
according to Robert Samber;
*Long Livers*

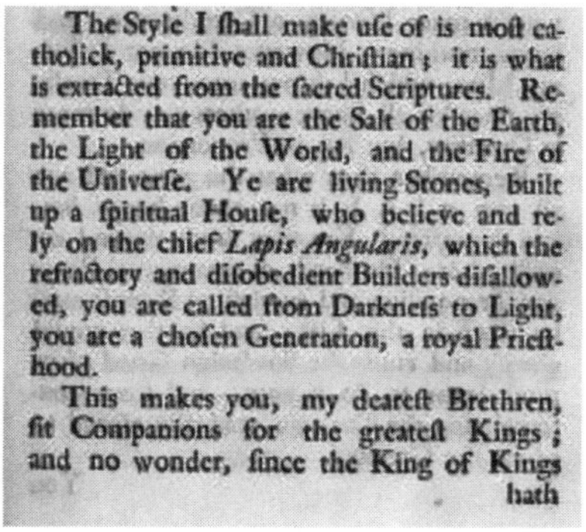

The Style I fhall make ufe of is moft ca-
tholick, primitive and Chriftian ; it is what
is extracted from the facred Scriptures. Remember that you are the Salt of the Earth,
the Light of the World, and the Fire of
the Univerfe. Ye are living Stones, built
up a fpiritual Houfe, who believe and re-
ly on the chief *Lapis Angularis,* which the
refractory and difobedient Builders difallow-
ed, you are called from Darknefs to Light,
you are a chofen Generation, a royal Prieft-
hood.

This makes you, my deareft Brethren,
fit Companions for the greateft Kings ;
and no wonder, fince the King of Kings
hath

Masonry's "uninterrupted Tradition" makes it meaningful that "ye are living stones, built up a Spiritual House," "exiled Children," "the Fire of the Universe," "Sons of Science . . . who are illuminated with the sublimest Mysteries and profoundest Secrets of MASONRY" (page li). Those secrets are clearly indicated as alchemical. The seeds of everlasting repose must be sown in this life, so that Man may ascend, first by contemplating the creature, then rising to his creator (page vi). Some are not illuminated; Samber addresses "a higher class who are but few."

In Masonic historian R. F. Gould's preface to an 1891 reprint of *Long Livers,*[2] he observed that Samber's letter suggested possible relations between Masonry and Rosicrucianism during and after the 1720s; perhaps, Gould suggested, some high-ranking Masons were joined to another "Hermetic Society"—Samber's terminology being inconsistent with stonemasons' lodges. Arguably, Gould entertained a common but mistaken conception of the seventeenth-century craft. The idea of so-called speculative or symbolic Masonry being fruit of Rosicrucian impulse was notably propounded in 1824 by Thomas de Quincey, by whose time a Masonic-style neo-Rosicrucianism had flourished and faded on the continent.*

The ground for linking Enochic themes with magic and Hermetic philosophy and alchemical practice had been laid the century before the "Rosicrucian Manifestos" appeared. According to Professor Gabriele Boccaccini: "The idea that magic and alchemy could provide a shortcut continued to fascinate European intellectual circles." In his *Introductio in divinam Chemiae artem* (Basel: Perna, 1572), Petrus Bonus repeated Roger Bacon's remarks that Enoch was the great Hermogenes [Hermes]."[3] Enoch's status as a patriarch of Rose-Cross ideology is evident from the *Fama Fraternitatis* itself, with a conclusion strongly reminiscent of the sphere theme in du Bartas's "The Columnes" (1584), printed in English in 1613—a year before the printed *Fama* appeared in Germany.

---

*The *London Magazine* (January 1824) published de Quincey's assessment of German historian J. G. Buhle's view that this transformation occurred between 1630 and 1640, the work of Dr. Robert Fludd (1574–1637), outspoken defender of the R. C. Brotherhood.

Our Philosophia is nothing new but is the same which Adam received after his fall and which Moses and Solomon applied. . . . Thus it should not be said: "This is true according to philosophy but false according to theology," for everything which Plato, Aristotle, Pythagoras and others recognized as true, and which was decisive for Enoch, Abraham, Moses and Solomon and which above all is consistent with that wonderful book the Bible, comes together, forming a sphere or ball in which all the parts are equidistant from the centre.[4]

Britain in the 1650s saw a vigorous network of writers familiar with Fludd and the figure of Enoch as perfected man, with "theomagical" emphases accommodating of Rose-Cross ideology. Early in the next century, Samber was himself a devoted reader of one of these writers, Thomas Vaughan ("Eugenius Philalethes," 1621–1666), who brought an English translation of the *Fama* to its first English printing in 1652.

Only one of Britain's Hermetic network is definitely known as a Free-mason, however: Elias Ashmole (1617–1692), "made a Free-mason" at Warrington in 1646. Ashmole's 1650s' circle included Dr. Robert Childe (ca. 1612–1654); physician Nathaniel Henshaw; Henshaw's brother Thomas, a lawyer; alchemist Thomas Vaughan (Thomas Henshaw's friend); and Dr. Levin Flood (Robert Fludd's nephew and inheritor of his uncle's library). Attempting to form both an ideal Christian community on the lines of likely *Fama* author J. V. Andreae, and a chemical club, these men revived sixteenth-century Hermetic enthusiasms, to which the persistent rumor of a secret Rose-Cross fraternity acted as leaven.*

---

*Dr. Levin (Livinius) Fludd's father was Thomas Fludd. Thomas Fludd's brother was Dr. Robert Fludd (1574–1637). Levin Fludd studied medicine at Leiden in 1634, graduating M.D. at Padua in 1639; he died in 1678. Robert Childe studied medicine at Leiden in 1635, graduating M.D. at Padua in 1638; afterward a member of the Royal College of Physicians, London (*Athenæ Oxonienses an Exact History of All the Writers and Bishops,* vol. 1, 819 (*Fasti Oxonienses*), 1691; see also Daniela Prögler, *English Students at Leiden University, 1575–1650: Advancing Your Abilities and Bettering Your Understanding of the World and State Affairs* (Routledge, 2013), 194. Dr. Childe introduced Ashmole to Levin Fludd at Fludd's home at Maidstone in 1651.

Fig. 11.3. Elias Ashmole (1617–1692)
by Cornelis de Neve

While Levin Fludd and Robert Childe studied medicine in Padua in 1638, King's Master Mason Nicholas Stone's son went to Rome to study the Italian masters' sculpture and architecture, sending home busts and architectural books via the English factory at Livorno. That same year, the Renter Warden's accounts for the London Company of "freemasons" reveal that Nicholas Stone *senior* attended a special event, a mere note of which has survived.

P[aid]d w[hi]ch the accompt [accountant] layd out w[hi]ch was more than I have received of them w[hi]ch were taken into the Accepcon [Acception] whereof xs [10 shillings] is to be paid by Mr Nicholas Stone, Mr Edmund Kinsman, Mr John Smith, Mr William Millis, Mr John Colles.[5]

All we can say for certain is that this "Acception" event was held under the auspices of the London Company of Freemasons (renamed from 1677 the London Company of Masons) with those "taken into the Accepcon" all members of that company. While the Grand Lodge of England for a long time held (and its successors generally hold) that the word *accepted* differentiated "operative" (craftsmen) from "speculative" masons (justifying the Grand Lodge's existence), this distinction is misleading if applied to seventeenth-century London Masonry. Anderson, for example, seems only to have understood the term *accepted* as one equivalent to the term *admitted* used of nonmasons (like himself) joining lodges of stonemasons in Scotland.

Sculptor of one of the century's greatest artworks (effigy of John Donne, Saint Paul's Cathedral), Nicholas Stone had been company master four years earlier, while Edward Kinsman succeeded him in 1635. John Colles (or Collis) would be company master in 1648. Whatever was involved in being "taken into the Accepcon," it was not to acquire practical knowledge of architecture! Important evidence regarding Stone was deliberately destroyed. In 1720, according to Anderson, "at some private Lodges, several very valuable Manuscripts (for they had nothing yet in print) concerning the Fraternity, their Lodges, Regulations, Charges, Secrets, and Usages (particularly one writ by Mr. Nicholas Stone the Warden of Inigo Jones) were too hastily burnt by some scrupulous Brothers, that those papers might not fall into strange Hands."[6]

The "strange Hands" may have been responding to a call of June 24, 1718, made by new "Grand Master" George Payne, when, according to Anderson, Payne "desired any Brethren to bring to the Grand Lodge any old Writings and Records concerning Masons and Masonry in order to shew the Usages of antient Times: And this year several old Copies of the Gothic Constitutions were assembled and collated [including the Cooke MS]."[7] One may wonder whether the "scrupulous Brothers" included Anderson's "old Masons" who believed in Enoch's pillars.

It seems likely some pre–Grand Lodge Free-masons suspected the new regime's intentions. Anderson may have had a hint of the content of Stone's burned manuscript. He refers to it in a side note comment to the following statement about Inigo Jones (1572–1652).

> The best Craftsmen from all Parts resorted to Grand Master [an anachronistic title] JONES, who always allow'd good Wages and seasonable times for Instruction in the Lodges, which he constituted with excellent By-Laws, and made 'em like the Schools or Academies of the Designers in Italy. He also held the Quarterly Communication* [side note:]
>
> *So said Brother Nicholas Stone his Warden, in a manuscript burnt 1720.[8]

According to Masonic historians Knoop and Jones, being taken into Acception was distinct from other admission ceremonies to the Company.[9] Anderson's oft-missed key detail about Inigo Jones and Nicholas Stone's ambitions to emulate academies of Italian designers itself warrants further study, especially when we recall how Francesco Giorgi's influential *De Harmonia Mundi* had regarded the architectural proportions of Vitruvius as being of significant theological and spiritual as well as scientific interest. Nicholas Stone sent his son to Italy to research Vitruvian architecture and sculptural values. "Harmony" is repeatedly asserted as an absolute characteristic of the early eighteenth-century Masonic lodge, relating the proportions of architecture to the amity shared among members, to the nature of the heavens, linked by what would be described by renowned early Freemason scholar William Preston (1742–1818) as "a peculiar system of morality, veiled in allegory and illustrated by symbols." The situation suggests that senior architects who valued higher learning were aware that their practical work on earth reflected, or relied on, higher dimensions than commerce. Was Enoch, whose pillars testified to the link of the arts and sciences to the heavens and to lost knowledge preserved by a few, a patron of such aspiration? Evidence exists suggestive of an esoteric link between the Acception ceremony and reception of anima mundi, (soul of the world) understood as Metatron, or Enoch transfigured (in III Enoch).

That working freemasons had pursued alchemy is clear from Elias Ashmole's publishing of Thomas Norton's *Ordinal of Alchemy* (1477) in *Theatrum Chemicum Britannicum* (1652), where Norton writes, "But we may wonder that weavers, Free Masons [Ashmole's phrasing], tailors, cobblers, and needy priests join in the general search after the Philosopher's Stone, and that even painters and glaziers cannot restrain themselves from it." A ceremonial intention of "Acception" is arguably discernible in an illumination to an original MS of Norton's *Ordinall* of 1477.*

It shows a scene redolent of Italian humanist Lodovico Lazzarelli's *Crater Hermetis* (1505) wherein Lazzarelli's master, called "Enoch" (Giovanni Mercurio da Correggio), effected Lazzarelli's spiritual regeneration; that is, Enoch imparts divine wisdom to his disciple, elevating him to a superior level of existence.†

The illumination to Norton's *Ordinall of Alchymy* shows a master in his chair. He holds a blue book in his left hand by the praying hands of his pupil, with a red book in his right hand close to the pupil's face (who may be about to kiss it). The pupil kneels on green tiles before the master's throne. Framed by a Gothic, floriated archway, the green-tiled floor extends behind to a blue night sky of golden stars. Above, angels bear scrolls, carrying the following messages in Latin. Top left is from Psalm 44: "Thou hast loved justice, and hated iniquity: therefore God, thy God, hath anointed thee with the oil of gladness above thy fellows." Top right, from Psalm 27:14: "Expect the Lord, do manfully, and let your heart take courage, and wait for the Lord." Also in Latin, the pupil swears: "I

---

*THE ORDINALL of Alchymy,* written in verse by Thomas Norton of Bristol in 1477, containing the first five chapters. On vellum, of the fifteenth century. Small Quarto. British Library, MS 10302.

†Wouter J. Hanegraaff, "Sympathy or the Devil: Renaissance Magic and the Ambivalence of Idols," *Esoterica* 2 (2000): 1–44, which reinterprets the Hermetic idol-making passage from *Asclepius* in the light of Lazzarelli's *Crater Hermetis;* that is, the highest adept, like the Egyptian sculptor who infuses divinity in a statue, creates souls; the anima mundi spiritualizes its projections. Making men divine has its heavenly analog in Enoch's transfiguration into Metatron in III Enoch, identified with the anima mundi.

Fig. 11.4. Thomas Norton's *Ordinall of Alchymy* (1477)

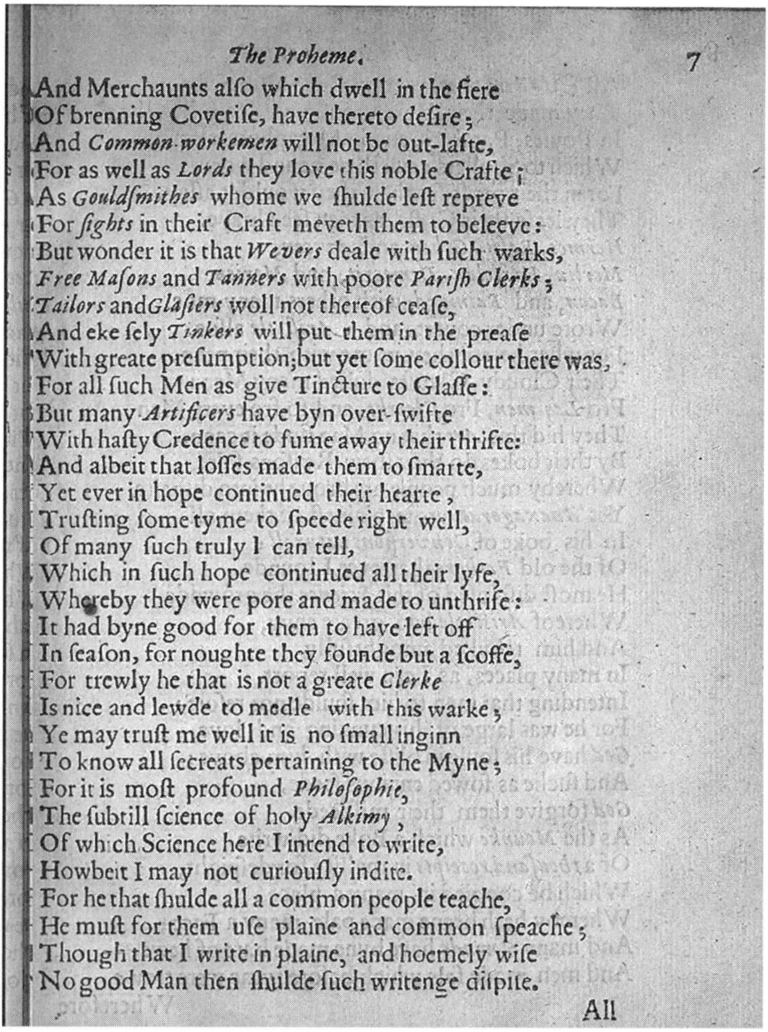

*The Proheme.*      7

And Merchaunts alfo which dwell in the fiere
Of brenning Covetife, have thereto defire;
And *Common-workemen* will not be out-lafte,
For as well as *Lords* they love this noble Crafte;
As *Gouldfmithes* whome we fhulde left repreve
For *fights* in their Craft meveth them to beleeve:
But wonder it is that *Wevers* deale with fuch warks,
*Free Mafons* and *Tanners* with poore *Parifh Clerks*;
*Tailors* and *Glafiers* woll not thereof ceafe,
And eke fely *Tinkers* will put them in the preafe
With greate prefumption; but yet fome collour there was,
For all fuch Men as give Tincture to Glaffe:
But many *Artificers* have byn over-fwifte
With hafty Credence to fume away their thrifte:
And albeit that loffes made them to fmarte,
Yet ever in hope continued their hearte,
Trufting fome tyme to fpeede right well,
Of many fuch truly I can tell,
Which in fuch hope continued all their lyfe,
Whereby they were pore and made to unthrife:
It had byne good for them to have left off
In feafon, for noughte they founde but a fcoffe,
For trewly he that is not a greate *Clerke*
Is nice and lewde to medle with this warke;
Ye may truft me well it is no fmall inginn
To know all fecreats pertaining to the Myne;
For it is moft profound *Philofophie*,
The fubtill fcience of holy *Alkimy*,
Of which Science here I intend to write,
Howbeit I may not curioufly indite.
For he that fhulde all a common people teache,
He muft for them ufe plaine and common fpeache;
Though that I write in plaine, and hoemely wife
No good Man then fhulde fuch writenge difpite.
                      All

Fig. 11.5. Thomas Norton's reference to "Free Masons"
(Ordinall of Alchymy, 1477), published by Elias Ashmole
in *Theatrum Chemicum Britannicum* (1652)

shall keep secret the secrets of Alchemy." Note especially how the master enjoins the pupil: *Accipe donum Dei sub sigillo sacrato;* that is: "Accept the gift of God under the sacred seal." "Accipe donum dei" would conceivably be an appropriate injunction to someone taken into an "Accepcon."

Fig. 11.6. Robert Vaughan's engraving to accompany
Ashmole's publication of Norton's *Ordinall of Alchymy in
Theatrum Chemicum Britannicum* (1652)

Ashmole had the design engraved by Robert Vaughan (1597–1663) for the printed *Theatrum Chemicum Britannicum*. In Vaughan's exquisite engraving, the master puts one book—possibly the Bible—before the one who swears to keep secret the "donum dei" he has accepted. Instead of a Gothic archway we now have two distinct pillars, differently decorated and constructed, with curious inscriptions of figures and a symbol resembling a door, while an arch, flanked by lions, adjoins the capitals. The left pillar displays illogical perspective and may be hollow. There is perhaps an inner shelf in darkness (the pillar on the right is light). The pillars appear to be tilted slightly off a checkered floor that recedes to a *veil,* above which the dove of the Holy Spirit hovers, emanating beams of light, flanked by angels. One may speculate whether Ashmole, in altering the original manuscript design, perhaps drew on personal experience of being asked to accept a secret. The authentic meaning of *acception* would not then be, in the first instance, *that a person is accepted,* but rather *that the initiate has accepted something:* a significant distinction and two-way process. Having accepted, the candidate is accepted; that is, becomes acceptable (see Romans 5:2 and 12:5). The one who enters the Holy of Holies, who passes through the veil, must be *acceptable* to the Lord. Recall Samber's point about true Freemasons being those who had passed the *veil.* Enoch "walked with God," acceptable to the Lord, for he accepted God, source of wisdom, and could thus approach the source (eternal life) untrammeled by the world.

The precise words exchanged by master and pupil in the engraving reappeared in 1698 in a work about the Philosopher's Stone, *THE GOLDEN AGE: Or, the REIGN of SATURN REVIEW'D,** in praise of the alchemical works of Eugenius Philalethes (Ashmole's friend Thomas Vaughan), particularly with regard to the anima mundi, the soul of the world, or "breath of God," which Vaughan says in his *Lumen de Lumine* must—*note*—be *received.*

---

*An Essay. Written by HORTOLANUS Junr.* Preserved and Published by R. G. M[ichael]. Sendivog[ius]. London, Printed by J. Mayos, for Rich. Harrison, 1698.

It [the animating soul that sustains or en-spirits all creation] is an Influence of the Almighty God, and it comes from *Terra Viventium,* namely the second person [compare with Metatron or "little Jahveh" in III Enoch], whom the Cabalists style the Supernaturall East.* For as the Natural Light of the Sun is first manifested to us in the East, so the Supernatural Light was first manifested in the second person, for he is *Principium Alterationis,* the Beginning of the wayes of God, or the first Manifestation of his Father's Light in the Supernatural Generation. From this *Terra Viventium,* or Land of the Living comes all Life or spirit, according to that position of the Mekubalim [kabbalists]: *Omnis anima bona est anima nova, veniens ab Oriente.*

Every good soule is a new soule, coming from the East: that is from Hocmah, or the second Sephiroth, which is the Son of God. . . .

This third Light from whence the souls descend, is Binah, the last of the three sephiroths [*sic*], and it signifies the Holy Ghost. Now that you may know in what sense this Descent proceeds from that Blessed spirit, I will somewhat inlarge my Discourse, for the Cabalists are very obscure in the point.

*Spirare* (say the Jews) *Spiritus Sancti proprium est,* to Breath[e] is the proprietie of the Holy Ghost. Now we read that God breathed into Adam the Breath of Life, and he became a living soule.

Here you must understand that the third Person is the last of the three, not that there is any Inequality in them, but it is so in order of Operation, for he applies first to the Creature, and therefore works last. The meaning of it is this: The Holy Ghost could not breathe a soule into Adam, but he must either receive it, or have it of himself. Now the truth is he receives it, and what hee receives, that hee breaths into Nature. Hence this most holy spirit is styl'd by the Cabalists *Fluvius egrediens è Paradiso,* because he breaths [*sic*] as

---

*It should be noted that in the earliest Masonic catechisms, the master's throne is in the east, for the master sets men to work with the rising sun.

a River streames. He is call'd also Mater Filiorum, because by this Breathing he is as it were delivered of those souls, which have been conceived Ideally in the second Person.

Now that the Holy Ghost receives all things from the second Person, is confirmed by Christ himself. When the spirit of truth is come, he will guide you into all truth, for he shall not speak of himself, but what soever he shall heare, that shall he speak, and he will shew you things to come. He shall glorifie me, for he shall receive of mine, and shall shew it unto you. All things that the Father hath, are mine; Therefore said I, that he shall take of mine. Here wee plainly see, there is a certaine subsequent order or Method in the operations of the blessed Trinity, for Christ tels us, that he receives from his Father, and the Holy Ghost receives from Him.

Againe that all things are conceived Ideally (or as we commonly expresse it) created by the second person, is confirmed by the word of God. The World was made by him (saith the Scripture) and the world knew him not. He came unto his own, and his own received him not.

This may suffice for such as Love the Truth, and as for that which the Cabalist speaks of the fourth and fifth Dayes, it suits not with my present designe, and therefore I must wave it. It is clear then that *Terra viventium,* or the Eternall Fire-Earth buds and sprouts, hath her fierie spirituall Flowers, which we call soules, as this natural Earth hath her natural Vegetables.[10]


Vaughan explicitly identifies the "East" with the second sephira, "Hocma" (Wisdom), which he calls the "Son of God." The third sephira, Binah (Understanding), Vaughan identifies with the Holy Ghost, which Adam must *breathe in* to make him "a living soule." Free-mason Ashmole was aware of the extant seventeenth-century Free-masons' catechism whereby the light of the East ("the jewel") first touches the master's throne in the east of the lodge before setting brethren "to work." Vaughan emphasizes that the Holy Ghost could not simply "breathe" the soul into Adam; Adam had to *actively* "receive it first."* The *formative creative principle* is stressed: the ability to construct by divinizing art requires an *acceptance*.

Hortolanus Jr. in *The Golden Age* of 1698 gives an account of what Vaughan knew of the anima mundi: "The Anima (he says) is an instrumental Agent, a seed or glance of Light, simple and without any mixture, descending from the first Father of Lights" (page 13). Even more central to our search is Robert Fludd's antecedent account of the anima mundi, which appeared in 1638, the year Nicholas Stone was taken into the Acception, a year after Fludd's death in 1637.

Fludd's *Philosophia Moysaica* (1638) identifies the anima mundi specifically with "Mettatron," into whom the Holy One in chapter 10 of III Enoch (ca. fifth century CE) transforms Enoch and makes him a throne like his own, that Metatron as a "Little Jahveh" may sit at the door of the seventh hall of heaven, it being announced through the Herald that Metatron henceforth is God's representative and ruler over all the princes of kingdoms and all the children of heaven (all that sustains creation), save the eight high princes called JHVH by the name of their king. Fludd writes:

> The more secret Theologians and those most expert in true Cabbala say that just as Mind has domination in the human Soul, thus does Mettatron in the celestial world, where he rules from the Sun, and the Soul of the Messiah in the Angelic world, and Adonai in the Archetypal. And to the degree that the active intellect of Mind is the light of the soul, even so the light of that same Mettatron or World's Soul is Sadai, and the light of the Messiah's soul is Elchai, which signifies the living God, and the light of Adonai is Ensoph, signifying the infinity of Divinity. The world's soul is therefore Mettatron, whose light is the soul of the Messiah or of the Tetragrammaton's

---

*Eugenius Philalethes, "The Prester of Zoroaster," in *LUMEN DE LUMINE,* 81–84.

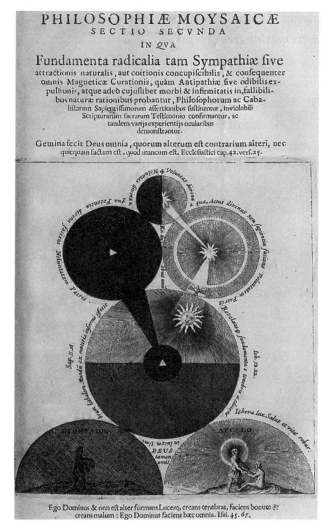

Fig. 11.7. Robert Fludd's *Philosophia Moysaica* (1638)

virtue, in which is the light of the living God, in which is the light of Ensoph, beyond which there is no progression.[11]

"Mettatron," writes Fludd, "is nothing else but that universall Spirit of Wisdome which God sent out of his own mouth, as the greatest gift and token of his benignity unto each world, and the members thereof:

to reduce them from deformity, and nonexistence, into act and formall being. . . . And this therefore was termed rightly in the eies of wise men Mitattron or *Donum Dei catholicum,* which reduceth the universall Nothing into a universall Something."[12]

Remarkably, in our context, Robert Fludd translates "Mitattron" as *donum dei,* or "gift of God," something that had to be received or *accepted:* the gift or inner life of creation. "Donum Dei" is of course the very expression given to what the initiate in Vaughan's engraving (see p. 172)—and Ashmole-Vaughan's version of it—is asked imperatively to accept: *Accipe donum Dei sub sigillo sacrato.*

We do not know whether Dr. Robert Fludd enjoyed familiarity with Masonic Acception, or even, as Buhle and de Quincey suggested, assisted in devising a transformed level of Masonry. After practicing as a physician in Fenchurch Street, Fludd lived in Coleman Street, a neighbor to the London Freemasons Company in Masons Avenue, where Acceptions took place. In fact, Masons Avenue joins Coleman Street to Basinghall Street, City of London. Furthermore, tantalizing, if inconclusive, evidence exists that links Fludd's name to the Accepted Masons and to the Acception.*

During the early 1890s, master of London's Masons Company Edward Conder examined old company records. His findings appeared in 1894 in *The Records of the Whole Craft & Fellowship of Masons* (facsimile edition, 1988) as well as the 1896 Transactions of the Quatuor Coronati Lodge of Research (AQC IX, 28–50). Conder inspected a Company Inventory of June 24, 1663, from the Quarterage Book of the Masons Company (Guildhall MS 5313, Folio 1). It indicates the dignity with which Acception records were accorded at that time. In 1663, the company kept the "name of the Accepted Masons in a fairly enclosed [probably gilt or silver] frame with a lock and key." The same inventory lists the following: "Item. One Book of Constitutions which Mr Flood

---

*I am very grateful to Masonic historian Matthew Scanlan for kindly sharing with me his research regarding what follows in the next paragraph concerning Fludd and "Accepted Masons."

[variant spelling of "Fludd"] gave. Item. One Book of Constitutions. Item. One Bible" (AQC IX, 38). A second inventory of 1676 listed the following: "One. Book of Constitutions of the Accepted Masons. One Book of the Ancient Constitutions. One great Bible. A faire large Table of the Accepted Masons. One Money Dish and One Ivory Hammer." We cannot be certain that "Mr Flood" (clearly someone familiar to the company) was the famous Dr. Robert Fludd. "Mr Flood" may have been Fludd's nephew, Dr. Levin Fludd, friend of Accepted Free-mason Elias Ashmole (1617–1692). Levin Fludd inherited his uncle's library. Perhaps it was neither, but the name connection is striking and, all things considered, I should say, significant.

According to Urszula Szulakowska's comment on Fludd's five-volume "History of the Microcosm and the Macrocosm" (*Utriusque Cosmi Historia,* published 1617–1621 by Theodore de Bry of Oppenheim) in her essay "Robert Fludd and His Images of the Divine":

> In his medicinal incantations Fludd used the Hebrew form of the name of Jesus, which, he claimed, possessed immense magical potency. He equated Jesus Christ with the kabbalistic angel Metattron, the heavenly form of the Jewish Messiah (UCH, 2 1621: 2–5). He was said to be the soul of the world, pervading it throughout as "anima mundi" or Anthropos (UCH, 2 1621, tract 2, sec. 1: 8–9). Fludd states that "Hochmah" (Wisdom in the kabbalistic Tree of Life) is the same as the "Verbum" (the "Word" in the Christian Gospel of John who is identified with Jesus Christ). The Christian "Word" is the same as the first letter of the Hebrew alphabet, "Aleph." This Christian Messiah is the most potent medicine for all human ills. The Verbum, or Metattron-Christ-Messiah, is the form of God himself, residing in the sun.[13]

Since III Enoch reveals Metatron as the transfigured Enoch, it would appear that Fludd may unknowingly have identified the Messiah

Jesus with Enoch!—an identification already made by Renaissance humanist Lodovico Lazzarelli's spiritual master, Giovanni Mercurio da Correggio, whom Lazzarelli called "Enoch," in 1484.* Such ideas were certainly of interest to learned Masons, and aspects of them have undoubtedly found their way into Masonic degrees.

Fludd was profoundly interested in the harmonies and spiritual basis of architecture, as well as architecture's practical utility, interests that would at the time have provided comfortable entrée into Freemasons Company Acception status, especially with questing minds like Nicholas Stone at the company helm. Fludd linked architecture to music, a key idea of Britain's late sixteenth- and early seventeenth-century cultural renaissance. According to Fludd, working on the cabalist and Pythagorean principles dear to Francesco Giorgi, the universe is a monochord. Making sense of its physical structure requires an understanding of music (one of the seven liberal arts). Fludd depicts the universe as an architectural Temple of Music in *Utriusque Cosmi Historia*. He harmonized this knowledge with his conception of practical anatomy and medicine. Emblematic images in Fludd's books present alchemy as the key to creation, with the sun as divine transformative agent. Cosmic creation, from the black stage of chaos, stirred into formative dynamism by Light, is a seven-step alchemical operation (as Genesis suggested).

Fascinatingly, Fludd's work on cosmic harmonies brought him into disagreement with astronomer Kepler, who had similar interests but from a less idealized perspective. Kepler called his own work on the subject (after Giorgi perhaps) *Harmonices Mundi* ("The Harmonies of the World," 1619). While disagreements probably seemed greater between one another than they appear to us, Kepler was nonetheless able to formulate his third law of celestial motion from a consideration of the proportional congruence of musical intervals and planetary movement,

---

*See my book *The Golden Builders* (2004), chapter titled "The Hermetic Philosophy," for more on Lazzarelli and "Mercurio da Correggio" (born 1451).

having found the difference between a planet's maximum and minimum angular speeds approximates to harmonic proportion. For example, measured from the sun, the earth's greatest angular speed, between aphelion and perihelion, varies by a semitone, with a 16:15 ratio, from *mi* to *fa*. Kepler discovered (or perhaps *rediscovered*) the mathematics behind an inherited intuitive knowledge familiar to medieval astronomers as "the harmony of the spheres." The solar system was a choir, and man would do well to mirror and echo it.

For example, the 3rd-degree Charge, used in the United Grand Lodge of England today, informs the Mason that acquaintance with the "hidden mysteries of nature and science" (accessed via the seven liberal arts recommended for a Mason's study in the Fellow Craft, or 2nd degree) have only brought him "*before* the throne" of God (intellectual apprehension of a necessary First Cause). This makes perfect sense when we consider the work of the likes of Fludd and Kepler, and of course, later, Isaac Newton. Passing *through* the veil, however, required existential confrontation with the spiritual dimension of the universe, mediated, in Greek terms, via transformative *nous* or *logos* (Hebrew: *neschamah*). To overcome the "King of Terrors" (fear of death), higher illumination is necessary, and *that* comes from beyond the limits of unaided reason (Hebrew: *ruach*). Ordinary reason takes one *before* the divine throne only. For while reason can recognize a lawful universe and can logically trace its existence to a first principle, such reasoning alone cannot raise the Mason to highest being. While noting the possible implication of Merkabah mysticism about the divine throne, we also note how the Mason is intriguingly informed in the charge that "the light of the Master Mason is darkness visible," wherein we may consider the dark cloud of divine presence that obscured the Holy of Holies to the priests' eyes when the Ark's staves were removed as it was placed there (1 Kings 8:10–13). "Darkness visible" is also the initiated capacity to see that what one formerly took for "light" was darkness, concealing light. Thus a *donum dei* is gift of sight and separation from the blind.

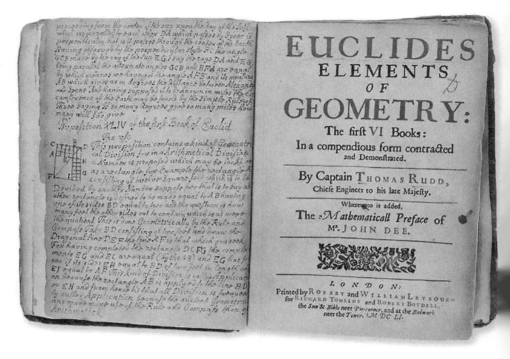

Fig. 11.8. Euclid's *Elements of Geometry* with
Dee's *Mathematicall Preface*

As H. Kvanvig observed: "In Jewish tradition Enoch is primarily portrayed as a primeval sage, the ultimate revealer of divine secrets."[14] That a more explicit role for Enoch (other than as pillar maker) may have been watered down or excised with the Grand Lodge reordering of symbolic Masonry might explain the return of Enoch as a figure of significance in the "Ancient and Accepted Rite" after the 1760s. Before we examine that development, we might observe briefly Enoch's role in John Dee's apotheosis of mathematics in his famous preface to Henry Billingsley's translation of Euclid's *Elements,* published in 1570, aimed at freemasons and all the nation's artisans who needed to calculate, or "speculate"—as the term was then employed to denote the practical process of "mirroring" nature using instruments like square and compass (from Latin *speculum,* or mirror).

## JOHN DEE AND PRIMAL MATHEMATICS

While recommending Euclid to artisans, as well as scholars and gentlemen, not only did John Dee (1527–1608) insist that architecture was a liberal art ("among the Artes Mathematicall"), never to be regarded as a secondary "trade" (sharing, it seems, the Old Charges' assertion that Euclid taught Geometry-Masonry to the sons of great lords), but Dee also insisted on there being two aspects of mathematics (which encompassed architecture): first, the earthly, concerned with mensuration; second, the heavenly, concerned with the Platonic realm of pure ideas and divine intelligibility—the completion of the arts. Such a view also has its place in assessing the kind of thinking that may have informed the "Acception." One thinks of Nicholas Stone's and Inigo Jones's desire to infuse Italian Renaissance philosophical practice into English Masonry as well as Ashmole's insistence in his *Theatrum* that Dee deserved recognition for

Fig. 11.9. John Dee (1527–1608)

his seminal role in raising mathematics to the highest level of classical learning, warranting, as Ashmole put it, the "commendation of all learned and ingenious scholars" (*Theatrum Chemicum Britannicum*).

Obviously, Dee is most remembered today for controversial angelic conversations and reception of what he called an "angelicall language," called "Enochian" by later aficionados of Dee's work. While Dee's status and relevance to our story is better understood in terms of his alchemical geometry and mathematical ideas, he held to another theme in common with Masonry; namely, the perfectibility of universal man, of which perfection Enoch was the prototype.

Anderson declared famously in 1723 that Masons, as Masons, held to "that religion on which all men can agree," consonant with a Lodge of *Harmony,* and an idea possibly descending from the belief that before Babel there was a unity of peoples and language, with patriarchs vouchsafed pristine science, religion, and art: Enoch's inheritance and legacy. Before resorting to what Dee was convinced was direct angelic contact, he worked on an "alphabet of nature" that would show that "without regard to person, the same most benevolent God is not only the God of the Jews, but of all peoples, nations and languages."[15] Before committing to the idea that the original language might resemble letters reproduced in Pantheus's *Voarchadumia* and compiling with Edward Kelley the "angelicall language" of *Liber Loagaeth,* sometimes called "The Book of Enoch," Dee made interesting work of finding a primal language through pure geometry, taking mathematics as indicative of purest ideas-communication, the language of creation. Looking at Greek, Latin, and Hebrew, Dee's *Monas Hieroglyphica* (1564) observes: "The shapes of all those letters were produced from points, straight lines, and the circumferences of circles, disposed by a wonderful and most wise artifice."[16] The essence of this idea appears at the start of Anderson's *Constitutions* when Anderson sees geometry written into Adam's heart by God from the beginning: it is God's signature, his breathed word (or *logos,* or anima mundi), so to speak, animating a dormant, earthy creation. Dee's dynamic symbol of cosmic unity, his "Monas," which, by the understanding of the time, synthesizes geometry, alchemy, astronomy, and language, is generated from a point, lines, and circle.

As Nicholas Clulee has observed, Dee's Monas symbol is essentially Hermetic, and Dee, in his defense of Bacon (*speculum unitatis,* 1557, now lost) followed Roger Bacon's view that Enoch and Hermes were essentially one.[17] Following Proclus's commentary on Euclid, Dee sees the line projected from the Monad as the dyad, the unlimited, or world of generation. The circle is heavenly. These concepts rather form an analogy with the familiar mason's square and dividers, where the square extends in earth measurement, and the dividers take one from the monad, or point, via a dyad to the heavenly or circular movement.

Fig. 11.10. Dee's *Monas Hieroglyphica*

Proclus associated the circle with "triadic god" Mercury or Hermes Trismegistus—inventor of writing and all arts and sciences. Dee calls his Monas the "Seal of Hermes"; it contains the Mercury symbol, for Mercurius (which may be compared to penetrating and sustaining anima mundi) is "rebuilder of all Astronomy" and "astrological messenger."[18]

If, as Anderson maintained, "the old Masons" had firm belief in Enoch's pillars, then some at least may have admired the Monas symbol for showing all things coming from the One, while incorporating and differentiating elemental and celestial dimensions visible in architecture with its straight lines and harmonizing curves. We know for certain that Ashmole did—with his motto "Ex Uno Omnia" and nom de plume, "Mercuriophilus Anglicus"—and numerous commentators would continue to illuminate Masonry with speculations of a Pythagorean and Neoplatonic kind on the mysteries of geometry and symbols as gateways to spiritualized consciousness, and many alleged links between matter and divine mind. Enoch in kabbalist tradition is Man restored wholly, and Masonry may be seen as an allegory of that.

Dee's "Mathematicall Preface" to Billingsley's translation of Euclid's *The Elements* (1570) is open to interpretation as a detailed vindication of the Masonic belief that geometry is key to the arts and sciences, making number the essential craft. However, while number would open all the secrets of the manifest world, Dee held contemplative mathematics ultimately superior to practical or applied mathematics, as it led to awareness of eternity and the source of the unifying principle, allowing one to trace manifestation back to pure idea. Dee called men to see the higher value of mathematics as the creative realization of divine powers. It was, perhaps, a conception at home in the Masons Company's "Acception," before London's Grand Lodge assumed control of lodges after 1716.

Since Dee's magisterial assessment of the dignity of mathematics and geometry within the "Mathematicall Preface" and the *Monas Hieroglyphica* was practically tailor-made for Freemasons' self-justification, we must suspect the only reason Dee was not cited as an authority by Anderson in 1723, or subsequently, was because of the reaction to Méric Casaubon's scandalous publication of Dee's diaries in 1659. That publication linked Dee's name forever to conjuring and unsound arts, with the practitioner a devil's dupe. "Free-mason" Ashmole (1617–1692) was one of the few who labored to defend Dee and preserve his papers. However, it seems likely that Anderson, or a source he relied on, had read the "Mathematicall Preface," for there is a telltale parallel of associations appearing in both Dee's "Mathematicall Preface" and in Anderson's 1723 *Constitutions*.

Referring to Vitruvius's ten books on architecture, Dee writes: "Vitruvius, the Romaine: who did write ten bookes thereof, to the Emperour Augustus (in whose daies our Heauenly Archemaster, was borne)"; while Anderson writes: "to Rome, which thus became the center of Learning, as well as of Imperial Power, until they advanced to their Zenith of Glory, under AUGUSTUS CAESAR (in whose Reign was born God's MESSIAH, the great Architect of the Church), who having laid the World quiet, by proclaiming universal Peace, highly encourag'd those dexterous Artists that had been bred in the Roman Liberty, and their learned Scholars and Pupils; but particularly the great VITRUVIUS, The Father of all true Architects to this Day."[19]

Apparently borrowing Dee's "Archemaster" parenthesis, Anderson perhaps sidesteps Dee's theologically risky sobriquet "heavenly Archemaster" with his paraphrase "Architect of the Church," but at the expense of losing Dee's precious advanced art of *Archemastrie*—Dee's word for the supreme skill in applied arts and science, with practical mathematics the highest point of mathematical aspiration: a complete use of conjoined gifts material and spiritual in the highest service of restored Man.

For Dee, the highest level of architecture indicates something higher than itself. The perfect architecture, Dee asserts, is by its nature "Immaterial." An architect in this league of magnitude was, according to Dee, Vitruvius's admirer, Leon Battista Alberti (1404–1472), who, synthesizing in his mind the liberal arts, was creative beyond existing bounds, becoming thus the true "Renaissance," or reborn, man. Two proverbial quotes attributed to Alberti suffice to justify Dee's encomium of the "Baptist": "A man can do all things if he but wills them"; and "When I investigate and when I discover that the forces of the heavens and the planets are within ourselves, then truly I seem to be living among the gods." Dee looked to Renaissance arts and a massively increased number of liberal arts for the future, not to a backward-looking veneration of patriarchs at the expense of tomorrow. Dee was futuristic. By ignoring the real Dee, it is arguable that Andersonian Masonry suppressed itself, unlike Enoch, who, by contrast, *went all the way.*

# TWELVE

# The Return of Enoch

Anderson's *Constitutions* and a subsequent 3rd "Master Mason" degree of substituted secrets (ca. 1730) failed to satisfy all Freemasons. Dissatisfaction with English Grand Lodge Masonry would eventually see Enoch Masonically revived: a difficult process since Masonry had become so closely associated with Solomon's Temple and its pillars that any revelation of Masonry's "lost word"—which Hiram Abiff in Masonic myth refused to surrender—was bound to be associated with a now established setting in Jerusalem rather than in the antediluvian period.

The first recorded appearance of something like a "Royal Arch" degree (or order) to reveal the lost word was in Ireland in 1743. Eight years later, Irishmen in London formed a rival Grand Lodge: the "Antients." Laurence Dermott became its second grand secretary in February 1752, the year that yields first evidence of the Royal Arch in lodge minutes. Cherished by the Antients, Dermott called the Royal Arch the "root and marrow of Masonry" (*Ahimon Rezon,* 1756). In 1757, a version of the Royal Arch was worked in Fredericksburg, Virginia.

The English version of the Royal Arch story is set in the time of Zerubbabel after promulgation of Cyrus's edict of 538 BCE permitting Jews to rebuild their temple in Jerusalem. (The modern U.S. version is set in the time of the reformer king of Judah, Josiah, ca. 648–609 BCE.) According to the central story, workmen clearing rubble for the foundations of the new temple encounter a hole. With pickax, shovel, and crowbar (compare with the three parts of Hebrew letter shin ש: symbol in Christian cabala for spiritual fire), workmen descend to a hidden vault below what had been the Holy of Holies of Solomon's Temple. They find a white marble pillar in the form of a double cube on which is a gold plate with a triangle and circle inscribed upon it, wherein is written the lost word.

It seems likely the original lost word was the tetragrammaton (the four Hebrew letters of God's name—yod, hé, vau, hé) with the Hebrew letter shin centered within as keystone—making "Yeheshuah" (Jesus), according to Reuchlin's Christian cabalist *de verbo mirifico,* 1494. Adding shin not only makes the Hebrew for "Jesus" but also renders the unspoken word of JHVH audible or manifest. Modern versions of the Royal Arch have de-Christianized the original ritual with substituted words. In England, currently, "Jehovah" has replaced "Jabulon" and thereby compounded a muting of potent symbolism in favor of a vapid universalism.[1]

The myth of the hidden vault seems a conflation of the discovery of Frater C. R.'s tomb in the *Fama Fraternitatis*—which revealed "The whole glory of God" on a brass plate in the tomb-vault—with a story first recorded of Philostorgius (born ca. 364 CE) in a work by Photius, patriarch of Constantinople in 853,[2] retold in Samuel Lee's *Orbis Miraculum or, The Temple of Solomon, Pourtrayed by Scripture-Light.* The depictions of high priest Zadok with his ephod and King Solomon on the frontispiece to Lee's book look like models for analogous roles in Royal Arch ritual.

Fellow of Wadham College, Oxford, Samuel Lee (ca. 1625–1691), learned in physics and alchemy, was friend to Wadham College Warden and Royal Society founder John Wilkins (1614–1672), author of *Mathematical Magick* (1648), which drew on John Dee's "Mathematicall Preface."[3] Lee's book displays mathematical and architectural learning shared with Wilkins.

Samuel Lee tells how Emperor Julian the Apostate sanctioned rebuilding Jerusalem's temple to prove Jesus's prophecy of its permanent destruction untrue—but the prophecy is vindicated.

Fig. 12.1. *Orbis Miraculum* by Samuel Lee

When the foundations were a laying, as I have said, there was a stone among the rest, to which the bottom of the foundation was fastened, that slipt from its place, and discovered the mouth of a cave which had been cut in rock. Now when they could not see the bottom by reason of its depth; the Overseers of the building being desirous to have a certain knowledge of the [*sic*] they tied a long rope to one of the Labourers, and let him down: He being come to the bottom, found water in it, that took him up to the midancles, and searching every part of that hollow place, he found it to be four square, as far as he could conjecture by feeling. Then returning toward the mouth of it, found a book lying there wrapped up in a piece of thin and clean linnen. Having taken it into his hands, he signified by the rope that they should draw him up. When he was pulled up he shews the book, which struck them with admiration, especially seeming so fresh and untoucht as it did, being found in so dark and obscure a hole. The Book being unfolded, did amaze not only the Jews, but the Grecians also, holding forth even at the beginning of it in great Letters (In the beginning was the Word, and the Word was with God, and the Word was God.) To speak plainly, that Scripture did manifestly contain the whole gospel.[4]

However, it would seem that for some Masons, even the Royal Arch with its lost word rediscovered offered insufficient revelation of the hidden glories of ancient Freemasonry. Besides, the pillars of Enoch had still to be Masonically rehabilitated. In the 13th degree of "Morin's Rite," called in England the "Royal Arch of Enoch," this task was cleverly undertaken by an ingenious blending of antediluvian and Solomonic myth.

Taking what he could from the work of Lyon-based Jean-Baptiste Willermoz (1730–1824), who began assembling elements for a 25-degree system about 1761, Creole trader Éstienne Morin (1717–1771) went to Port au Prince in 1763 with authority from Écossais Masons from the

Fig. 12.2. Jean Baptiste Willermoz (1730–1824)

Council of the Grand and Sovereign Lodge of Saint Jean de Jerusalem, to promote Masonry in the Americas. In about 1766, Morin completed a Constitution (backdated to 1762), a foundational document for what would eventually become the Ancient and Accepted (Scottish) Rite.[5]

The 13th degree offers another slant on the Royal Arch, first by addressing the problem of how first to connect the lost word of the Royal Arch with Enoch, and second, how to connect Enoch to the Temple at Jerusalem. The solution to the first issue lay in Genesis 4:26: "And to Seth, to him also there was born a son; and he called his name Enos: then men began to call upon the name of the LORD." The *Name* then was vouchsafed to Seth's progeny, so it was a small step to insist that Enoch preserved the true Name from the Flood in a (new) pillars story. The second issue was addressed through novelties in the pillars story, inspired by the Royal Arch and other sources.

The degree legend informs initiates how, seeking revelation, Enoch experienced a vision that took him to a mountain to see God's Name impressed in a triangular, golden plate. Manifest to Enoch in the vision, God forbade him pronounce the sacred name. Enoch was then carried underground perpendicularly, finding nine levels, each with an arch above it. In the ninth arch, Enoch saw the plate, again surrounded by flaming light. Filled with God's spirit, Enoch built a subterranean temple in Canaan with the nine arches he'd envisioned. He had a triangular plate made, each side a cubit, and had gems set within the gold and inscribed the Name. It was placed on a triangular pedestal of white and black marble, deposited in the deepest arch. The temple completed, he made a stone door and put a ring of iron in it and placed it over the opening of the first arch, to save the temple from impending deluge.

Enoch then made two pillars, one of brass to withstand water, the other of marble to withstand fire, engraving on the marble pillar hieroglyphics signifying a most precious treasure concealed in the arches underground, while on the pillar of brass were inscribed the principles of the liberal arts, particularly of masonry. In the degree legend, a Masonic account of Lamech, Noah, and the ark followed.

Moving on to Solomon's wish to establish a Temple, potential "Knights" were informed that when digging its foundations, an ancient ruin was found with many treasures, duly carried to Solomon. Fearing its pagan provenance, Solomon moved the project to Mt. Moriah, where a vault beneath the Sanctum sanctorum was constructed, supported by a large pillar, which he called the Pillar of Beauty, to support the Ark of the Covenant. Solomon later sent three craftsmen to search the ruins for more treasures. They discovered a stone door with an iron ring. Undeterred, they lowered by rope one of the three who found the ninth arch, leading to the precious treasure's retrieval and delivery to Solomon, who made them Knights of the Royal Arch. The plate was taken to the Pillar of Beauty, while the vault's name was changed from the secret to the sacred vault.

Thus did Enoch's pillars return to Freemasonry, "like a nubile Cinderella: sparsely clad, and much interfered with."*

I should say that the contrived nature of the legend of the 13th degree amply demonstrates that something had indeed been lost, when we compare the degree's rather conventional religious moralism with the spiritual and alchemical depth enjoyed by Fludd, Vaughan, Dee, and Ashmole.

## "OUT OF EGYPT I HAVE CALLED MY SON"
### James Bruce and the Book of Enoch

By the time Charleston saw a "Lodge of Perfection" in 1783, Scottish explorer—and Freemason—James Bruce, laird of Kinnaird (1730–1794) had been back in Great Britain for a decade following years of pioneering exploration in Egypt and Ethiopia in quest of the Nile's source.

Initiated into Freemasonry at Scotland's famous Cannongate Kilwinning Lodge No. 2 on August 1, 1753, Bruce's adventurous career

---

*An appropriate simile from David Sherwin's script for Lindsay Anderson's movie, If . . . (1968), where a pompous British public school headmaster describes "education" in these terms.

was crowned by the bestselling *Travels to Discover the Source of the Nile in the Years 1768–73* (five vols.) in 1790. Bruce, whose name will forever be joined to the "Bruce Codex" of Gnostic literature (the Books of Jeu and an unnamed Gnostic work on the passage of the soul through the powers of the Archons), was the man who brought four large quarto Ge'ez versions of the Book of Enoch to the pope, the king of France, the king of England, and the last, home to Scotland, a text that had not been seen in its entirety outside of Ethiopia since late antiquity, though fragments from Syncellus and other sources had been gathered in the sixteenth century and whetted appetites of biblical scholars and other learned persons concerned with the origins of knowledge, who would have likely linked the missing book to Josephus's pillars of Sethite knowledge, whose account, as we know, was embellished subsequently and joined to Hermetic traditions.

Given that when British Museum librarian Carl Gottfried Woide

Fig. 12.3. James Bruce (1730–1794)

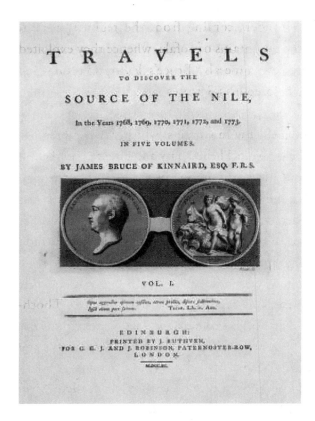

Fig. 12.4. *Travels to Discover the Source of the Nile, in the Years 1768–73*, vol. 1, by James Bruce

was alerted to the Book of Enoch's presence in Paris he immediately crossed the Channel to transcribe it, one might have thought learned Freemason Bruce would have found more delight in the long-lost Book of Enoch's text than appears from his witty, if dry, comments in *Travels*. One might also have expected Bruce to have extrapolated more about the Old Charges' Hermes-son-to-Cush relationship—after all, Cush's progeny (Cushites) were, as he recognized, regarded as ancestors to Ethiopians, Sudanese, biblical Shebans, and even Libyans in the eighteenth century, when it was customary to see the world's races all descended from Noah's sons, Ham, Shem, and Japhet—eventually giving us such unfortunate, imaginary racial categories as "Shemitic" or Semitic.

Bruce was aware of the Ethiopian tradition that Cush's descendants went south beyond Egypt, Saba, and the flatlands of Atbara, and—

fearing another flood (reminders coming from the region's tropical rains)—lived in caves in the mountains of Sofala, whence they exploited to their profit plentiful precious minerals.[6] Bruce's description following here bears comparison with Josephus's Sethites.

> The Cushite then inhabited the mountains, whilst the northern colonies advanced from Meroë to Thebes, busy and intent upon the improvement of architecture, and building of towns, which they began to substitute for their caves; they thus became farmers, traders, artificers of all kinds, and even practical astronomers. . . . Letters too, at least one sort of them, and arithmetical characters, we are told, were invented by the middle part of the Cushites.[7]

The creation of writing was traditionally attributed to Thoth-Hermes in Egypt. Bruce takes the "prodigious fragments of colossal statues of the dog-star" still to be seen at Axum as evidence of architectural prowess as well as devotion to Sirius, saying that in the Troglodyte's language *seir* meant "dog," explaining why the province was called "Sirè" and the river bounding it "Siris." As we shall see, these observations are pertinent to Josephus's intended siting of the surviving Sethite pillar. Bruce believed the Cushites moved from Axum in the Abyssinian mountains to Meroë for better views of the stars, calling ancient Meroë "that first seminary of learning."[8] Thence they established Thebes, evinced by caves above Thebes that he believed made their first accustomed dwelling there, still haunted by memory of Noah's Flood.

Bruce has interesting things to say about Thoth (equated traditionally with Hermes and Enoch) in the context of Cushite astronomy and philology that would have fascinated learned Masons, though perhaps oaths of secrecy prevented Bruce from linking his conceptions to Masonic tradition, if in fact he was aware of the Old Charges' Cush-Hermes tradition, Anderson having excised it many years earlier. Bruce does not accept the classical contention that Osiris was once king of Egypt and "Tot" (Theuth) his secretary, or that they could have communicated the invention of writing to all peoples of Europe in "very different periods." Thebes, Bruce maintains, was built by Ethiopians from the city of Sirè, or the Dog Star. While Diodorus Siculus believed Osiris came from putting an O before Siris to make it intelligible, Bruce asserts, *contra* Diodorus, that that could not make Osiris the sun. No, "Osiris" was simply the Dog Star, "Syrius," not a man: called after a dog because the star's becoming visible at its heliacal rising gave warning, as in a dog's bark, that the Nile's inundation was imminent. This, Bruce believed, was the first hieroglyphic, and Isis, Osiris, and Tot were inventions relating to it.[9]

From a Masonic point of view, what Bruce could be said to have been doing was what, to an extent, Anderson did with his *Constitutions* more than sixty years earlier: bringing ancient lore into conformity with contemporary, rationally enlightened methods, achieved by experience and patient recording of local records and visible evidence, applying common sense; Bruce shared his era's educated tendency to be indifferent to obscure spiritual meaning or abstruse metaphysics. "I know," he writes, "that most of the learned writers are of sentiments very different from mine in these respects. They look for mysteries and hidden meanings, moral and philosophical treatises, as the subjects of these hieroglyphics."[10] He dismisses the idea of eternal knowledge, "which must have appeared by every man finding it in his own breast." This is almost a paraphrase of Anderson's first paragraph of history in the 1723 *Constitutions* where he says that Adam must have had geometry written in his heart by God. If so, asks Bruce, why go to the trouble of writing it with much "labour on a table of porphyry or granite?"[11] This is some irony, for Anderson's *Constitutions* has been considered a kind of manifesto of the "Enlightenment"! Presumably, Bruce would have been rather skeptical of the idea of antediluvian pillars containing the knowledge that hard experience alone was teaching the descendants of Cush! However, a kind of symbolic link between Cush and Hermes is still discernible in the movement from Flood to Cushites, to Thebes, to "Tot," though it is expressed as a rational, logical conjecture over time, without anthropomorphism, based on observations on the ground. Bruce interpreted repetition of glyphs by supposing their practical purpose, having to do with the Nile, sharing the enlightenment philosophy of his era that people learned not by revelation but principally through sense-engagement with ever more challenging circumstances, amid appropriate climactic conditions. Bruce gives an example of what he is getting at with respect to "Tot," supposed secretary of Osiris.

> The word Tot is Ethiopic, and there can be little doubt it means the dog-star. It was the name given to the first month of the Egyptian year. The meaning of the name, in the language of the province of Sirè, is an *idol,* composed of different heterogeneous pieces; it is found having this signification in many of their books. Thus a naked man is not a *Tot,* but the body of a naked man, with a dog's head, or ass's head, or a serpent instead of a head, is a *Tot.*[12]

The different forms of the idols suggested to Bruce different phases of observed astronomical phenomena of public utility. Likewise, he defers from the views of Iamblichus and others that the *Crux Ansata* (or ankh) commonly in Thoth's hand was a symbol of divine being proceeding through the heavens, or of eternal life. Rather, Bruce reckons it simply a monogram of his name: TO (with the *O* above the *T*). Of course, without realizing it, Bruce provides more possible meat for the deep seeker of astral symbols; that is, if *Tot* is Sirius, and Enoch is *Tot,* then that could explain Enoch's assumption to the heavens, his transformation into a divine light source, and manifest link with knowledge of the Flood, especially if it be considered that the phrase "sons of God" might refer to the stars (or Watchers)—and perhaps we make the additional step of identifying Seth, the son of Adam in Genesis, with ancient Egyptian god Seth, son of Geb!*

---

*Depicted as the so-called Sethian animal, identified by this author in *The Babylon Gene* (2013; under nom de plume "Alex Churton") with the Egyptian desert hare—or as a man with an Egyptian desert hare's head. Incidentally, the bilateral hieroglyph of the desert hare means "to be."

Thus, Bruce may possibly have rationalized the legend of Enoch's pillars by automatically conflating them in his mind with the stelae of Egypt, assessed by Bruce as objects giving useful information about flooding, designed to withstand nature's erosions. In other words, like a good man of the age of reason, he assumes the rational fact of sense obviates obscure myth. For example, Bruce refers to a stele of hieroglyphics (14 × 16 inches) showing a naked man standing on two crocodiles holding both a serpent and a scorpion in either hand and being brought to his attention by Abyssinia's generous king at Axum in 1771. Bruce calls it "one of those private Tots, or portable almanacs."

Fig. 12.5. "No. 1 A Table of Hieroglyphics, Found at Axum 1771";
from Bruce's *Travels* (1790), bk. II, ch. III

Fig. 12.6. "No. 2 A Table of Hieroglyphics, Found at Axum 1771" (Reverse of "No. 1"); from Bruce's *Travels* (1790), bk. II, ch. III)

One of the serpents is the tail of a lion. Above the figure is the head of a bearded man with a curious striped cap. Bruce takes it for the "Cnuph or Animus Mundi," though Apuleius, whom Bruce doubts, says this latter was made in the likeness of no creature whatsoever. On the reverse Bruce observes not only the crux ansata (ankh) and Tot but also what he takes to be plain numbers, such as 1,119; 45; and 19 and other arithmetical figures.

202 of Hermetic Philosophy

He reckons it an almanac displayed for public guidance in the seasons, the state of the heavens, and of diseases prevalent under such influences. Into this context, he then introduces Hermes, whose literary prowess he takes from Iamblichus's *de mysteriis.* "Hermes," Bruce writes, "is said to have composed 36,535 books, probably of this sort, or they might contain the correspondent astronomical observations made in a certain time at Meroë, Ophir, Axum, or Thebes, communicated to be hung up for the use of the neighbouring cities."[13] Bruce then quotes from Iamblichus's fellow Neoplatonic philosopher Porphyry that what the Egyptian almanacs contained is but a small part "of the Hermaic ["Hermetic"] institutions; all that relates to the rising of the moon and planets, and of the stars and their influence, and also some advice upon diseases."

Bruce goes on to hypothesize about the origin of language, believing it was unlikely to have been invented before the Flood (*good-bye Enoch's pillars!*), but probably, by necessity, soon after. He proposes hieroglyphics the first form, developed by Cushites and later simplified into the Ethiopian language, which appeared to have some hieroglyphic remnants to Bruce's eyes. One naturally speculates whether the Hermes-son-of-Cush theme may not be a kind of shorthand for the development Bruce believed took place historically in Ethiopia and Egypt, where writing, architecture, and geometry were all, he believed, combined in a kind of perpetual battle over fear of rising water.

Taking all of this on board, we are not surprised to find Bruce more amused than surprised by the contents of the Book of Enoch, for which learned Europe had been waiting since late antiquity. Bruce makes no allusion to Enoch in Masonic terms. He may not have known, or have been interested in, the use made of Enoch in the Ancient and Accepted Rite and would probably have been unimpressed if he had. Other than that, Enoch had practically disappeared from common Grand Lodge–type Masonic practice (Bruce was a member of the Grand Lodge of Scotland). Indeed, had Bruce been faced with the question, he would certainly have insisted that Enoch could not have inscribed the name of God on a plate, or anything else, because there existed no means to do so, there being no writing before the Flood, in Bruce's opinion, and as he states boldly, "it is very clear, God did not invent letters, nor did Moses."[14]

Bruce is content with the idea that the Book of Enoch—though it went before Job in the Abyssinian canon—was yet an apocryphal book and used as such, he argued, by Saint Jude as a rhetorical example of what Jude's opponents accepted; that is, "your own prophet tells you . . ."[15] In fact, the plain sense of Jude's epistle does not support Bruce's view and is quoted by the "brother of James" (most likely Jesus's brother) as authoritative.

> All that is material to say further concerning the book of Enoch is, that it is a Gnostic book, containing the age of the Emims, Anakims, and Egregores, supposed descendants of the sons of God, when they fell in love with the daughters of men, and had sons who were giants. These giants do not seem to have been so charitable to the sons and daughters of men, as their fathers had been. [Bruce describes the descent into cannibalism, which makes the giants' victims cry to God] and God sends a flood which drowns both them and the giants.[16]

This curt summary accounts, Bruce says, for about four or five of the first chapters and is but a quarter of its contents, "but my curiosity led me no further. The catastrophe of the giants, and the justice of the catastrophe, had fully satisfied me." Bruce then relates how Dr. Woide left London for Paris with letters from the Secretary of State to Lord Stormont, ambassador at the court, for permission to peruse the manuscript in the French king's care, "but I know not why, it [the translation] has nowhere appeared. I fancy Dr. Woide was not much more pleased with the conduct of the giants than I was."[17]

Bruce's anti-enthusiastic testimony must conclude our investigation into Enoch's influence on the formation of Masonic mythology, for much of the lava of that mythology had, by the time of Bruce's death in 1794, solidified, with "regular" Freemasonry constitutionally unable to supplement, or exploit, its knowledge of Enoch, such as it was.

While the mid to late eighteenth century saw the greatest flourishing of Masonic experimentation, when many roads were followed in quest for the lost word, it is arguable that the meaning Enoch may have had to some "old Masons" was itself lost, as "regular" Freemasonry embraced a moralizing, rationalistic, Newtonian celebration of Solomon's Temple that shaped subsequent Freemasons' mental furniture. Nevertheless, Freemasons continued to base their legendary lineage upon a nuanced notion of an "ancient theology" derived from Adam and transmitted by initiation.

# THIRTEEN
# Enter Isaac Newton

Let's backtrack some seventy-five years from the time of Freemason James Bruce's death in 1794 to the period in which London's Grand Lodge was formed. In 1719, John Desaguliers became the Grand Lodge's third grand master.* Serving as "Deputy Grand Master" from 1722–1723 and again in 1726, it was Desaguliers, in league with Scottish clergyman James Anderson (author of the *Constitutions*) and Whig courtiers to the relatively new Hanoverian regime such as John, 2nd Duke of Montagu (grand master, 1721) and the Duke of Richmond, master, from 1723, of the Rummer and Grapes Lodge, Westminster, who would initiate the transformation of Freemasonry into its primary modern form.

Now divorced institutionally from the masons' trade, a key aspect of the philosophy underpinning the new "Craft" emerged from Desaguliers' personal devotion to Sir Isaac Newton, who would die at the grand age of eighty-four on March 20, 1726.† Desaguliers's worship of Newton was revealed in 1728 in an "allegorical poem," *The Newtonian System of the World, the Best Model of Government,* in which Desaguliers presented the orderly Newtonian universe as perfectly

---

*John Desaguliers (1683–1744), originally Jean des Aguliers, Huguenot refugee from France. Raised in England from age two, he was educated at Christ Church, Oxford; lectured on experimental philosophy at Hart Hall in 1710; and graduated M.A. in 1712. In 1714, he was elected Fellow of the Royal Society, becoming curator of experiments, in which time he invented the planetarium for public education, while writing on physics, astronomy, and mathematics.

†"Old style" Julian calendar, when the New Year started on March 25, the spring equinox.

Fig. 13.1. Isaac Newton
(1642–1727)

representative of God ("the Almighty Architect"), as Newton wished
the universe to be seen. Desaguliers waxed lyrical as to how "with
Newton's help" men could now see that it was "attraction" that governed the world's machine and, by extension, the perfect fraternity.
Parallels with a spruced-up idea of the lodge were practically explicit,
as Desaguliers extolled "Harmony" as the principle not only of the universe but also of the system of government, now established by tolerant
Hanoverian authority, worthy of respect, not rejection, as Tory Jacobites
(supporters of exiled Stuarts) were wont to think.*

While reminiscent of Neoplatonic conceptions of Harmony dear
to those who followed paths delineated by Pico, Ficino, Giorgi, and
the Renaissance "ancient theology," Desaguliers's conception is more
coolly mathematical, social, and political, more "modern" in the rational
sense. Desaguliers believed that Newton offered clear demonstration,
a practical system rather than supposition based on ancient authority
superseding logic. Desaguliers desired to educate his audience to the
amazing shift Newton had accomplished—a shift very much in the
direction of Godly knowledge, against fanatical superstition.

---

*Evidence suggests a majority of the "old Masons" of London were Tories with possible
Jacobite sympathies.

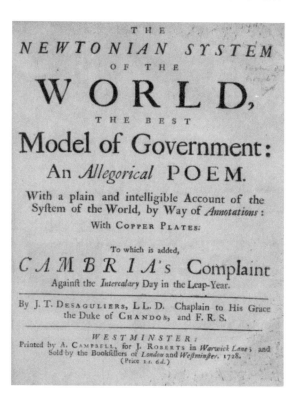

Fig. 13.2. Desaguliers's
*The Newtonian System
of the World*

Nevertheless, as we shall see, Newton would have been uncomfortable were his *Philosophiæ Naturalis Principia Mathematica* ("Mathematical Principles of Natural Philosophy," 1687) and *Opticks* (1704) taken to be truly "new." Newton stressed how his work only confirmed mathematically what had once been central to the knowledge of an ancient civilization. In deference to his master, Desaguliers respected this view when in his notes to the first verses of his poem, he maintained that

> the System of the Universe, as taught by Pythagoras, Philolaus, and others of the Ancients [that the planets go round a center], is the same, which was since revived by Copernicus, allow'd by all the unprejudic'd of the Moderns, and at last demonstrated by Sir Isaac Newton.[1]

And further in verse:

> What made the Planets in such Order move,
> He [Pythagoras] said, was Harmony, and mutual Love.
> The Musick of the Spheres did represent
> That ancient Harmony of Government:
> When Kings were not ambitious yet to gain
> Other's Dominions, but their own maintain . . .[2]

*Attraction,* Desaguliers observed, directed but did not dictate planetary movement, and "attraction" was the basis for wise government. The new King George I ruled by love of his people, declared Desaguliers, a love of (anti-Catholic) liberty in tune with the planets, themselves guided by harmonious mutuality, a pleasing music, as opposed to discordant strains of tyrannical compulsion; namely, the papacy and the French monarchy. It is thanks to Newton, Desaguliers seems to say, that the cause of British liberty is now in tune with the cosmos, set firmly on a system of sacred love expressed in number and equable harmony.

The Enlightenment had arrived, and with it, the modern lodge: radix of harmonious building, or "raising" of men.

Newton's own enlightenment did not, however, come from the rationalist assumptions that came to typify the eighteenth century. Much to the anger, embarrassment, and not infrequently blank or hostile indifference of twentieth-century historians of science, it has become increasingly clear since the 1930s that Isaac Newton did not subject his religion to mathematics but instead received his mathematics as God-given ally of revelation, within the context of a divinely created order. For Newton, mathematics promoted knowledge of God, and served God. Natural philosophy (science) was not "objective"; that is, outside of the system it undertook to understand. Its interest was truth and by definition therefore consistent with God, who would always be found to have "judged aright," having fathomed all proportions, and "without him was not anything made that was made" (John 1:3). The mathematician sought God's harmonious intelligence expressed in creation. Indeed, the very nature and experience of mathematical discourse bore witness to that intelligence; it was not a matter of human opinion. A mathematical proposition, properly calculated, was unassailable and of the nature of truth, which was divine. Genesis witnessed a creation undertaken with respect to number: there being seven days, divided equally according to first principle.

Born on Christmas Day, a few months after the beginning of the English Civil Wars (August 1642) and a generation after the birth of astrologer and mathematician Elias Ashmole (who fought for the king in the wars), young Newton enjoyed the full benefit of Kepler and Galileo's discoveries, which built on Copernicus, as well as a classical education in the sciences at Cambridge. He also had ample opportunity to develop within himself an annoying disquiet over contemporary disharmonies in theology. The civil wars, which shaped his world, were fueled by mutually inconsistent, violently competitive religious convictions that drove men into mutual enmity, generating death, destruction, misery, and perpetual contention.

Like many intelligent, sensitive individuals coming into maturity in such conditions, Newton eschewed the vulgarity of his times and sought solace in knowledge rooted firmly in the past. When Newton compared that inherited knowledge to the man-made world he saw around him, he saw man's chief problem was ignorance of the true God whose creation was manifestly *not* at war with itself. To Newton, the natural world was innocent, conforming harmoniously to law, without dispute. If only man could do the same! Man was given ten rules, and one of love that summed the others up, but still veered astray like the blind to the destruction of himself and his fellows.

When Newton looked at the "how" of natural things, he looked to things as they presented themselves to him, and he looked into what men in the past had said about those things. Very frequently, he observed that the views of the ancients conformed to what he himself suspected and attempted to test systematically. So much so, in fact, that he would in time embrace the firm conviction that practically all important discovery of natural law was *rediscovery* of a once pristine knowledge of the past that had since become garbled by ignorance multiplied through the generations: a process he also observed in the deformation of Christian truth into competing religious sects, and of religion in general. Like the Renaissance sages we have discussed, he was also bitten by the idea of a prisca theologia, only we may say that in Newton's case, he more firmly identified the essence of ancient spiritual knowledge with knowledge of the cosmos—like Josephus's Sethites—that the ancient religion and science were inseparable at the root, though not indivisible in the course of time. Time, then, represented to Newton a process of deformation of knowledge, which suggested to him the essence of his life's work: to arrest that deformation and reintroduce humanity to core truths of divine law with respect to nature, which might then lead to reformation of religious practice and universal cleansing of conscience.

For example, when Newton approached the extraordinarily difficult question of how gravity worked, he, as Kepler had done with respect to planetary movement, took Pythagoras's cue, comparing the lengths of musical strings with the distances of the planets, convinced that Pythagoras understood by means of the relation of the "harmony of the heavens" to musical intervals that the weights of the planets toward the sun were reciprocal as the squares of their distances from the sun.

As Michael White noted in his *Isaac Newton: The Last Sorcerer* (1987), an early version of Newton's Query 23 for his *Opticks* records Newton's observation: "Whence it seems to have been an ancient opinion that matter depends upon a deity for its laws of motion as well as for its existence."[3] To understand gravity, Newton was sure that God was not simply a deus ex machina (as "Enlightenment" deists would suppose) but was involved spiritually in the sustenance of cosmic structure. He took his cue both from Genesis and the arrival on earth of God's creative intelligence as testified by the New Testament. According to Michael White, Newton came to believe that Christ had a spiritual body that became flesh for his earthly operation and became spiritual again at the Resurrection. This conception informed his insight into the maintenance of gravity, so that "the incorporeal ether which facilitates the phenomenon of gravitation (and perhaps other forces) is actually the body or spiritual form of Jesus Christ."[4] This idea seems consistent to a significant extent with Robert Fludd's identifying Metatron with the anima mundi, and the anima mundi with Christ, for the anima mundi (or world soul) is the invisible sustenance of life in the universe, into which, or whom, according to III Enoch, the heaven-dwelling Enoch ultimately becomes transfigured. Newton was of course aware that in Genesis the creation is undertaken by "Alhim" (or "Elohim") or "Gods," hence the momentous decision: "Let *us* create man in our image and likeness" (Genesis 1:26).

For Newton, Christ is the agent by whom God created all things (John 1:1–4), and therefore, the spiritual body of Jesus is the medium by which celestial mechanism is maintained. Scriptural testimony to this conception is abundant in the Wisdom literature (where "Lady Wisdom" herself plays this role) and particularized to Jesus Christ in Matthew 28:20: "Teaching them to observe all things whatsoever I have commanded you: and, lo, *I am with you always,* even unto the end of the world. Amen" (my italics).

The idea of a spiritual dimension in, and sovereign to, creation, participating in change and transformation, predisposed natural philosophers in Newton's time to pursue alchemy, and Newton was exceptional in this pursuit only by the degree of zeal and experimental exactitude he invested in it. He left a veritable library of the most extensive notes of his alchemical experimentation to a largely disinterested posterity. In 1675, in the midst of his long preoccupation, Newton communicated with a

"Mr. F" (alchemists used simple code names for each other). *Mr. F* might have been Ezekiel Foxcroft (ca. 1633–1675),* recently retired Fellow of King's College, Cambridge, remembered as translator of Johann Valentin Andreae's *Chymical Wedding of Christian Rosenkreutz,* written in 1606 and sometimes erroneously called the "third Rosicrucian manifesto," since it was pirated in Strasbourg in 1616, a year after the *Fama* was republished with the *Confessio Fraternitatis.* Foxcroft's translation was printed posthumously in 1690. Foxcroft's mother, Elizabeth (sister of Benjamin Whichcote, 1609–1683, leader of the Cambridge Platonists), was friendly with Cambridge Platonist Henry More and theosophist and alchemical enthusiast Anne Finch, Viscountess Conway of Ragley Hall, Warwickshire. Elizabeth Foxcroft was herself an alchemist and aficionado of "Teutonic Theosopher" Jacob Böhme (1575–1624), shoemaker-mystic (or gnostic) of Görlitz in Saxon Lusatia. Böhme envisioned the universe—and Man and Christ's role in it—as manifesting a vast spiritual-alchemical process, centered on the human heart, receptor of divine knowledge. Newton admired Böhme too. Newton's communication with "Mr. F" referred to an alchemical document titled "Manna" that "W.S." had sent to Mr. F, and which Mr. F had sent to Newton. Newton noted on the manuscript:

For alchemy does not trade in metals as ignorant vulgars think, which error has made them distress that noble science; but she has also material veins of whose nature God created handmaidens to conceive & bring forth its creatures. . . . This philosophy both speculative & active is not only to be found in the volume of nature but also in the sacred scriptures, as in Genesis, Job, Psalms, Isaiah & others. In the knowledge of this philosophy God made Solomon the greatest philosopher in the world.[5]

---

*This is the date of death given in the Cambridge Alumni registers, whereas the previous year is given in the Eton School registers, which may or may not cast doubt on the ascription of "Mr. F" to Foxcroft.

Like fellow adepts, Newton had his own alchemical pseudonym, an anagram of his Latin name, whereby Isaacus Neuutonus became alchemist *Ieoua* (Jehova) *Sanctus Unus* ("God, Holy, One," or One Holy God), reminiscent of Elias Ashmole's alchemical, Neoplatonic motto *Ex Uno Omnia*, "From the One, All," and the Smaragdine Tablet of Hermes Trismegistus—which Newton found inspiring—in which the cosmic alchemical process is to "work the miracle of the One Thing." Our modern equivalent, or analogy, to that One Thing might be said to be a unified field theory of physics that so tantalizingly eluded the elder Einstein.

Newton followed Rosicrucian apologist Michael Maier (1568–1622) in seeing ancient myths as sometimes expressing alchemical knowledge. Indeed, he made copious notes from Maier's *Symbola Aureæ Mensæ duodecim nationum* (Frankfurt, 1617) and from Maier's other works on alchemy and mythology. A myth found in Ovid's *Metamorphoses* and in Homer's *Odyssey* attracted Newton's attention. It described Apollo giving Vulcan a view from afar of his wife Venus abed with Mars. Smithy to the gods, Vulcan fashioned a fine net of ironlike strength in which the lovers were caught *en flagrant* and hung from the ceiling for the Olympians' entertainment. As Venus means "copper" in alchemy, and Mars "iron," and Vulcan "fire," their participation in the net suggested an experiment to Newton, which he undertook. The experiment of cooking copper and iron in a slow fire, resulting in a purple alloy with a streaky surface resembling a net, has since been repeated. Newton saw this kind of knowledge as prisca sapientia knowledge he called "astronomical theology," a staple attainment of antediluvians. The work of Böhme and others would have stimulated Newton to think of alchemy as coming from the divine process of original creation. The quest for the Philosopher's Stone, then, was at the least an analogy for the return to the elementary formula or formulae of that which precipitated constellation of primal elements.

Such knowledge Newton did not think should be universally available, but secreted among those who had demonstrated worthiness, and he was always on the lookout both for that quality and any perceived slip from that state in those he knew. On April 26, 1676, for example, he wrote to Henry Oldenburg, editor of the Royal Society's Transactions, to commend Robert Boyle's discretion in restricting communication of matters to do with "philosophical mercury": "Mr Boyles uncommon experiment about the incalescence of Gold & quicksilver . . ." wrote Newton, "may possibly be an inlet to something more noble, not to be communicated without immense danger to the world if there should be any verity in the Hermetick writers."[6] Those "Hermetick" verities were spelled out in Elias Ashmole's introduction and translation of *Fasciculus Chemicus or Chymical Collections. Expressing the Ingress, Progress, and Egress, of the Secret Hermetick Science out of the choicest and most famous authors* (London, 1650), in which Ashmole makes it piously plain that the alchemical adept should separate himself from the bulk of humanity to live a wholly virtuous, celibate life of spiritual dedication, to be a vessel of spiritual inspiration. This life Newton was happy to aspire to whenever he could, remaining, by all accounts, a perpetual virgin.

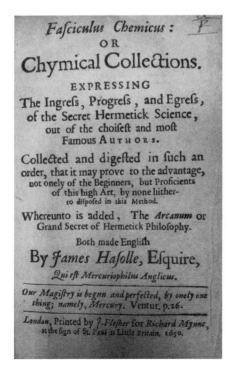

Fig. 13.3. *Fasciculus Chemicus or Chymical Collections* by Elias Ashmole

# FOURTEEN

# "A History of the Corruption of the Soul of Man"

According to the late John Chambers, the title above would be appropriate to the five million words or so contained in two trunks of Newton's notes auctioned in 1936. Their contents are now in process of being revealed at newtonproject.ox.ac.uk. "Everywhere," writes Chambers, "Newton is charting the descent of man's soul from perfection through constant falling-off and fretful renewals until, not far in our own future (Newton suggests a *diluvium ignis,* or deluge of fire, in 2060) everything ends with an apocalypse followed by a radically transformed world."[1]

Stephen Snobelen, director of the Newton Project, Canada, insists that Newton's theological writings were of equal importance to Newton as his natural philosophy and should be seen as components of Newton's great *overarching* concern: "the restoration of man's original pristine knowledge of God and the world."[2]

Union of the physical sciences and man's spiritual destiny is clearly visible in the way Newton approaches his theory of ancient temples. For Newton, the ancients didn't go to such feats of engineering simply to exhibit their culture. Their monumental structures, he believed, represented the universe on earth. As is well known, Newton was deeply embroiled in the symbolism and geometry of King Solomon's Temple, holding Solomon as antiquity's most profound figure, worthy of his time-honored link with Lady Wisdom.

## THE TEMPLE OF WISDOM

As far as Newton was concerned, Solomon recognized that geometry could represent God and the universe, a notion to which sacred architecture through the ages gave testimony, being incidentally the valued possession of master masons who constructed the greatest examples. Indeed, it is likely that London's Grand Lodge, under Desaguliers's mastership (after 1719), specifically emphasized this aspect of practical and symbolic geometry by elevating King Solomon's Temple, whose symbolism—related allegorically to geometry and morality—now permeates regular Freemasonry's three degrees. For Newton, Solomon's Temple was key to the wisdom of the ancients, its proportions encoding prophecy for the future.

Struck by the coincidence of the Copernican heliocentric theory with the view of Pythagoras's pupil Philolaus that at the center of the cosmos was a great fire, Newton believed the "sacred flame" central to many surviving temple sites proved that the ancients were mirroring knowledge of the heavens on earth; that is, they already knew what Galileo was forbidden by the church to assert. Newton took the Greek name "prytaneum"—given to the ever-burning fire in a town's center (from *prytaneis,* or "executive seat," where authorities gathered)—for such temples. Newton believed the wise of the ancients recognized the heavens above to be the true and real temple of God, so they mirrored its central life-giving force by the prytaneum, which they framed with reference to the heavenly bodies. The confines of the structure were then naturally regarded as sacred, due to what they represented, the spirit of which the structure and space embodied. Thus, *knowledge of the universe and knowledge of the divine were one.* According to Michael White, "Newton perceived himself as the new Solomon and believed it was his God-given duty to unlock the secrets of Nature, whether they were scientific, alchemical, or theological."[3] Furthermore, it now appears that Newton specifically held to the conviction of those whose testimonies animate part 2 of this book, that as Michael White puts it, "he was convinced that the ancients had once held the key to all knowledge and that this had been dissipated into the arcane philosophies."[4]

## THE ANCIENTS KNEW ALREADY

Now, the formal elegance of Newton's *Principia* already suggests a kind of apotheosis of geometry, and this work in particular encouraged a kind of deism in the eighteenth century—that God had set a basically perfect machine in order and let it run, impersonally. The other interpretative possibility was a pantheism, or identification of God with the universe, where the mind of God was so expressed in the natural philosophy of creation that mind and creation, being so identified, were substantially inseparable. That seems to have been the vision of Bruno, but even in the mathematical oasis of *Principia,* Newton was emphatic about the mysterious transcendence of God's ways, writing in the "General Scholium" that ends the work that "the supreme God is all power to perceive, to understand, and to act, but in a manner not at all human, in a manner not at all corporeal, in a manner utterly unknown to us . . . nor ought to be worshipped under the representation of any corporeal thing."

If God should choose to transform his creation by deluge of fire, which is not something necessarily willed by the structure of the universe itself, though it may be, as it were a possibility, or probability, "programmed in" from the beginning. It is the sovereign, ultimately incomprehensible will of God that decides the destiny of the whole, not the logic of mathematics alone. Naturally, then, the figure of Noah interested Newton, for Noah was entrusted with a secret of the first great deluge willed by God to punish wickedness. Furthermore, Noah had of course brought with him the antediluvian knowledge of the Sethite, Adamic inheritance, which Josephus records was inscribed on the pillars subsequently ascribed to Enoch. In his unpublished paper *Theologiæ Gentilis Origines Philosophicæ* ("The Philosophical Origins of Pagan Theology," chapter 2), Newton identifies Noah with Saturn, king of the first Golden Age, "and by far the happiest."[5]

Therefore since the golden age is the first of the eras, Saturn, who was ruling at that time, must be Noah, and his son Jupiter in the next age must be Noah's son Cham, and therefore Jupiter's sons—Hercules, Osiris, Typhon and Vulcan—must be sought among the sons of Cham. I am now speaking about the Egyptian Gods. For the Chaldaeans, the Assyrians and the Greeks worshipped various different men under the names of the same Gods, adapting them to their own nations. For since they said that Jehovah, whom the Greeks called Ιαω, the Latins father *Iaon* or Jupiter, was the name of the supreme God—etc. . . . As long as all men lived under the government of Noah in Babylonia, the golden age endured. With the division of the earth and the government of Cham in Egypt the silver age begins. When the sons of Cham subsequently set off for the different lands which were granted to them by their father and established new kingdoms separately, then began the age of bronze. In the fourth stage, Belus, the grandson of Cham, founded the government of the Assyrian Shepherds by violence and bloodshed.[6]

Newton related the Flood story as told by Chaldaean historian Abydenus (ca. 200 BCE), allegedly taken from primordial texts wherein King Sisithrus plays the Noah part, having been warned of a flood by Saturn, the god Newton believed derived from Noah. Completing his mission, Sisithrus is swept into heaven, like Noah's grandfather Enoch.[7] Newton believed the gods of the pagans were natural phenomena, the chiefest being the planets, but that their names came from revered men who contributed something to posterity, only God's chosen vessels avoided this fundamental error of idolatry.

So the ancients knew the Earth went around the sun, and this astronomical theology was allied by Newton in his treatise "On the Church" to the moral point that men love the Lord God with all their hearts, souls, and minds, and their neighbors as themselves, just as the planets traveled peacefully about the fire that warmed them and kept them in order by attraction. Noah, after making a burnt offering fol-

lowing deliverance from the Flood (an assembly constituting a prytaneum), received seven laws of conduct found in Genesis 9, binding on
humanity, descendants of Noah.

Having perceived the religion of the prytaneum alone might have
led people astray; a "manual" of the seven Noachide laws was given to
specify the purity God desired. In his "Irenicum," Newton observes
that "all nations were originally of the religion comprehended in the
precepts of the sons of Noah, the chief of which were to have one God,
& not to alienate his worship, nor profane his name; to abstain from
murder, theft, fornication, & all injuries; not to feed on the flesh or
drink the blood of a living animal, but to be merciful even to brute
beasts; & to set up Courts of justice in all cities & societies for putting
these laws in execution."[8]*

The purified religion fell, according to Newton, not long after
Cush went to Egypt, when polytheism emerged from the error of confusing the symbols of religion with the substance: "For 'tis agreed that
idolatry began in the worship of the heavenly bodies and elements."†
The fire of the prytaneum also came to be worshipped, as in Persian
Zoroastrianism. In Newton's *Theologiae Gentiles Origines Philosophicae*,‡
ancient peoples worshipped the same twelve gods based on Noah, his
children, and grandchildren, giving them different names in accordance
with their histories, so Newton compared twelve Greek gods with those
of Romans and Egyptians: "all of a kindred. . . . They lived all at the
same time, which is called the age of the gods"; that is to say, after
Noah's golden age: decline. Nevertheless, the ancient truth came down
in fragments that left tinctures of true philosophy, if garbled.

---

*This stress on the religion of the Noachide law likely explains why Rev. James Anderson
in the 1723 *Constitutions* of the Free and Accepted Masons states that Masons in times
gone by were called "Noachidae," holding to the first principles of religion, which,
Newton believed, were of immutable reason and eternal in nature. See page 158.

†From a draft chapter 2 of a treatise, "On the Origin of Religion & its Corruption."

‡See endnotes 5 and 6.

The Planets & the Elements which are signified by the names of Gods were enumerated by the Egyptians in this order: a Saturn, Jupiter, Mars, Venus, Mercury, Sun, Moon, Fire, Air, Water, Earth (Terra). The Earth (Tellus) which is represented/produced/foreshadowed by the four Elements is the Fifth essence and completes the number twelve. The whole of Philosophy is comprehended in these twelve, provided that the stars indicate Astronomy, and the four Elements the rest of Physiology.[9]

There is a reductionist aspect to Newton's logic that, for better or worse, was much imitated by disciples. Thus, William Whiston, for example—the man who translated Josephus into English and got the "Sesostris pillar" story wrong—also wrote a Newtonian-influenced "New Theory of the Earth" (1696) in which he "explained" the Flood as the effect of the gravitational pull of a passing comet, while the Genesis creation story could be explained as issuing from the vantage point of a passing comet. Predictably, the world's end would also likely come from comet collision or one nudging the Earth from its orbit. A little knowledge can be a dangerous thing. How dangerous, then, an abundance of knowledge? In 1701, Newton eased Whiston's path to taking over Newton's Lucasian professorship of mathematics at Cambridge, but when Whiston's heretical Arianism excluded him from office, Newton, deeply wary of religious controversy, distanced himself—especially as he held views similar to Whiston's on the Trinity—something Newton kept secret lest he lose his academic position. In 1716, Newton blocked Whiston from Royal Society membership, true to a lifelong tendency to favor no one for very long.

Newton was of course wary of philosophical novelties unsupported by sober mathematics, convinced his own discoveries were confirmative only of what records suggested had been lost or corrupted through time. In his own mind he was a restorer, not an innovator. Leading Jacobite, Lord Francis Atterbury, dean of Westminster, echoed this view in a lecture delivered shortly after Newton's death, to wit, that the ancients were "men of genius and superior intelligence who carried their discoveries in every field much further than we today suspect, judging from what remains of their writings. More ancient writings have been lost than have been preserved, and perhaps our new discoveries are of less value than those we have lost."[10]

It might be considered that Newton went to extremes in modestly assessing his work, but he was convinced the ancients knew about the atomic structure of the universe, while even his law of universal gravitation long had been anticipated by Pythagoras's conception of spherical music, which involved, as he saw it, the principle of a gravity whose force diminishes in inverse proportion to the square of the increasing distance.*

Newton believed the raw science was expressed by the ancients as a great mystery, that being a way to transmit to the worthy while concealing from the vulgar, but it only required a weak link in the chain, or a contradiction along the way, or corruption, or disaster, to reduce a coherent mystery into incomprehensible myth. Also, the sense of mystery attached to natural philosophy might come naturally from the sense of awe experienced by those first privileged to glimpse some working of the divine mind, which ultimately is a mystery and divine prerogative. This is not our modern view, and it is certain that if Newton returned to earth in this age, he would want many scientific voices to be arraigned for impiety and heresy as well as perverse deviation from his own expressed intentions. It would make a most interesting spectacle to see Isaac Newton return and address some of our more conceited "geniuses" with the finger that exclaims: "J'accuse!"

---

*Through experiment, Pythagoras discovered an inverse-square relation in string vibration, expressed in the unison of two strings when tensions are reciprocally as the squares of lengths. Newton believed Pythagoras extended this relation to the weights of planets and their distances from the sun. From pursuing this line, Newton numerically calculated gravity from the relation of distance from an object to a gravity source, such as a planet to the sun, or the moon to the earth. Newton reckoned this was true knowledge passed on esoterically but lost in its essence and universality through later posterity's misunderstanding, dulled by moral devolution, or, we might say, consciousness contraction, in subsequent generations.

Of course, it was recognized in his own time by men like natural philosopher Christiaan Huygens (1629–1695) that Newton had in fact far exceeded the ancients in mathematically sequenced deductions and logically unassailable conclusions; he had invented calculus and formulated the laws of gravitation, motion, and light. He had not re-created myths or vague "forces." However, claims made for Newton's primary inventiveness could only be argued upon what had *survived* from the ancients, involving an assumption that what had survived corresponded to what was once known and understood. On the purely evidential demand of science, the claim is sound. However, Newton regarded surviving evidence differently. Newton trusted his intuition, or rather, it must be said, his imagination, which enabled him to perceive that what he envisioned had existed before the predations of time had reduced the legacy of the past, of which legacy only fragments and ashes remained, though enough in his view to justify confidence in an unseen antediluvian world whose knowledge exceeded our own.

On the other hand, it could be that had Newton been witness to some of the current achievements in applied science in technology, he might have been suspected of projecting backward what was in fact *still to come* and that, contrary to what he thought, his vision was more attuned to what had *yet* to come than what had once been. This is all rather circular, however, for Newton could still assume that whatever might come, had in fact been known before him, perhaps in a superior manner, in an uncorrupted past, which past he definitely believed in. And I suspect this would have been the crux of his argument; that is, that the moral and spiritual state of a people is reflected in their access to the profoundest knowledge. It is doubtful, had he seen these times, that he would have concluded that humanity had in fact so advanced from a state of corruption and ignorance and moral wantonness as to imagine it could enjoy the fruits of a knowledge that was, to him, ultimately divine in origin. He would have associated our culture's addiction to technology in warfare and defense as a clear indication of knowledge gone wrong, akin to the corruption of the "giants" who waged war with the gods in ancient Greek myths he wrote about as he found in Diodorus Siculus and Apollodorus, and the slipping into an age of lead, of bloodthirsty ingenuities pursued to bitter ends.

It is also worth adding the thought that by presenting his discoveries as, effectively, "rediscoveries," he was in fact legitimizing them, rather like the image of a postdiluvian younger Hermes finding the Sethite pillar of knowledge, as retold in the Old Charges of Freemasonry; it didn't do Trismegistus's reputation any harm! His stance elevated Newton to the position of a historic archetype, entitled to dispense favors, or retract them, on, or from, whom he wished, which in fact is what he did, as his professional life left a trail of disappointed, hurt, and embittered fellow natural philosophers as well as eager disciples. On the other hand, while that take may satisfy the suspicions of cynicism, it may just be the case that Newton absolutely, genuinely believed that human beings had devolved from a former state of expanded consciousness, and the best we could do was to pick up the pieces. Such is implied in that now famous quote of Newton's that his discoveries represented his choosing the odd pebble on a seashore for examination, only too aware of the vast number of unexplored or formerly unseen pebbles all about him: an "ocean of truth" or endless beach remaining unexplored. This may not have been polite humility only, but rather an indication of how much he considered had already been *lost* to the compass of the human mind. One must bear in mind that for Newton, knowledge ultimately came from God, and God is eternal. Man's finitude—the consequence, Newton accepted, of sin—restricts his operations, and ordinary consciousness, severely.

## NEWTON AND THE "DAIMON"

Regarding access to higher consciousness, John Chambers drew attention to Newton's keen interest in the myths about Rome's alleged second king, Numa Pompilius (dated 753–673 BCE), who, according to legend, had two chief "daimons" as inner guides, among others. Chambers suggests the daimon ("genius," or guardian angel)—a conception Plato associated with Socrates—seems in Newton to be identified with the prisca sapientia (ancient science), in that the daimon is believed to exist outside of ordinary, bounded consciousness, and may be beyond the material universe altogether.[11]

One of Numa's daimons was woodland goddess Egeria, whom legend said Numa married. He also enjoyed the service of muse Tacita, who linked his mind to other geniuses, resulting in the production of "sacred books" that Numa insisted be kept in memory and passed on by their guardians. *Tacita* means "the silent one"—one thinks of the Pythagorean injunction to silence. Newton's interest in Numa lay particularly in his bringing Vesta's virgins to Rome, Vesta's temple being, to Newton's view, a perfect example of an antediluvian prytaneum, for Plutarch (ca. 46–120 CE) observed the temple's simplicity, and its absence of images of God, for it was idolatrous to liken the "highest" to a created thing. The "highest" might then refer to a state of consciousness, or spiritual gnosis. Newton inherited the view that the first principle of being was passionless, pure, invisible, apprehended by abstract intelligence. Newton appears to have experienced such personal exaltations of mind; indeed, it would be difficult to account for his life without such experience. When smaller minds judge such a mind, we know we're going to lose something vital.

Newton believed he had inherited the ideas of Pythagoras, Philolaus, and Aristarchos of Samos—men who had, he perceived, received knowledge from the prisca sapientia—of the "gravity" of the center, of which the sun was an image, suspired by power of the invisible God, delegated to the Son. The idea of the sun as "visible god," attributed to the Thrice Great Hermes, Newton certainly read in Copernicus, and of course in the Hermetic literature imbibed on his alchemical quest. This is the key to seeing how modern science has seriously deviated from Newton's beliefs.

The mathematics of gravity was not his "explanation" of the universe; it was simply a mode of intelligibly perceiving its mechanics, its law. How gravity actually could be sustained in existence brought out what for Newton was the essential metaphysics of creation, and he believed he had scriptural and classical warrant for these beliefs and that the mathematics also suggested the imperative of believing them, for the beauty and pristine qualities of the mathematics could not have occurred randomly, or of itself, but rather mirrored the intelligible nature of the invisible but ultimately inscrutable God. Newton believed the universe itself testified to the way in which men should relate to God, and to one another, and if pure observation and contemplation were insufficient, then one had the personal example of Jesus as set forth providentially through the medium of the gospels and prophecies inspired by consciousness of the highest, yet communicated in ways apprehensible to ordinary minds.

A mathematical account of the universe was also not, in Newton's view, his own invention. It was Pythagoras who had seen that number provided unity amid nature's divers phenomena. Philolaus had seen how, without number, the universe loses form, becoming a phantasmagoria without limit, obscure and indiscernible. Geometry itself could not be man's invention, for it was inherent to the creation, whose harmonies were demonstrable, and must preexist it in the creator's mind. Man may see only an aspect of it, appropriate to his sensory apparatus at his time. Newton felt he had only applied what was there already to be applied. Originality was the prerogative of origin.*

Newton valued most those he considered were in touch with origin.

---

*We may see Newton's faith in harmony in Anderson's *Constitutions* of the Free and Accepted Masons, where it is written: "Let Harmony rule the Lodge"; that is, in distributing the members in harmonious arrangements like the planets, while using the geometer's tools of square and compass to analogize all movements within the lodge, from the heart to the heavens (this is in essence what may be called "the Newtonian Lodge," although existing lodge arrangements, *before* Anderson, Desaguliers, and the "Grand Lodge," may already have been symbolically ripe for acquiring a Newtonian gloss). A late seventeenth-century Masonic catechism gives in answer to the question "How high is your lodge?" the answer: "Without foots, yards or inches, it reaches to heaven." See Churton, *Freemasonry: The Reality* (2009), 61; *Sloane Ms.* 3329 (British Library).

Thus, he respected Moses, familiar with the mysteries of Egypt. Newton believed Moses left a description of the creation in numbered sequence fitted for ordinary minds. The real, or interior, knowledge was reserved for those judged fit to receive it, for Moses had seen from the circumstances surrounding the Great Flood what happened when infantile or malevolent minds accessed knowledge beyond their capacity. Instead of making them wise, it rendered them dangerous. Democracy was emphatically not, in Newton's estimation, a principle of infinite extension.

Amid a wealth of fresh Newtonian material now available to a seeking public in the Newton Project (one wonders if he would have approved!) are Newton's notes from the work of "Cambridge Platonist" and Royal Society Fellow, Rev. Ralph Cudworth (1617–1688). We may observe closely from these notes that Newton sees the ancient wisdom of the universe as having been transmitted specifically through initiatic, not publicly accessible, traditions. In this instance, he is interested in what he believes was a link in the chain of tradition between Pythagoras and the Orphic Mysteries, a Greek mystery cult traced back to the magical lyre of Orpheus, promising knowledge of the gods' origins, and union with "god."

> The Pythagorick principles are the Orphick traditions. For what things Orpheus delivered mystically those Pythagoras learned when he was initiated by Aglaophemus [a *prisca theologus* according to Ficino] in the Orphick mysteries. Pythagoras himself affirming as much in his book called the Holy oration (with yet perhaps not Pythagoras's but writ by one of his scholars) p 296. Proclus upon the Timæus.
>
> Pythagoras as we are informed by Porphyrius & Iamblichus, learned something from all these four, from the Ægyptians, the Persian Magi, the Chaldæans & Orpheus or his followers. And accordingly Syrianus [MS. Coll. Caj. Cant. p. 14] makes the Orphick & Pythagorick principles to be one & the same.

It is Pythagorical to follow the Orphick genealogies. For from the Orphick tradition downward by Pythagoras was the knowledge of the Gods derived to the Greeks [Proclus in Timæum p 289, Cudw. p 299.][12]

That Newton believed not only that superior knowledge of the universe was held in antediluvian times but that elements of that knowledge were handed down esoterically as well is quite explicit from miscellaneous draft portions of his *Theologiæ Gentilis Origines* ("The Philosophical Origins of Pagan Theology"), now held in the National Library of Israel. Newton writes in chapter 1:*

The ancients developed two philosophies, a sacred philosophy and a common philosophy. Philosophers taught the sacred philosophy to their disciples by types and enigmas; orators committed the common philosophy to writing openly and in a popular style. Sacred philosophy flourished especially in Egypt, and was based on a knowledge of the stars. This is evident from the annual procession of the priests instituted in honour of this Philosophy. Clement of Alexandria described the pattern of this procession, which he had seen with his own eyes, as follows.

The Egyptians practise a philosophy all their own; their sacred procession shows this clearly.

The singer comes first, carrying one of the symbols of music. They say that he should learn two of the books of Mercury, one of which contains the Hymns of the Gods, the other the rules of the Royal life.

---

*Titled "That Pagan Theology was Philosophical, and primarily sought an astronomical and physical understanding of the world system; and that the twelve Gods of the major Nations are the seven Planets together with the four elements and the quintessence Earth."

After the singer comes the Caster of Horoscopes, holding in his hand a timepiece and a palm, Symbols of Astrology. He must have the astrological books of Mercury on the tip of his tongue. There are four such books, one of which is about the order of the Stars that appear as Fixed, another about the conjunction and luminosity of the Sun and the Moon, while the remaining two are about the rising of the stars.

Then follows the scribe of the sacred things, with plumes on his head, and in his hands a book and a ruler [or basket], in which there is both ink for writing and a reed with which they write. (10 books pertain to him.) He has to know the so-called Hieroglyphs, 2 Cosmography and 3 Geography, 4 the order of the Sun and Moon and of 5 the Five Planets, 6 the Chorography of Egypt and 7 the Description of the Nile, as well as 8 the organisation of the apparatus for the sacred rites and of the consecrated places.[13]

You get a feeling that Newton was very impressed by Clement of Alexandria's (third century CE) description of an Egyptian religious procession, ordered by the disposition of knowledge of the heavens. For him, it pointed far back to a lost golden age.

And what might we think today of Newton's estimation of the multitude being incapable of coping with profound knowledge, given to downward-tending corruption? Well, I pen this chapter's coda at 10:49 a.m. on Saturday, July 20, 2019. It is today fifty years since Apollo 11's *Eagle* spacecraft landed safely on the moon. I, like millions of others, recall being awestruck at the sight of this unparalleled, astounding achievement relayed by television around the world. When initiating the moon program, President Kennedy saw it as vital that what men undertook, "free men must fully share." The achievement was not hidden from the multitude, but open and declared. Many of us felt on that early July morning fifty years ago that the world had just gone up a notch on the evolutionary scale, that human consciousness could now rise to only greater heights and that those who landed in the Sea of Tranquility might bring some of that tranquillity home with them.

And here we are . . . fifty years later. Because the Western world is determined to prevent the Islamic Republic of Iran from developing nuclear weapons, the Iranian Revolutionary Guard has hijacked a British-flagged oil tanker in the Straits of Hormuz, threatening a global conflict that we all pray will not erupt. Should such people be permitted to exploit knowledge of the atom? *Should anyone?* The bird has flown . . . and the Eagle has landed.

Astronauts Neil Armstrong, Buzz Aldrin, and Michael Collins left a message on the surface of the moon: "We came in peace for all Mankind."

It is still there.

# FIFTEEN
# Antiquarianism
## Stukeley and Blake

*Life is a pure flame, and we live by an invisible sun within us.*

SIR THOMAS BROWNE, *RELIGIO MEDICI*, 1642

Son of a Lincolnshire lawyer, William Stukeley was born in 1687, five years before Elias Ashmole, grand old man of British antiquarianism, died in London. In some respects, Stukeley picked up work that senior Free-mason Ashmole and his antiquarian father-in-law, Sir William Dugdale, had commenced in the seventeenth century, the century that saw antiquarianism's emergence as a serious gentleman's interest and discipline. And with antiquarianism came archaeology. It was probably Ashmole who was first to use pottery finds as a dating method for ancient sites. A great collector, Ashmole donated his collections to the University of Oxford, organizing the first-ever public museum in the country, still known as the "Ashmolean" and currently sited on Beaumont Street, attracting huge numbers of visitors every year.*

It should now be clear what stimulated men to start digging and

*Readers wishing to know more about the remarkable Elias Ashmole might consult my biography, *The Magus of Freemasonry: The Mysterious Life of Elias Ashmole, Scientist, Alchemist, and Founder of the Royal Society* (2006).

Fig. 15.1. William Stukeley
(1687–1765)

observing and collecting. Interest in antiquity represented a profound need to recover what was lost and to bring it to light for people's improvement. We thus see a clear analogy to rediscovering the pillars of Enoch. Antiquarianism properly started after the dissolution of Britain's monasteries in the 1530s, during the long Protestant backlash against the Roman church. A prime mover in the field of knowledge recovery was John Dee. In that "deluge," as Ashmole notably and poignantly described the monasteries' cruel destruction, so many treasures disappeared forever—including an estimated 98 percent of monastic libraries—that gentlemen of a certain sensitivity began to wonder not only how to save what remained but also to consider what might lie beneath the surface of a changing world, where records of ancient families were disappearing because the old clerical and aristocratic orders had become dislocated by religious and political conflict, in addition to the ordinary ravages of time and change. Antiquarians sought the "Enoch's pillars" of another age of lost wisdom. Thus, antiquarianism went hand in hand with archaeology, the exploration of beginnings (from the Greek *hē archē* = the beginning). How many invaluable secrets lay beneath soil and stone? Answering the question was profoundly stimulated by the prisca theologia and prisca sapientia impulses imported from the continental Renaissance, developed across the Channel in uniquely English ways.

232 of Hermetic Philosophy

British antiquarianism was pursued by country gentlemen, clergymen, lawyers, and doctors. We may recall how physician Sir Thomas Browne (1605–1682)—friend of Ashmole and of John Dee's son Arthur (also a doctor, and alchemist)—wrote in "The Doctor's Religion" that he would love to discover the pillars of Enoch, were it not for doubt over their ever having existed. And here we see a point: What of the past was true, and what was false?

Good people felt a rare but powerful urge to separate fact from legend and myth. An earnest hunger grew for true knowledge of the past, for authentic identity, though cynics then as ever ridiculed the interest. The bringing to bear of disciplined historiographical methods was a feature of the time, and a relatively painstaking, forensic approach to data is notable in Ashmole—trained lawyer and mathematician—evinced in his antiquarian masterpiece, *The History of the Most Noble Order of the Garter* (1672), regarded as a wonder for depth of learning and factual discrimination: qualities eminently manifest in its pages to this day.

William Stukeley followed in the footsteps of Ashmole and Ashmole's friends Robert Plot, John Aubrey, and William Dugdale, and of their illustrious predecessor, Sir William Camden (1551–1623), author of antiquarian and chorographical game-changer, *Britannia* (1586), a study of Britain in its topographical entirety. It is no surprise to learn that ordained minister Stukeley was also trained as a doctor, concerned to improve the nation's health by removing scotomas of obfuscation with sharpened pen.

Stukeley's *Memoirs of Sir Isaac Newton* appeared in 1752. Containing research into Newton's early life, it also told of Stukeley's own relations with he who had presided over Stukeley's Royal Society fellowship in March 1718. Fellowship was one thing, but Newton was dismayed when in November 1721, Sir Hans Sloane and other society dignitaries suggested that Stukeley take Sir William Halley's place as society secretary.* Considering it presumptuous, Newton cold-shouldered Stukeley

---

*Halley is famous for accurately tracking Halley's Comet.

for two or three years. By Christmas 1725, however, Newton relented, and indulged Stukeley with a long conversation.

We had some discourse about Solomons temple [remembered Stukeley]; a matter which I had studyed with attention, & made very many drawings about it, which I had communicated to my Lord Thomas, earl of pembroke, to Mr. Martin Folkes, & some more of my friends. I found, Sr. Isaac had made some drawings of it, & had consider'd the thing: indeed he had studyed every thing. We did not enter into any very particular detail about it. but we both agreed in this, that the architecture was not like any designs, or descriptions yet publick. No authors have an adequate notion of antient, & original architecture. Sir Isaac rightly judged that it was older than any other of the great temples mentioned in history; & was indeed the original model which they followed. He added, that Sesostris in Rehoboams time, took the workmen, from Jerusalem, who built his Egyptian temples, in imitation of it; one in every Nomos [division of territory in Egypt]. & that from thence the Greeks borrow'd their architecture; as they had a good deal of their religious rites, their sculpture, & other arts.

Sir Isaac thought, the Greeks, according to their usual ingenuity, improv'd architecture into a higher delicacy; as they did sculpture and other arts. I confirmed his sentiments by adding, that I could demonstrate (as I apprehended) that the architecture of Solomons temple was what we now call Doric. Then, says he, the Greeks advanced it into the Ionic, & the Corinthian, as the Latins into the composite.[1]

In Stukeley's *Memoirs,* we see him visiting the wide-eyed genius in old age to discuss the infinitude, or otherwise, of the universe, with Stukeley willing to speculate, and Newton interested in his ideas, pondering them warmly. Indeed, from Stukeley's account of Newton we should have little idea that Stukeley is mostly remembered today for

*A direct view of the Remains of the adytum of Stonehenge.*

Fig. 15.2. William Stukeley's *Stonehenge*

lifting John Aubrey's investigation of Stonehenge and Avebury prehistoric sites in Wiltshire to wider historical interest, publishing a systematic theory of their origins.

Stukeley believed that Celtic Druids built Stonehenge. They were, he believed, part of a Phoenician colony who'd received monotheist religion from Abraham. Thus the Druids inherited a portion of the ancient wisdom on which human civilization was founded, which of course, to subsequent theorizers, made Britain something of a providentially touched place, whose very topography was open to mystification. By 1730, Stukeley was prepared to see the massive Avebury site of standing stones in relation to Pythagorean number symbolism, encoding a belief in the Trinity. The legend that Joseph of Arimathea brought Jesus to Britain long after the patriarchal period only made the central idea that much more potent as a new, subtly influential phase of national mythology and occult ideology. For Stukeley, Britain reflected part of God's chosen design, and British history was an archetype for the world.

None of this was lost on revivalists of Druidism in the eighteenth century, and of course much of the spiritual revival stimulated by

Fig. 15.3. A British Druid depicted in
William Stukeley's study of Stonehenge

William Blake's enthusiasm for Stukeley's books on Britain's (alleged)
ancient religion, which persisted through Blake's younger disciples,
and onward through the Victorian era to British Theosophy enthusiasts, to the revival of magic and a "Celtic Church," and on to the
intense reaction against materialism that grew in the 1960s, which

flourishes still in enthusiasm for a spiritually revived Britain as an epitome for the planet.

Visionary artist William Blake (1757–1827) accepted Stukeley's view that the Druids built Stonehenge, and the idea of the original, pristine religion and science being centered in the British Isles, with ultimate apotheosis occurring when the spirit of "Albion" finally heeds his "sister, Jerusalem." "Jerusalem" represents spiritual liberty and the recovery of the whole Man to former glory, at one with the universe and its infinite spiritual life: apocatastasis.

Blake was fully aware of the idea of a pristine religion and science, subsequently corrupted in time, but attributed its corruption in Britain to the Druids themselves, having read in Roman writer Tacitus about Druidic human sacrifice—and the biblical account of Abraham almost sacrificing his own son—a practice scandalous even to Romans, for whom sustained cruelty was frequent state policy. Blake saw human sacrifice as spiritual corruption recurring in his own time, where a union of church and state pressed men into army and navy against Napoleon Bonaparte. For Blake, this call for war and empire was another phase of "human sacrifice," sanctioned by religion—he referred in his prophecy

Fig. 15.4. A self-portrait by William Blake (Essick Collection)

*Jerusalem* to "Druid temples," and "serpent temples" governed by King George—against what he saw as the true interests of human liberty (Blake had also been an enthusiast for American independence).

Personally inspired by the legend of Joseph of Arimathea's coming to Glastonbury with the Christ child, Blake saw the child Jesus as the return of a descendant of innocent patriarchs who united all knowledge before its fall and the Flood's subsequent destruction—which Blake interpreted less as righteous judgment than as a "flood of time and space," or saturation of the human mind with the bindings of materialism. Blake saw the patriarchal period of antediluvians as one involving Britain, land of purity and mirror of heaven, until Druids slipped from divine understanding, instituting an oppressive, knife-bearing priesthood, failing the sweet promise of the original. For Blake, the Fall meant loss of divine consciousness, of the spiritual eternity of the "divine imagination," of full human identity. Formerly, cosmic Man contained in himself the "worlds of eternity," a happy innocence corrupted by the enclosing of higher mind in shackles of rational, logical constraints, believing only in what was demonstrated, amid brooding on mere matter to the detriment or obliteration of clear vision of God within and the infinite *through* Nature "without." What the European Enlightenment saw as Reason, Blake saw as a harbinger and counterfeit savior of materialism. Reason had its place but should never stand alone, abstracted from higher spirit. There were "more things in heaven and earth than dreamt of in your philosophy," he would have quoted to the rationalist literalist.

While his attempt to understand the myth of an ancient corruption of pristine science and religion continued to drive Blake's adult life, it happens that the same can be said of his predecessor Stukeley, though Stukeley's perception of the fall from ancient awareness was definitely not attributed to a usurpation by reason. For Stukeley, as for Newton, reason was one of the faculties corruptible by a diet of falsehoods but was nonetheless a corruption that only reason, furnished with demonstrated knowledge, could cure: reason enlightened by divine vision could interpret knowledge in perspective. In fact, Blake was not so far from Newton as he would think, but of course Newton, by Blake's time, had come to represent a movement of European thought inimical to Blake's spiritual vision, a conception that in fact represented a highly selective interpretation of Newton's true mind, as we have demonstrated.

Stukeley is linked to Blake in curious ways. In Stukeley's book *Stonehenge,* for example, van der Gucht's portrait engraving of the author includes Stukeley's nickname around the oval medallion: "Chyndonnax," a supposed Gaulish Druid. The name also appears on a rock or stone in front of the engraving of a British Druid in the same work. This engraving inspired one of Blake's own earliest engravings, executed when apprenticed to James Basire, engraver to the Society of Antiquaries, whose prestigious ranks Stukeley had dignified before his death in 1765—about the time Blake entered apprenticeship. Blake's engraving of Joseph of Arimathea—for Blake the true, modest image of an ancient Christian—is depicted with the same arms, shape, and position as that of van der Gucht's "Druid." The fact that the left arms form squares may symbolically refer to the claims of Accepted Free-masons of the time; namely, that Druid "architects" were their ancient brethren. Stukeley had been initiated into a London lodge at the Salutation Tavern, Tavistock Street, on January 6, 1721, less than two years after Desaguliers had become the Grand Lodge's grand master, while Stukeley's friend John, 2nd Duke of Montagu, became grand master six months after Stukeley's initiation, on June 24, 1721. Stukeley became master at a new lodge at the Fountain Tavern in the Strand (close to where Blake would spend his last years, in Fountain Court), but when London's Grand Lodge attempted to stimulate a rush of new initiates, Stukeley demitted to form his own lodge in his hometown of Grantham, Lincolnshire. When Anderson's *Constitutions* asserted in 1723 that "Celtic Edifices" evinced the craft's spread from the East, one senses Stukeley's thought behind it, the *Constitutions* being dedicated to the 2nd Duke of Montagu.

Blake's distinctive take was that Joseph of Arimathea was the builder of Gothic cathedrals, and Blake idiosyncratically denied any

Fig. 15.5. *Joseph of Arimathea among the Rocks of Albion*

superiority to Greek architecture, as held by Stukeley in conversation about Solomon's temple with Newton. "Gothic form is living form," Blake famously declared, in contradistinction to Anderson's published belief that Gothic was, at best, inferior to Roman and Greek styles, constituting "rubbish" from an unenlightened past.

## STUKELEY, FREEMASONRY, AND THE *PRISCA SAPIENTIA*

In Stukeley's account of his life, penned in 1753 (four years before Blake's birth), he recorded his suspicion that Masonry, however much it may have changed over time, yet represented the "remains of the mysterys of the antients."

While serving as editor of journal *Freemasonry Today* during the late 1990s, I was fortunate to be approached by Stukeley-scholar David Boyd Haycock with a story he had unearthed from studying Stukeley's 1735 essay *Palæographia Sacra,* in which Stukeley set out to discover "a

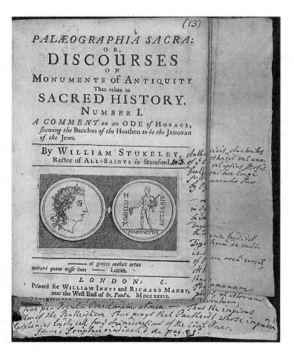

Fig. 15.6. *Palæographia Sacra,* Stukeley's 1735 essay, annotated by Reverend Thomas Hughes

scheme of the first, the antient, and patriarchal religion that had first existed before the birth of Moses and Christ." It is pleasant, as I write this, to know that Stukeley had already formulated the theme of this book some 285 years ago!

Stukeley was aware of Newton's view that lost knowledge of the ancients had come down in "mysterys." Stukeley endeavored to understand the origin of the mysteries of which Masonry was a remnant, arriving at the following conclusion.

> The origin of the mysterys (as we hinted before) is no other than the first corruption of true religion, when they began to deviate from the patriarchal religion, into idolatry and superstition, and this was as nigh as early as the renovation of mankind, after the Noachian deluge.

According to Haycock, the mysteries persisted throughout the ancient world "and it was this secret religion—a fragment of the primeval patriarchal religion—which Stukeley believed the Druids had possessed, and which he hoped to discover in the secrets of Freemasonry."[2] Therefore, Freemasonry existed because of the loss of knowledge incurred through past corruption of an ancient, pristine, and patriarchal religion.

At first, according to Rev. Stukeley, the patriarchs enjoyed "the most excellent gift from heaven," but "its native charms were miserably defac'd, obscur'd and perverted into superstition and idolatry." Moses and Jesus's teachings were intended to *restore* the original religion. This was going quite a lot further than Saint Augustine's belief that while the thing now called Christianity was known to the ancients, its promise had yet to be fulfilled in the person of Christ. Stukeley took the prisca sapientia's implications to their logical conclusion. What was in the distant, obscured past was better than what followed. One might add that Enoch's pillars would have constituted the appropriate visual emblem of this ancient knowledge if Josephus's pillars story had come from scripture, but the essential *idea* is there, and Stukeley undoubtedly knew about the pillars and thought about them, both from a Freemasonry perspective and from his historical and scriptural knowledge.* Blake's own view was consistent in the main with Stukeley's, though Blake remythologized the idea of antediluvian corruption, rendering it directly applicable to political and social realities in the "Albion" of his lifetime. This Blake did by dramatizing the conflict of what we may call "patriarchetypes," akin to Gnostic aeons who battle it out spiritually for possession of Albion's psyche: the results mirrored in actual conditions "on earth"; that is, in the realm manifest-to-senses.†

Blake understood that access to primal, antediluvian knowledge—called "paradise" by Blake—was attainable through poetry, painting, and music, which for Blake constitute the primary arts of divine imagination and his version, so to say, of the seven liberal arts, for Blake had an aversion to mathematics and geometry and the "law of the numbers." This aesthetic and temperamental aversion set him apart from Stukeley and Desaguliers and, of course, Newton, whom Blake represented in his famous print as a human compass, dwelling insouciantly beneath an ocean of watery (material) time and space, obsessed with abstract formulations, his rationally constrained mind focused coldly on abstractions rather than spiritual reality. To Blake, abstracted reason suppressed poetry, painting, and music. As a student at the Royal Academy of Art, Blake experienced firsthand rational, academical strictures on "Art" delivered by know-all of acceptable taste, the regally patronized, academically secure Sir Joshua Reynolds. Blake never forgot a personal slight on his artistic intuition made insouciantly by Reynolds, whose word was artistic law.

Blake held that the original *art* was the original science, which was divine knowledge—not the deism of the rationalists, but the living spirit

---

*Stukeley attended Roger Cotes and William Whiston's experimental philosophy course at Cambridge, run after Whiston succeeded Newton as Lucasian professor of mathematics in 1702. Whiston's translation of Josephus into English was published in 1737.

†For details of Blake's personal mythology of corruption and return, see my Blake biography, *Jerusalem! The Real Life of William Blake* (2015).

of the prophets of old, rejected by the worldly. Newton accepted that the original science was the original religion, but then, as Blake wrote: "Christianity is Art." And, for Blake, Jesus *is* the divine Imagination, for imagination is the bridge or way to eternal, inner realms, boundless. Imagination redeems the world's abstraction and mortality, which is the enemy of the true Christian, typified as "Joseph of Arimathea," an innocent follower of the dictates of pure inspiration.

For Stukeley, the antiquarian's job was more defined. He was to restore to light what ignorance had allowed to decay. Blake would have said as much for the poet, painter, and composer of music. But unlike Stukeley, as far as we know, Blake, perceiving the tenor of his times, felt a growing oppression and darkening of mind that would engender, as he prophesied, a situation where the "scientist" of the nineteenth century could not tolerate the imaginative man or woman daring to utter anything of substantial value to knowledge. The visionary was to be dismissed as hysterical or worse, while the factories of industrialized misery and mental slavery were tolerated as necessary. It was, by the end of Blake's life, common to consider him a sometime resident of Bedlam,* or what we know as "psychiatric care," a being to be pitied or ignored.

We cannot afford to ignore him.

---

*The famous Bethelehem Hospital for the insane, London.

# SIXTEEN

# Blake and the
# Original Religion

*All had originally one language, and one religion: this
was the religion of Jesus, the Everlasting Gospel. Antiquity
preaches the Gospel of Jesus.*

WILLIAM BLAKE, *DESCRIPTIVE CATALOGUE* (1809)

To understand Blake's conception of what he believed to be the primordial truth inherent to all religions, we need to grasp some ideas that to him were axiomatic.

In December 1788, interested persons were informed by London's followers of late Swedish visionary scientist Emmanuel Swedenborg (1688–1772) that a meeting would be held in Eastcheap, London, in April 1789 to formulate a "New Jerusalem Church" based on Swedenborg's teachings. Followers believed this new church would replace adherence to those founded before a "New Age" had begun in heaven (dated by Swedenborg to 1757, the year of Blake's birth). Thirty-one-year-old Blake and wife, Catherine, attended the meeting in 1789* but nevertheless remained in the Church of England. However, one

---

*Some three months before the storming of the Bastille that launched the French Revolution.

ancient Hermetic idea greatly elaborated upon by Swedenborg had become part of Blake's mental furniture: the idea of "correspondence," a fundamental idea, according to French scholar Antoine Faivre (born 1934), of Western Esotericism.

We may recall the Hermetic aphorism dear to John Dee: *mundus imago dei*—the world is the image of God. As the stars project rays of light-energy that penetrate the inner alchemy of nature, so earthly events manifest spiritual causes. Thus, according to the theory of correspondences, earthly events can be interpreted as signs of higher spiritual activity. For Blake's eidetic imagination, this realization involved moving habitually amid a world of symbolic meanings, continually vivified by spiritual correspondences and visual images formed by divine analogies. Fortunately, Blake knew very well how to distinguish the two principal planes of vision, between what he called the "vegetable eye" and the spiritual eye of inner vision—when all interior faculties were fused in harmony. He thus retained his sanity despite the depth of his sensitivity.

Since the conception of two worlds was fundamental, Blake accepted, in his own way, the message of the Hermetic sin par excellence; that is, that love of the body causes humanity's downfall (remember the Narcissus myth in the Pimander). Blake did not interpret this warning in the orthodox ascetic, or "Encratite," manner; that is, that pleasures of the flesh were sinful, or that sensual pleasure was bad. It meant that one should not mistake physical image for spiritual substance. One should not confuse "body" as vehicle with what "bodies" appear to contain. The "real man" is the spiritual body, not its natural reflection.

For Blake, Man is a spiritual being in a spiritual and living universe, whose perceptions have shrunk, or fallen, to the level of the five senses. These close him in. Blake follows Neoplatonic doctrine in that "the body is that part of the soul perceived by the five senses," a position strongly at odds with the intellectualism of his contemporaries' "Enlightenment," which generally held the senses to be the chief, or even sole, source of our knowledge of reality. Blake saw the senses as

faculties of the soul, their data perceived by mind as "body" or the material world, or objects. If the perceiving mind is overwhelmed by sense
data, it "falls" into the world characterizing that data. Such, according to Blake, is the awful predicament of the *real* unenlightened: they
cannot see spiritual "wood" for sense-data trees. In fact, to be subject
to sense is to miss the best, most enriching boon that the sense-world
has to offer. Instead of experiencing true *joy* and eternity in love, for
example, the "once-born" experiences a let-down when senses decrease
in stimulation, followed by a dissatisfied hunger. The problem of sex
in Blake's time (and ours doubtless) goes back to the view of the sexual
organs as wicked, and best avoided: gateways to hell.

So I hope we are getting closer to glimpsing Blake's idea of the original
"religion" from which he believed Man had fallen. Blake did not demur
from the Hermetic notion that the original Man was androgynous, or
that God (meaning divinity) was "bisexual," but held, along with Jacob
Böhme, that the *division* of the sexes was a result of the Fall, and for that
reason, the sexes' spiritual reunion was emblematic of an upward move,
returning to a state of bliss—and Blake's *original religion* is characterized
by just that: *bliss,* spiritual liberty, with "right beliefs" being those tending
in that direction. The original religion is direct knowledge of the life of
heaven, eternity, when the limits of sense are expanded infinitely inward
and outward so that we may see "heaven in a wild flower" and "eternity
in an hour," as Blake puts it so powerfully in words that tantalize us—we
who are on the cusp of realizing what Blake was getting at.

In ethical terms, falling into love of the body is to identify with a
limited, corporeal "self," or false ego, bound to sense and matter. The
true being is, like the daimon or guardian angel, beyond that world,
and the angel may call to us through voice of conscience or in dreams,
inspired art, or through circumstances that reflect heavenly will: "Thy
will be done, on earth, as it is in heaven," as the Paternoster expresses it,
though in ways the orthodox Christian has, according to Blake, failed
to understand and appropriate, thereby perverting what Blake calls the
Everlasting Gospel" into an everlasting torture.

The "natural man" of materialist science and forensic biology is but an image of the real. This is the fundamental spiritual critique of the idol: mistaking image for reality. This is most pertinent to our visual culture, pathetically on its knees, awestruck or "awe-stuck" by so-called iconic imagery. We can be sure Blake would be disturbed by the digital revolution's opaque and repetitive reflectiveness.

For Blake, the Fall is expressed as worship of Nature, and is expressed *in* worship of nature. Such was his truck with Stukeley's Druids, who saw that nature eats of itself and so instituted human sacrifice to placate the uncertainties and apparent capriciousness of natural processes, attributing that capriciousness to their god, ever hungry, or as Blake would paraphrase the Gnostics, a false god, an "Old Nobodaddy" who was jealous because he could not understand there was a spiritual source greater than himself.

According to Blake, corporeal vision leads to corporeal war. The true saints, among whom he included his roughly dressed Joseph of Arimathea, do not bear arms. They are involved in the "Mental Fight," the one we hear or sing about in the famous hymn "Jerusalem," which employs Blake's words from his poetic epic *Milton* (ca. 1804). The idea is implicit to John Bunyan's wonderful hymn advocating what it takes "to be a Pilgrim," so dear to the real Blake. As we know bitterly from history's burning pages, corporeal struggles only change appearances; fundamental and causative spiritual conflicts are left unresolved.* If you ignore the gifts of the spirit, you become a slave to history, trampled by time, a passive player, he or she who thinks him- or herself active, trusting in a house of cards built on sand—which metaphor rather sums up our present state of affairs, viewed through the vegetable eye with the benefit of high-sight.

---

*As an illustration of this principle, I should recommend seeing the film *The Fog of War,* a brilliant exposition of the professional life of Presidents John F. Kennedy and Lyndon B. Johnson's Secretary of State for Defense Robert McNamara (1916–2009), who reflects with clarity and power a series of vital lessons he learned from his activity during the Vietnam War, until he had to quit office in 1967.

So who is the subject of the One, original religion? Who is the "real Man"?

Blake calls the "Real" Man—the essential being—the "Poetic Genius"; that is the generating source of *poiēn* (Greek: "to make/create"; the origin of "poetry"). We are right if we call the source of creativity "God." Without the creative source, nothing can be allowed or "let to be." God's *modus* is expressed in the word, or authorization, *Fiat!*—let it *be:* what is created is existence.

## ALL RELIGIONS ARE ONE

In 1788, Blake created a series of two-by-two-and-a-half-inch copperplates under the title *All Religions Are One/There Is No Natural Religion.* What he meant by "Natural Religion" was that view held by some philosophers and clergy at the time that religion could be deduced without revelation, from sense experience alone; being in the world, they thought, necessitates belief in a God who made it and respect for fellow creatures in the interests of survival. Curiously, when exponents of scientism today argue against theism, they tend to argue against this

Fig. 16.1. *All Religions Are One,* copperplate by William Blake

conception of natural religion, asserting to the contrary that nature does not need, or even suggest the need for, a God or absolute morality. When Anderson wrote in the 1723 Masonic *Constitutions* "Charge" on religion that Masons held to "that religion on which all men can agree" (while forbidding religious arguments in the lodge), it has been thought Anderson was influenced by natural religion: a point unproved, I think; the ambiguity was probably intentional, intended for inclusive harmoniousness.

Anyhow, Blake was having none of this unspiritual natural religion stuff. Nature alone did not contain the essence of religion, if by nature we mean the evidence of sense experience. Creation does not come from its appearance; nature is not to be worshipped.

Blake attacks natural religionists using their own philosophical postulates. For the sake of argument, Blake accepts the principle taken from Francis Bacon (1561–1626): knowledge comes from experiment. So, Blake treats of "the faculty that experiences." What is *in* men that can experience? For Blake, the answer is the Poetic Genius, the true man. The outward form is derived from it (man made in the image of God). Man derives his form from God, as in Platonic philosophy, where all outward forms derive from the "genius," or transmitting principle (from the Greek *genes* = becoming). Becoming comes from being. God's name is given in Exodus as "I am that I am."

Let it be.

According to Blake, the ancients called the Poetic Genius "an Angel and Spirit and Demon." Creativity is the essential sign or manifestation of genius ("as above, so below") or, we may say, being in touch with the genius. The genius is the friend of Man, and this friend may come in many forms depending on the mind on which that coming is registered. But whatever form is apparent, there will always be an essential unitive experience that can be shared across different well-meaning cultures.

Blake was influential on the thought of Aleister Crowley, whose Thelema system (or religion, if you will) requires first the "knowledge and conversation of the Holy Guardian Angel" as a primary step to realizing cosmic consciousness, the liberation of what we may call "Hermetic Man," who breaks free from the spheres to the spiritual beyond. The Angel does not die.* We may see the "Angel" as the light beyond reason that is the goal of Kabbalah and authentic Freemasonry, and, as Blake shows, of all mature religion. *Why do we need this Light?*— "All the better to see you with, my dear," as John Lennon put it.

The false image stands in our way, obstructing the light. Why do philosophies conflict? All philosophies aim at truth, Blake maintains, but they derive from divers capacities for truth. He means, follow no "school of thought"! Take what you know is true from any source, if it helps.

Blake's Principle 4 introduces his challenge to Reason. No one ever discovered the Unknown by traveling through the Known. Acquired knowledge has its limits. Without the vision to go further, without imagination, we should be stuck with data, like Neil Armstrong minutes from the moon's surface when his onboard computer was overwhelmed by data—he *looked to himself*, taking manual control to find a previously unknown place to land, and safely. In the light of the limits of the known, Blake asserts the existence of the Poetic Genius, the inner fire.

According to Blake, then, the different religions of different nations come from different reception of the Poetic Genius, known everywhere as the "spirit of prophecy." Blake trusts the biblical prophets over the philosophers; likewise, the Gothic over the Grecian; the heart over numbers; imagination over reason. Those in touch with the Poetic Genius speak the divine word, the living *logos*. They *know*. True science is spiritual truth. In this context, the Poetic Genius corresponds to the Stoic Logos, the intelligible principle sustaining all things, akin to the Metatron (or heavenly Enoch) of Robert Fludd and the Christian Cabalists. As the Gospel of John says of the Logos/Word, "through him all things were made." If Blake had written John 1:1, it would read:

*This realization came to me personally as a boy in the summer of 1965, around my fifth birthday. This book is not *all* theory!

*In the beginning was the Poetic Genius.* Being becomes becoming. Hence Blake's "Jesus the Imagination" is audible being, the life of heaven creating.

Please note that Blake does not, like so many of today's comparative religionists, blur differences and say "all religions are *the same.*" It is the *source* of prophecy that is One. *Ex Uno Omnia,* as Ashmole insists. Scripture is mediated through the limitations of the embodied, and scripture is received according to such limitations, though we shall find identity of principle should we seek it. The author of Genesis did not use a telescope to envision the creation of the heavens and the earth—still less a passing asteroid as Whiston surmised! The capacity to grasp essence relies on the individual's access to the same Poetic Genius from whence scripture's principle derives. We need not conflict over incidentals. When the spirit is shared, conflict dissolves.

Regardless of the historical or scientific knowledge limitations of scripture writers, *spiritual meaning* is absolute and inexhaustible, coming, as it were, afresh to all who experience it, sometimes overwhelmingly. If the mind is unstable, access to the Poetic Genius may involve a period of insanity, or confusion of planes. Cultivation over time of the Poetic Genius is essential to spiritual understanding, and to science, or true knowledge of the world. ("Seek and ye shall find," as Jesus enjoined.) We are free to seek, and there is something to be found. According to Blake, "The true Man is the source, he being the Poetic Genius."

As ought to be clear by now, Blake identifies Jesus's divinity with the Poetic Genius. Having concluded that once we see the Poetic Genius we may grasp that all religions are one, Blake moves on to show that "there is no natural religion"; that is, one that conforms to nature and reason. As Samuel Taylor Coleridge would realize, after Blake, natural religion opens the way to reason's rejection of it.

It was a principle of natural religion that nothing can be a truth of natural religion if it is mysterious or not demonstrable. Here we see what I would call the abuse of Newton. Newton demonstrated the principle of the heavenly bodies, thereby confirming a "natural religion"—and, to be sure, there is something of the natural religion idea in Newton's attention to the prytaneum as the basis for ancient religion; that is, observation of nature determining cult. By *mysterious,* the natural religionist means "beyond human reason." Blake has already shown that reason is the slave of the known, and a good dose of mystery should open the cavern of the strict rationalist! Blake ridicules philosophy associated with "father of liberalism" John Locke (1632–1704). "Naturally," Blake says, echoing Locke, Man "is only a natural organ subject to sense." *Au contraire,* redounds Blake, Reason reduces every thing, and every one. The senses tell us very little about a flower compared to what the poet may reveal: "heaven in a wild flower"; or Jesus's rhetorical question when confronted by the lilies of the field, "was Solomon in all his glory arrayed as one of these?" (Matthew 6:29). Blake insists that the object of desire comes from the Poetic Genius, which transcends Reason and is not subject to sense perception: "The desire of Man being Infinite the possession is Infinite and himself Infinite."

Having demolished his opponents' postulates, Blake expresses his "Application." "He who sees the Infinite in all things sees God. He who sees the Ratio sees himself only. Therefore God becomes as we are, that we may be as he is." Each person has Christ potential, but we need to desire it if we should go beyond the known. NASA would never have reached the moon had they relied only on what was already known in 1962, when a great many people with a little or even a reasonable knowledge of science and technology should have said such a wonder was impossible, at least by the decade's end. The *desire* had to be there, and maintained. When the desire waned, so did the program.

"Bring me my arrows of desire!"

Development of Reason, therefore, is an evolved state, which can in fact become a devolved and separating condition: a reverse of the liberal consensual notion that Reason is an improvement "by" the brain. Rather, Blake sees his age's offering primacy to Reason as diminution of "the Ancient Man," who, as kabbalists maintained, "contained in himself all things"; that is, Man was a microcosm who tragically became

Fig. 16.2. *Newton,* as portrayed by William Blake
in an experimental print (1795)

absorbed in the image. He had lost divine reason and erected a lesser deity in its place.

We may compare Blake's conception of the Poetic Genius, if we will, with the "Names" or "dignities" that Ramon Llull sees expressing the divine being, which may be compared to the spiritual aspect of the kabbalist's sephiroth down to Malkuth, where the vegetable eye rules perception. And what are all these dignities combined as One, but what Pico della Mirandola called the dignity that is *Man*? So we find in Blake what we keep finding among those who have looked to the ancient original as a model: we see Man returned to magian dimensions through the recovery of spiritual knowledge from the uncorrupted *fons.* He couldn't dream of it if he had not at some point known it, for nothing comes from nothing.

# SEVENTEEN

# From the Enlightenment to Theosophy

## Persistence of Antediluvian Unity of Science and Religion

William Blake was not entirely alone in his conviction that giving unaided Reason primacy would leave Man in the cold, "outside of himself." In France, Louis Claude de St. Martin (1743–1803) was fired by a similar vision of the need to return to a primordial state of true knowledge. Building on the work of mystical high-grade Freemason Martinès de Pasqually (1709?–1774), author of a gnostic "Treatise on Reintegration" and founder of the Elect Cohens of the Universe (which St. Martin joined in 1768), St. Martin called for a "restitution" or reintegration of the shattered divine image of Man: his return to his true being.

To begin with, St. Martin followed Pasqually's theurgic, ceremonial path to recovering the pristine faculties enjoyed by Adam before the Fall. The mind was to familiarize itself with angelic realms. In his vital work *Of errors and truth, or men recalled to the universal principle of science* (1775), St. Martin criticized ordinary reason on the lines that it usurped a higher function. True enlightenment is a supernatural gift, not a product of mental calculations. The lower function is in no posi-

Fig. 17.1. Louis Claude de St. Martin
(1743–1803)

tion to comprehend its superior. Religion is the means of transmitting wisdom to those willing to receive it. The True Cause is capable of things unimaginable and beyond mental calculation and cannot ever be a philosophical principle cut and fitted to the rational brain's dimensions, dimensions proved perennially to be inconsistent.

Like Blake, St. Martin insisted that the Fall could be overcome. The scattered fragments of the true image still exist; they can reflect the light, so long as they are joined through the process of man's reintegration. Reintegration is rendered possible by the sacrificial act of the *Réparateur,* Christ the Word, epitome of the restored image of antediluvian Man's innocence. The Réparateur repairs the breach, restoring "man-God." Regeneration, note, will also involve the natural, physical world, which, through reintegration, will also recover an Edenic state when "the wolf also shall dwell with the lamb" (Isaiah 11:6–9).

In 1790, St. Martin abandoned all theurgical and Masonic rites. He'd learned from Jacob Böhme's works how the divine Sophia enables rebirth into true life. Spirits visible through Pasquallian rites were now regarded by St. Martin as relatively impure; Lady Wisdom possessed the authentic goods. St. Martin applied himself to Christian mysticism, encountering Madame Guyon, Jane Lead (author of *Enochian Walks with God*, 1694), Caspar Schwenckfeld, and Valentin Weigel, among other luminaries of the Western spiritual tradition. Through broadening his palette, St. Martin's "Illuminist" beliefs spread to Russia, where Christian thinkers struggled with the logical effects of the French Enlightenment. For St. Martin, history, properly considered, reflected a process of Return. Any progress worth the name was a reflection of Reintegration through divine Wisdom—a process he believed to be sole justification for the terrible events of the French Revolution. In time, men would learn a new language, in fact, the original language of Adam, by which Adam called the animals: a fundamental medium of pure communication, this being just one of the promised benefits of overcoming the Fall.

St. Martin, like Madame Guyon (a favorite also of Blake), praised the "men of desire," those who panted after the highest, to be sated with nothing less. The more the people of desire were reintegrated into the Fullness of God (the Pleroma), the more divine signs they would be empowered to decode, and the greater would be their knowledge of creation's original language. The full embrace of the Sophia would represent full integration in the creative life of the Word. Here was an ideal beyond the earthly, violent promises of social revolutionaries!

## THE TRADITION

Around the time St. Martin left this world, self-proclaimed neo-Pythagorean Antoine Fabre d'Olivet (1767–1825) underwent a religious crisis, resolved in 1805 when he committed to theosophical wisdom, having discovered a Pythagorean Unity behind all phenomena that was both source and end of All. This unity, the quest for which d'Olivet believed represented the essential drive of the good life, is directly comparable to Pasqually and St. Martin's Reintegration. Fabre d'Olivet was aware he was not the first person to have achieved such a gnosis. To explain how that could have been, he invented, or devised from exist-

Fig. 17.2. Antoine Fabre d'Olivet
(1767–1825)

ing, suggestive thoughts, a conception that would, many years after his death, become a vital idea in Western mysticism.

D'Olivet's experience had brought to him the essence of what he called the "Tradition"—a word that is hardly new, being a possible translation of the Islamic designation *Sunni,* or of the Hebrew *Kabbalah,* for example. The Tradition, d'Olivet reckoned, must exist in all people at some level because it has come down with our species through the changing times, and independently of them. It was, he concluded, a primitive, ancient revelation, a gift of providence or divine foreknowledge. *Primitive* here does not mean what we think now by the term— "elementary" perhaps, in that the essentials of truth were known, but certainly not lacking anything important. *Formative* might express it better. D'Olivet posited the existence of a primal civilization that had once mastered life, living wholly by the Tradition that was pristine, pure, original, simple in essence and of the nature of the harmonious garden of dream.

In thinking about this ancient civilization's location in time, d'Olivet believed it had to have existed before 4500 BCE; that is, before the Egyptian civilization revealed by archaeology and scholarship. It was evident to d'Olivet that such had to have once existed as it explained why so much that was essential can be seen repeated subsequently in so many forms, and were it not for the imposition of priestly and political authorities, this shared inheritance would be properly proclaimed. The Tradition was passed down from the Egyptians to Moses, from Pythagoras to Orpheus and Jesus: divine men steeped in the wisdom of the Tradition. In d'Olivet's terms, they knew how to bind Will with Providence and therefore knew the way back to Unity. ("I and my Father are One," John 10:30.)

Having contacted followers of the late St. Martin, d'Olivet proceeded to compose his own illuminist works through the second and third decades of the nineteenth century, while Blake lived the simplest life in Fountain Court, London, largely ignored but "with mental health and mental wealth." D'Olivet believed he had discovered sufficient of the "original language" to be able to decode aspects of the Hebrew Bible and of religious history. He also held to what he called the "volitive faculty," sensing, through acquaintance with the latest theories of mesmerism, that many diseases had their roots in a lack of will and that the "will" faculty could restore health. He cured a deaf boy by putting him in a "magnetized" sleep where the volitive faculty could be awakened, whereat d'Olivet applied his own will by sympathetic magnetism, resulting in the "miracle" of hearing restored to the boy. History, too, d'Olivet believed, needed magnetizing; that is, superficial viewing did not reveal its true meaning. Meaning had to be extracted by sympathetic engagement with its spiritual essence.*

D'Olivet's spiritual achievements led him to contend with the philosophy of Immanuel Kant, as regards Kant's conviction that spiritual truths were not justifiable by reason alone, a conception that encouraged many to think that religious belief was not really rational. Kant only wished to assert that philosophy was not equipped to judge the truth value of revealed statements. Whatever Kant meant, he had effectively divided faith from reason, something d'Olivet saw as disastrous because it would push religion out of science, making science the dominant power.

---

*D'Olivet's interesting conception would eventually help to inspire my writing *The Spiritual Meaning of the Sixties* (2018), which I hope has restored some people's belief in the best of the era.

D'Olivet surmised that had Kant been in touch with the Tradition, he would have recognized the ancient conception of Man's tripartite nature: body, soul, and spirit. Kant, d'Olivet believed, confused rationality with reason. Rationality belongs to the soul, whereas reason, or intellect (corresponding to the Greek *nous*), being linked to the divine intelligibility of the universe, appertains to the spirit. This intellectual spiritual faculty is what enables man to receive knowledge from the source of being. It is the apex, or crown, of the triangle and is vital to full understanding. This knowledge was what the Tradition had, what it had tried to pass on through time, which was discernible in many other bifurcated traditions, and which needed to be restored so that Man could become a unity in himself once more, and not, as Blake saw, a divided being of conflicting faculties, with no center—with the aching lack of one being filled by false ideals of "unity" such as all-embracing socialism, or mere satiety of flesh-wants. As Blake delineated, and as Carl Jung would follow, the psyche is fourfold and may be expressed in terms of four faculties in harmony: reason, intuition, feeling, and sensation. When harmonized dynamically, the awareness will have the character of the elusively spiritual, and one knows it when one is aware of it. There is a great deal more in the thought of Fabre d'Olivet of vital interest than space allows to adumbrate here.*

## SAINT-YVES D'ALVEYDRE

We should have known little or nothing of Fabre d'Olivet were it not for the efforts of another Frenchman, one central to what Dr. Christopher McIntosh called the "French Occult Revival," which emerged from the late 1880s to the first decade of the twentieth century. He was Joseph Alexandre Saint-Yves d'Alveydre (1842–1909), known as "Saint-Yves" or "the Marquis" to friends and disciples.

---

*The thought of the French Illuminists of this and the later period is explored in more depth in my books *The Invisible History of the Rosicrucians* (2009) and *Occult Paris* (2016).

260 of Hermetic Philosophy

Fig. 17.3. Joseph Alexandre
Saint-Yves d'Alveydre
(1842–1909)

Saint-Yves had met an old lady, Virginie Faure, who had known Fabre d'Olivet, when Saint-Yves was exploring spiritualism in the household of Victor Hugo (1802–1885), then exiled in Jersey. In fact, Saint-Yves has been accused of plagiarizing d'Olivet's original ideas, which were certainly incorporated into Saint-Yves's doctrine of synarchy, which was supposed to transform the political, social, and spiritual life of the West.

Whereas *anarchy*—which seemed to be threatening Europe's inner and outer structure—means "without rule," *synarchy* is its antithesis: return to an order tending to unity. Following d'Olivet, the head of this ideal order would be theocratic, men of desire chosen by God, elected, as it were, by consciousness only, dedicated to fulfilling the role of ensuring the passage of the Tradition through government and society.

Behind this social program, which Saint-Yves advocated in a number of "Mission" works published during the 1880s, was a belief system built upon d'Olivet's idea of a primal civilization, backdated some seven thousand years before Christ. This belief system appeared as Madame Blavatsky brought her Theosophical Society to Paris after its founding in New York in 1875 and subsequent re-siting to Adyar, Madras, in India. Blavatsky and Saint-Yves's ideas meshed at certain critical points. Certainly, they both believed in an ancient unified consciousness of essential knowledge having resided pristinely in antediluvian times, knowledge that had since been shattered into different traditions, and they believed that only through understanding and reconstituting this knowledge could humankind overcome a ruinous divide that had exploded between science and religion. In other words, spirituality, properly understood, was at one with true science, or knowledge of the universe, and was itself science, with what most people might consider "science" being understood as the practical or technical side of the deeper, or higher, experience. Blavatsky herself had no time for organized religion, or for the religion of Christianity. She had thrown in her lot with an idealized ultimate Truth, much of which she found represented in the late Vedic traditions of India, in yoga, and in her interpretation of Buddhism. To read Blavatsky, you might imagine that the pillars of Enoch were inscribed in Dravidian or Sanskrit and sited in Sri Lanka or the Himalayas.

While Western esotericists generally looked to ancient Egypt, Babylonia, and Syria-Palestine, the new schools inspired by Blavatsky and Olcott's Theosophy looked farther east, to India, and to the Himalayas, many accepting at face value Hindu traditions and legends indicating that the Vedas were far more ancient in composition than the Hebrew Bible.* *Véda* means "knowledge or wisdom."

As Saint-Yves, from a combination of reading, spiritism, and imagination, "filled in" the ideas of d'Olivet regarding the nature of a supposed primal civilization, leading Theosophists embraced his writings (as they reflected their own belief zone), and key ideas became swiftly

---

*The Vedas are generally considered to be oral traditions, only written down in the late Vedic period (late sixth century BCE to the first century BCE), with the *Samhitas* plausibly dated 1700 BCE–1100 BCE, a very broad surmise. The oldest complete texts are only some five hundred years old, on account of the climate negating preservation. Given that the stories of Genesis and Exodus likely go back to traditions passed from the late second millennium BCE, with the prophetic writings dated from the eighth century BCE to the second, it would seem there is little to choose between Sanskrit and Hebrew scripture as regards antiquity.

incorporated in Theosophical Society lore, to a point where it was difficult to tell what was Hindu or Buddhist legend and what was Saint-Yves.

Saint-Yves believed there had once been a universal legislator called Ram, his name echoed in Abraham, or "Ab Ram." Thus, Jews, Christians, and Muslims accepted Abraham as spiritual father to their traditions, and thus those three religions were joined to that of the Hindus, via Ram. This then was the root of religion and the basis of the fundamental unity (and goal of synarchy). Ram asserted the divine Unity. And here Saint-Yves was inspired by some old Indian legends of a lost world of perfect governance called Shambhala from whence would come the Golden Age as from a root. According to Saint-Yves, Ram still exercises spiritual direction for humanity from a subterranean city called Agarttha through his successor, the "king of the world."* From this city, hope in the world springs. If modern industrialized society tunes in to "the universal Trinitarian synarchy," real progress back to the One will be initiated. The full, eccentric detail of his *Mission of India in Europe* (attacked for heavy plagiarism), though first printed in 1886, did not see light of day until 1910.

## THE SECRET DOCTRINE

Two years after Saint-Yves put his ideas about ancient India to print, Europe was "hot" with Theosophy, for while the Jack the Ripper murders rocked London's East End in the summer of 1888, Helena Petrovna

---

*See my *Occult Paris,* 106–9. Scholar Joscelyn Godwin believes it likely that "Agarttha" came from Saint-Yves and his wife's Sanskrit teacher, called "Hardjii Scharipf." When lessons began, Scharipf indicated his *bona fides* as "Professor H.S. Bagwandass of the Great Agartthian School." There were other sources available for a legendary city of priest-kings in French travel books about India, such as Louis Jacolliot's *Le Fils de Dieu* (1873), which refers to Asgartha, City of the Sun, giving the source as the "Vedamarga." In Asgartha, readers are informed that Brahmatras ruled for more than three thousand years before an "Aryan" conquest, more than eight thousand years BCE.

Blavatsky's *The Secret Doctrine* appeared. Its two volumes presented Blavatsky's acquired notions of an ancient civilization from which the world's races were derived. Among numerous unacknowledged sources, she has been accused of taking from Fabre d'Olivet's *Histoire philosophique du genre humain* (1824), in which d'Olivet revealed his ideas of prehistoric races within an "occult" context.[1]

What is perhaps interesting is that we find late nineteenth- and early twentieth-century Theosophists very conscious of contemporary scientific theories—particularly regarding the latest geology—which, feeling they should best accommodate by absorption or reference, required pushing the date of earlier supposed, though historically unattested, civilizations far further back in time than would have been permissible to historical models common during the eighteenth century or earlier.

According to Blavatsky, "root races" emerged on continents now lost to time (in impressive anticipation of the continental drift theory of 1912 that led in the 1950s to plate techtonics), one of which was Atlantis, which allegedly occupied a good bulk of the Atlantic before dividing

Fig. 17.4. Helena Petrovna Blavatsky
(1831–1891)

into seven. Other lands arose just in time for survivors of a sinking Atlantis to move into the newly formed Americas, Africa, Europe, and parts of Asia. Blavatsky's ideas would be swiftly enhanced by her successors, including Rudolf Steiner in his book *Atlantis and Lemuria* in 1904. So far, according to Blavatsky, five of seven root races have emerged, with the sixth tipped to appear in the twenty-eighth century of our era.

Blavatsky seems to employ the gnostic idea of a primal "spiritual Man" when asserting that the first root race (Polarian) was etheric (or ethereal) and androgynous, reproducing asexually like amoeba. One notes the bit of science—microbiology this time—but we're soon back in Eastern lore, for the first mountain to rise was "Mount Meru," sacred, spiritual center of the universe according to Hindus, Jains, and Buddhists, thought by some to denote the Central Asian Pamirs.*

The Polarians were followed by the Hyperborean, golden-yellow race of the continent of "Plaksha," where now is the Russian Far East, north Canada, Greenland, Iceland, Scandinavia, and Siberia. *A science tidbit:* the earth had not developed an axial tilt, so the place was hot. The Lemurian, or third root race, inhabited Lemuria, now occupied by the Indian Ocean, Australasia, and South Pacific. Volcanic eruption led to its submergence. The public shock at Krakatoa's great eruption in Indonesia in 1883 does not seem unconnected to this detail. It should be noted that the dating of the earth's formation by late nineteenth-century "geologists" to something like two hundred million years enabled Theosophy to put the Lemurians' appearance some thirty-four and a half million years ago, which would have made them contemporaries with the dinosaurs. Dravidians and Australian Aboriginals were considered descendants of Lemurians.

---

*It appears G. I. Gurdjieff (1877/78–1949) was inspired by the Blavatskyan story when he has his "Seekers after Truth" explore the Pamirs in search of the "Sarmoung Brotherhood" in his *Meetings with Remarkable Men,* begun in 1927. Gurdjieff also dropped a hint of his thoughts on a great pre-Egyptian civilization when in the same work he referred to "pre-sand Egypt," a thought pounced on lately by researchers convinced that the Sphinx of Giza's oldest layers show signs of extreme exposure to rain over long periods. See my biography of Gurdjieff, *Deconstructing Gurdjieff* (2017).

According to Blavatsky's doctrine, the Atlanteans appeared about four and a half million years ago from a seventh Lemurian subrace who lived in what is now southern Ghana, later home to the Ashanti Empire. Originally bronze skinned, Atlanteans evolved into skin shades now associated with Native Americans, Malays, and Mongolian races.

Not surprisingly, given the ancient established source material for Atlantis, re-idealized allegorically by patron of experimental method Francis Bacon (*New Atlantis,* 1627), much descriptive space is accorded Atlantis's great civilization, beginning nine hundred thousand to a million years ago. Amerindian civilizations emerged out of Atlantean origins, with sun worship a common feature as well as socialistic political organization. Toltecs who had mastered Atlantis gave in to black magic some 850,000 years BCE (rather like the fall of the antediluvians in Genesis), corrupted by a dragon identified with the Buddha's opponent, Devadatta, with the people sinking into moral turpitude and incapable of valuing anything but the immediacies of sense perception and personal possessions. (*We know who Blavatsky's getting at, don't we?*) White magic resistance crystallized around the incarnation of Blavatsky's own spiritual guide "Morya." As Atlantis's emperor in 220,000 BCE, Morya opposed black magicians, who summoned armies of chimeras: human and animal combined warriors of fearsome mien. White magicians received mental messages to flee a coming conflagration. The messages came from Blavatsky's version of the "Great White Brotherhood" of neo-Rosicrucianism, Masters of Ancient Wisdom. Having been undermined by earthquakes, Atlantis collapsed into the ocean in 9564 BCE, with white magi escaping in ships, just in time.

Echoes with the Noah's Flood story are obvious, but Blavatsky will also have been familiar with the parallel Hindu myth of Vivasvana's son, Shraddhadeva "Manu," or *Archetypal Man,* father of our current humanity, seventh of fourteen manus of the current aeon ("kalpa"). According to myth, Shraddhadeva was king of the Dravida kingdom before the Great Flood (*Pralaya*). Warned of the flood's coming by Vishnu's avatar Matsya, Shraddhadeva saved the race by building a boat

to hold his family, the Vedas, *and* the "seven sages" (*saptarishi,* referred
to in the Vedas) above the worst of the cataclysm. We find again here
the idea of special knowledge (the Vedas) being saved from a precata-
clysm civilization on which a new one may be built. Thus, the Vedas
find analogy with Josephus's Sethite pillars. Shraddhadeva is not surprisingly given the epithet *Satyavrata* ("ever truthful"), rather like the
veneration accorded to Noah in pseudipigraphical Jewish lore.*

Current humanity, according to Blavatsky, is of the fifth root race,
the "Aryan" race. They emerged from Atlantean roots some 100,000
years ago. And here again we find our Hindu flood hero Shraddhadeva,
for his other name is Vaivasvata Manu, Master of Ancient Wisdom,
progenitor of "moon-colored" (white) Aryans.[2]

A coterie of Aryans enter the Sahara, but it is more like Gurdjieff's
pre-sand Egypt than today, being verdant and suitable for building a
"City of the Sun." Other Aryans traverse the earth to what is now the
Gobi Desert. We now enter Saint-Yves territory with the Thesophical
belief that Aryans built a city below an etheric city, Shambhala, home to
the divine "Lord of the World," Sanat Kumara, evolutionary race-guide.

Blavatsky did not believe everyone in this aeon was Aryan. There
were peoples deficient in spirituality, and some more like animals than
evolved, or evolving, humans, among whom she identified Tasmanians.
Semihuman stock, she thought, had intermarried with elements of
Lemuro-Atlantean races, accounting for the wilder-looking and "sav-
agely" behaving peoples. These ideas would not have been altogether
frowned on either by science or philosophy in the late nineteenth century, as everyone was intrigued to know why divergent characteristics of
race and cultural advancement (or lack of it) could be so marked about
the world. However, we know, such speculations could easily be taken
to dangerous extremes among disciples of pseudoscience motivated by
fear, hatred, and ethical indifference. After Hitler's gang sank the pre-

---

*In the Bhagavad Purana, Shraddadeva's father, Vivasvana, is one of twelve "Adityas," a
sun god. It is interesting to note the coincidence of the Gnostic Anthrōpos, or primal
Man, also being son of a deity.

war European continent, of course, we don't like to hear the word *race* outside of sport, and speak of "culture" instead, which implies everyone's got something to offer, which I suspect Blavatsky and her followers would accept in principle, unless the individual were spiritually corrupt.

Not all Aryans are white, for subraces of the Aryans include Hindus (Aryans, according to Blavatskyan theory, went from the Gobi to India in about 60,000 BCE); Arabians, who went to Arabia in about 40,000 BCE; the Persians, who of course went to Persia ten thousand years later; and the fourth subrace, the Celts. They migrated west from the "City of the Bridge" (built below Shambhala) in about 20,000 BCE, with the Teutonic race also heading west about the same time (Slavs are regarded as an offshoot of the Teutonic subrace). A sixth subrace is predicted to arise about now in the western United States, especially in California, an "Australo-American subrace," derived from British, Canadian, Australian, and New Zealander stock. They will have psychic abilities, and intelligence, and combine the best qualities of the fifth race with the emotional faculty of the fourth.

To read of the emergence of the sixth root race in Baja California in the twenty-eighth century, one should read Blavatsky successors C. W. Leadbeater and Annie Besant's work, *Man: Whence, How and Whither* (1913).[3] It could serve as basis for an interesting sci-fi movie. Suffice to say, this sixth race will, as we might have predicted from the general drift of Blavatsky's picture, have realized considerably more of the spiritual potential of humanity.

The classic return to purely spiritual mode underlies the whole dynamic: *apocatastasis*.

Blavatsky undoubtedly regarded spiritual development as more significant than racial origin. Her Theosophical Society's primary aim was to "form a nucleus of the Universal Brotherhood of Humanity, without distinction of race, creed, sex, caste, or color." Aware that human beings shared a common origin, she was also as aware as the Genesis story of Babel was, that it wasn't that simple. How could one account for the conflicts that exist, and have long existed, and the multitudinous differences, attractions, and antipathies between individuals and groups? Blavatsky held that while religions contained authentic knowledge, our species had often been ill served by those who saw themselves as guardians of religion, all too ready to emphasize differences over common attributes. It is a familiar slogan among Theosophists that "there is no religion higher than truth," but that still leaves "truth" up for the claimant. In this respect, Blavatsky encouraged something of a scientific attitude to history and religious conviction but also realized that much that she held dear was not demonstrable under laboratory conditions—at least not yet—and she was not above elaborate trickery to get attention, knowing that "miracles" had always been great attractors. A big and wily character, Blavatsky was not an academic.

Theosophy is undoubtedly notable for taking up the view reflected by Pico, Newton, Blake, and others that some primal truth once recognized openly was now dispersed among esoteric doctrines, on which Blavatsky drew heavily herself, on account of the evidence within esoteric traditions for direct *experience* of spiritual things, rather than reliance on religious dogma, untested and ring-fenced with authoritative prohibitions lest one find the priest exposed and the deity a scarecrow.

Blavatsky understood experiment in the original sense; that is, that one needed to *experience* things to find if they worked. The idea tested by experiment was true. The word *knowledge* in Sanskrit has the same root as the verb "to see," reflected in the Latin *video*. When something is made sensible to us, we say, "I see," or "Now I see!" Where spiritual experience is concerned, we are ourselves sole instrument, and we are not machines, no matter how much technocrats might like to turn us into their dream. In Blavatsky's time, however, Western culture was on the verge of extraordinary scientific discoveries that made people realize the old materialism of solid atoms, of stable substances, ever predictable once you had the "law," was over. Roentgen's discovery of X-rays and Curie's discovery of radioactivity, for example, taken for granted now, truly shook things up, and Theosophists were among

Fig. 17.5. Gérard Encausse "Papus"
(1865–1916)

the first to see the implications for spirituality and for future science.

This realization was particularly evident to Gérard Encausse (1865–1916), a remarkable Paris-based physician who called himself "Papus," the demon guarding health in Apollonius of Tyana's *Nuctemeron*. In October 1888, Papus cofounded the magazine *L'Initiation*, the literary Hermes of his and Lucien Mauchel's Librairie du Merveilleux occult and mystical shop at 29, Rue de Trévise, Paris: radix for "occult" knowledge, which housed a lecture room for any number of orders spinning off from Papus's Groupe Indépendant d'Études ésoteriques, including the Gnostic Church and the Martinist Order, named after Louis-Claude de St. Martin. *L'Initiation*'s masthead declared it the "Independent Philosophical Review of the Higher Studies," listing some of them as Hypnotism, Theosophy, Freemasonry, and Occult Sciences.*

---

*See my *Occult Paris* (2016) for a comprehensive account of Papus and all his endeavors, within the context of the entire French Occult Revival.

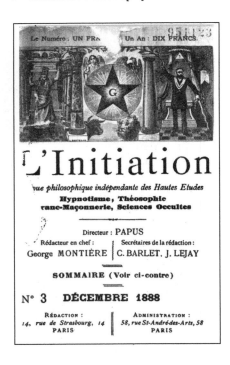

Fig. 17.6. *L'Initiation,*
December 1888

Future issues would carry the bold announcement at the head of the magazine's program: *Les Doctrines materialistes ont vécu* ("Materialist Doctrines have had their day"). These materialist doctrines have, the program continues, "wanted to destroy the eternal principles which are the essence of Society, of Politics, and of Religion, but they have only led to vain and sterile negations." This is Papus's great, largely forgotten war cry. His absolute faith in this message—arguably premature, or prescient—made him publish any intelligently written material in the magazine that held theoretical or practical ammunition to counter materialist doctrines.

Having emerged out of a Parisian Theosophical Lodge, Papus was familiar with the range of esoteric material explored by Theosophists as part of what they considered a scientific search for spiritual truth in obscure places. Subjects under theosophical inspection included Western magic, Neoplatonism, Hermeticism, and Gnosticism. However, Papus, like many other European Theosophists would soon balk at Blavatsky

Fig. 17.7. Col. Olcott and
Helena Blavatsky

Fig. 17.8. *The Secret Doctrine*

and her assistants A. P. Sinnett, Col. Olcott, and C. W. Leadbeater's overwhelming interest in Hinduism and Buddhism and the manifestation of a distinct, speculative Blavatskyan doctrine, evinced in *The Secret Doctrine* and elsewhere. Nevertheless, the latter work represented a kind of clarion call to action, and though Papus himself lost interest in Theosophy alone, he nonetheless refused to alienate the theosophical market and instead added to it anything that for him seemed to contain, however diverse, those proverbial scattered elements of spiritual truth that suggested a path to a new, spiritually aware civilization, enthusiasm for whose perceived imminence he shared with others longing for vast social improvements in the civilized, and as yet uncivilized, world.

From its beginnings in autumn 1888, serious articles appeared in *L'Initiation* on Freemasonry, Rosicrucianism, Kabbalah, ancient Gnostics, unusual discoveries in science and psychology, magnetism, mesmerism, Neoplatonism, Hermeticism, Paracelsian alchemy, St. Martin, Fabre d'Olivet, spiritualism, Taoism, Theosophy, synarchy, chiromancy, Egyptology, mythology, Buddhism, spiritualism, magical correspondences, psychic forces, esoteric music and art, literature, poetry, and Sufic, Chinese, and Hindu esotericism. It was all there—a veritable library of the "Marvelous," and the magazine ran successfully for twenty-four years, promoting a worldwide movement that only died (temporarily) amid the carnage of World War One, in which Papus himself succumbed to wounds and exhaustion suffered as a medic on the bloody Western Front in 1916. Martinists in Paris remember him today, and rightly treasure the lodge chair from which this good man once presided.

As it turned out, the doctrines of materialism have not quite had their day, but some messages take some getting through density of resistance. Practically nobody could have predicted how two world wars would change so much. "Reality," as John Lennon once opined, "leaves a lot to the imagination."

## PROBLEMS WITH THEOSOPHICAL INFLUENCE

It seems the majority of twentieth- and twenty-first-century people who have either investigated or advocated the view that there existed a primal, antediluvian civilization where science and religion were one, have fallen to greater and lesser degrees under the theosophical spell. This is not the place to go into reasons why that might be the case, but we can examine some of the pitfalls of that position.

When Stukeley and Newton looked into the issue of what the ancients knew, and how much more of what they knew they, and we, have yet to discover, they were effectively manufacturing science. They were on the apex of knowledge in their time, working to a number of preconceptions built into the higher learning of their day. It was still respectable science to hold the views Newton did about Pythagoras and Philolaus, despite astonishment in some quarters. While many scholars had by the end of the seventeenth century come to abandon the kind of hope in Hermes Trismegistus that so fired up Cosimo de' Medici, Giordano Bruno, and Marsilio Ficino, there was still serious interest in seeing what antiquarianism and its sister archaeology might tell us about the ancient world, and the still generally accepted accounts of the Bible. However, a rational, critical attitude had grown that wanted tactile facts first, traditions and opinions after. Blake may have rebelled against the philosophy holding that reality was a product of sense experience but he was going very much against the grain of the times, as were St. Martin and Fabre d'Olivet—which is why the philosophy of these men, interesting as it is, is not taught at our schools or in most mainstream university courses. The assumption has been that reaction to Enlightenment confidence could be safely dismissed without losing anything important.

Such was the materialistic confidence of nineteenth-century science—supported by sensory impact of the mighty constructs of industrial "progress"—that with the appearance of the "testimony of the rocks" (which blew Genesis's creation chronology to smithereens), and an alternative theory of human development (Darwinism), the established churches tended to shy away from the kind of aggressive overassertion that had come naturally to the Catholic Church in Galileo's day.

Unfortunately, the best philosophers against materialism were generally not acceptable to the churches. They tended to come from esoteric traditions, which the churches disliked on account of the historic battle with the independence of mystics.* Their defense tended to

---

*There were exceptions among intelligent churchmen, prescient of changing times. William Ralph Inge (1860–1954), Dean of St. Paul's, for example, pioneered Anglican interest in mysticism in Britain and America and listened to what mystically minded laypeople had to say, interpreting his times with exceptional sagacity in many highly readable books.

be dogmatic, sometimes fundamentalist, but weak to many scientific minds who had no choice but to believe the evidence of their senses.

The problem with Theosophy is that it was established precisely out of the conflict of fundamentals in belief. Madame Blavatsky first encountered her future assistant Col. Olcott in connection with a controversy in America over poltergeist phenomena in a rural farmhouse— the kind of test-case scenario that at the time was thought to justify, or invalidate, belief in God, spirits, souls, the afterlife, providential action, and the like. The problem was that science was not prepared to take spiritualistic phenomena seriously; as such apparent phenomena violated known laws of natural behavior and encroached on the sensitive, controversial area of religious opinion. Olcott and Blavatsky, on the other hand, were of a temperament unwilling to be cowed by human theory based on measurable phenomena, and the Theosophical Society was launched in 1875 as one means of investigating psychic phenomena as data requiring investigation to expand existing science's horizons by putting spiritual researches on a par with "material" researches. And the basis of their program was that spiritual ideas are common, at root, to all humankind, and this testimony far outweighed a relatively small number of professional "scientists" who, from the theosophical point of view, had almost completely hijacked the plane of what constituted knowledge. In other words, from the "scientistic" point of view (that is, the point of view that *believes* in science, as a belief system), Theosophy was consciously going *against* the science of its time, defending an openly spiritual interpretation of human welfare, accommodating unfounded theory received without strict sequential logic of measurable evidence.

# EIGHTEEN

# The Aim of Religion, the Method of Science

*Aleister Crowley and Thelema*

After all the Blavatskyan ideas of root races and subraces and lost continents and vast cycles of devolution and evolution, it is refreshing to come to the thought of probably the most significant "occultist" of the twentieth century. Aleister Crowley (1875–1947) was an admirer of Blavatsky, read her and her leading acolytes' works with attention, and regarded the founding of the Theosophical Society as a key

Fig. 18.1. A drawing of
Aleister Crowley by Augustus John
in the *Equinox,* March 1912

event in "new aeon" preparation. For Crowley, Blavatsky was herald. Nevertheless, he made it plain to anyone interested that root-race theory was, as far as he was concerned, unscientific bunk, designed to entertain its creator with the credulity of the credulous, and that Theosophy *as a system* was "Toshosophy."

It is odd then that Crowley's reputation is still for many who have not investigated the matter that of a "dabbler in black magic," presumably prepared to believe in anything. This is emphatically not the case. Crowley received an excellent classical and scientific education from good schools, tutors, and as an undergraduate at Trinity College, Cambridge, with particular interest in chemistry (he spent time in scientific laboratories among friendly chemists, theoretical and industrial). He enjoyed the company of leading scientists and leading writers on science, with whom he could hold his own, and pursued his researches into mysticism, yoga, and occult phenomena in a rigorously scientific spirit, even though he was dealing with areas of the mind for which there were but few to no ready scientific guidelines.

When he launched his magazine series the *Equinox* in 1909, it had as its masthead "The Aim of Religion, the Method of Science."

Fig. 18.2. *The Equinox,* March 1909

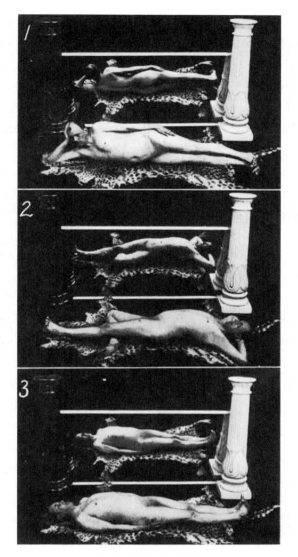

1. The Dying Buddha
2. The Hanged Man
3. The Corpse

*These three recumbant positions are more suitable for*
*repose after meditations than for meditation itself.*

Fig. 18.3a. Aleister Crowley doing poses of Asana yoga,
the *Equinox,* March 1912

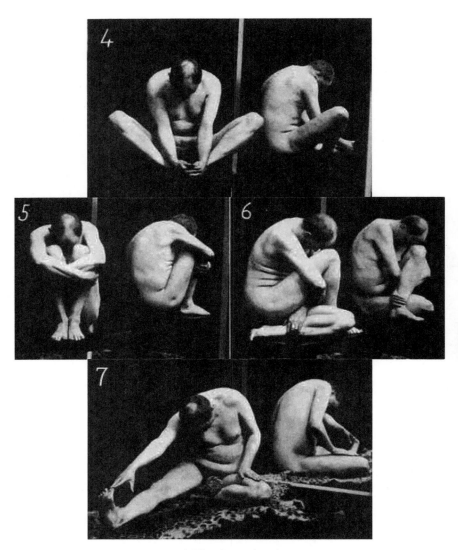

4. The Arrowhead
5. The Bear
6. The Ivey
7. The Parallelogram

*These positions with bowed head are suitable for
Asana and for meditation, but not for Pranayama.*

Fig. 18.3b. Aleister Crowley doing poses of Asana yoga,
the *Equinox,* March 1912

Fig. 18.4. (Left) Aleister Crowley featured in the *Equinox,* March 1910;
(right) Aleister Crowley in the *Equinox,* September 1913

People who followed his guidelines for magical and mystical training were expected to subject their thoughts to austere skepticism, dismissing imaginative speculation and suppressing the egotistic tendency to consider a personally moving experience, or thought, some great revelation for humanity, with oneself as hierophant. Sadly and predictably, people who have "gone off the deep end" have not taken sufficient notice of Crowley's many warnings. Playing with fire has always been dangerous. Crowley didn't play; he *worked*—then he played.

The question we must address is whether Crowley accepted the idea of a primal civilization whose awareness has come down to us in esoteric doctrines in the sense of a "Tradition."

First, Crowley would have disliked speculating on an issue as yet unresolved scientifically speaking. He worked with the knowledge available to him at the time and where he gave an opinion, insisted that was all it was, an opinion, not a vital factor of belief. By and large, he valued highly the science of the time, which held that the earliest civilization worthy of the name was that of the Sumerians in the Tigris-Euphrates

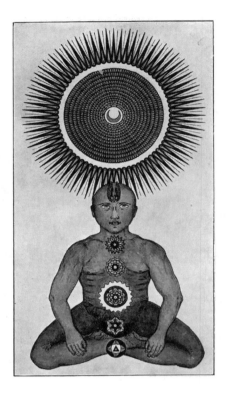

Fig. 18.5. The Yogi,
the *Equinox,*
September 1910

Valley, who gave us writing and the first evidence for extensively organized religion and legally based government.

In January 1917, while Crowley was running a literary magazine
called the *International* on Broadway, New York, an Assyrian immi-
grant reader, Samuel Aiwaz Jacobs (1891?–1971), wrote Crowley at his
office to assure him he had found the gematria of Crowley's magical
name, "Thērion" (Greek for "Great Wild Beast"), and it added to 666.
A typesetter from Patterson, New Jersey, Jacobs also showed how a
Hebrew spelling of Crowley's "Holy Guardian Angel" Aiwass added to
93, key number in Thelemic symbolism, it being the Greek gematria for
*Thelema* (Will) and *Agape* (Love), combined in the watchword "Love is
the law, love under will."

That was for starters, but it appears to have been Jacobs who also
informed Crowley that two Egyptian deities of Crowley's famous

Fig. 18.6. Samuel Aiwaz Jacobs
(1891?–1971)

*The Book of the Law** known to him and by ancient Egyptian orthography as Nuit and Hadit, as then understood,† were identical to the mother and father deities of the ancient Sumerians, Anu and Adad.‡ Furthermore, and more interestingly, Aiwass was the secret name of the "god of the Yezidis."§ In Crowley's opinion, this suggested that the message of *The Book of the Law*—known as Thelema—had genuine roots in human evolution, for it was believed by some at the time that the religion of the Yezidi Kurds of northern Iraq and Asia Minor had somehow inherited beliefs from ancient Sumer, the place Crowley himself described as "the earliest home of our race."

---

*The work was voice-dictated by "Aiwass" to Crowley in Cairo in April 1904.

†Today "Hadit" would be rendered as *Hor-behdetite:* "The Behdetite the great god Lord (of) the sky." Hor-behdetite was a form of the sun god Horus worshipped in the city of Behdet, a district of ancient Edfu, and depicted in the form of a winged solar disk.

‡Jacobs was not exactly right about this. Anu (Akkadian) or "An" was supreme sky god of the Sumerians, father of many gods, and worshipped in later Mesopotamian religion: a king and male. Anu has a female consort; however, she is not "Adad" but appears in early Sumerian texts as Uraš, later known as Ki and, in Akkadian, Antu, whose name is a feminine form of Anu. "Adad" is also male, a god of rain and thunder.

§This phrase could be misleading. In Yezidism, supreme deity created seven angels, of which Melek Tawus is chief, governing life on earth, through whom all tradition about God is mediated from wherever it may derive. The Yezidis' angel is called Melek Tawus, where *melek* means "angel" and *tawus* "peacock" (the latter his symbol). The "awus" syllables are analogous to "Aiwass" or "Aiwaz" or "Oiuz," as Jacobs spelled the name for gematric purposes.

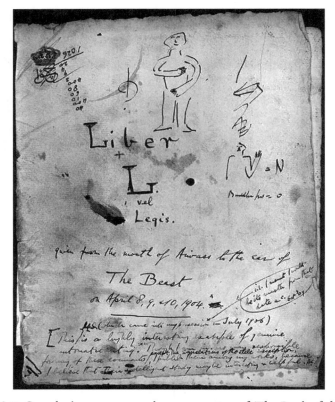

Fig. 18.7. Crowley's wrapper to the manuscript of *The Book of the Law* (courtesy of Ordo Templi Orientis)

Yezidis today believe theirs the most ancient religion in the world and that all religions in some way derive from it, and whatever is good in those religions is mediated to them through the spiritual governance of Melek (or Malak) Tawus or Taus. It should be borne in mind that Yezidism is primarily an oral tradition taught by "pirs," though there are writings that may be consulted, including a good number of impressive hymns still sung on religious occasions that express community faith in Melek Tawus.* Crowley wondered if his own spiritual experience

*See my paper "Crowley and the Yezidis" in *Aleister Crowley and Western Esotericism: An Anthology of Critical Studies*, edited by Henrik Bogdan (Oxford: Oxford University Press, 2016).

was leading him to a primary source of spiritual inspiration of civilized humankind.

This issue of ancient roots mattered to Crowley because he was suspicious of innovation and novelty in occult matters. An idea, he believed, ought always to have some historic authority behind it if it was to be taken as something more than the mental experience or guesswork of an individual. For example, Crowley insisted on using the word *Magick* for his religious system, because he looked to the past, to the knowledge of the magi, tribe of astrologers and sages of ancient Persia (Pico della Mirandola's thought was marked by similar respect for a magian ideal). Crowley viewed the magi as scientists of their time, albeit with different premises to modern scientists, concerned with knowledge, a unified knowledge understood as unifying spiritual and created planes of being for purposes of acting or willing objectives, or understanding phenomena. For Crowley, Magick is science, an open-ended quest for truth by disciplined, evidential method; he was unhappy with the whole notion of "occultism." Crowley found similar practical interests visible among ancient Egyptians. When explaining the meaning of Nuit and Hadit, for example, Crowley saw these "gods" as forces, laws or fundamental principles of nature, ancient representations of abstract realities; namely, Nuit represented *Space,* and Hadit represented *Motion,* that which occupies space, and the combination of these factors dynamized the known universe, with vital analogies in the metaphysics of sexuality and physical dualism generally.

File K.1. of the Yorke Collection ("Cephaloedium Working, Abbey of Thelema, Villa Santa Barbara, Cefalu, Sicily, 1920/21, Warburg Institute") contains Crowley's notes for a New Commentary on *The Book of the Law.* A portion of the notes speculates as to the identity of the author of the work.

LXXVIII [78]. The number of Aiwass, the Intelligence who communicated this Book. Having only hearing to guide me, I spelt it

AYVAS [איואס [Hebrew] samekh = 60; aleph = 1; vau = 6; yod = 10; aleph = 1], LXXVIII, referring it to Mezla, the Influence from Kether, which adds to the same number. But in An. XIV [1918] there came unto me mysteriously a Brother, [Samuel Aiwaz Jacobs] ignorant of all this Work, who gave me the spelling OYVZ [עיוז] zain = 7; vau = 6; yod = 10; ayin = 70 which is XCIII, 93, the number of Thelema and Agape, which concentrates the Book itself in a symbol. Thus the author secretly identified himself with his message.

But this is not all. Aiwaz is not (as I had supposed) a mere formula, like many angelic names, but is the true most ancient name of the God of the Yezidis, and thus returns to the highest Antiquity. Our work is therefore historically authentic, the rediscovery of the Sumerian Tradition. (Sumer is in lower Mesopotamia, the earliest home of our race) [presumably, Crowley is referring to what was then known as "Indo-Aryan" civilization].

Several paragraphs later, Crowley begins his commentary on the first verses of *The Book of the Law,* the principal deities of which (Nuit and Hadit) he further relates to the "Sumerian Tradition," the latter supposed to be at the root of Yezidi religion.

1. Had! The manifestation of Nuit. [*Liber AL vel Legis,* 1, 1]

The theogony of our Law is entirely scientific. Nuit is Matter, Hadit is Motion, in their full physical sense. They are the Tao and Teh of Chinese philosophy or . . . the Noun and Verb in grammar.

Our central Truth—beyond other philosophies—is that the two infinities cannot exist apart. . . . I must mention that the Brother previously mentioned [Samuel Aiwaz Jacobs] identifies them with ANU and ADAD the supreme Mother and Father deities of the Sumerians. Taken in connexion with the Aiwaz identification, this is very striking indeed.

## SCIENCE AND ANTEDILUVIAN MYTHOLOGY

While there has been change within the scientific community from the hostile materialist dogmatism of the nineteenth century, especially in the wake of X-rays, radioactivity, relativity, quantum physics, and other observations of phenomena not directly anticipated by Newton, it is still the case that people today who write sometimes ingenious popular books interpreting ancient archaeology, such as Robert Bauval (born 1948) and Graham Hancock (born 1950), are sometimes dismissed as purveyors of pseudoscience on account of employing a nonacademic methodology and playing hunches; that is, being selective in evidence according to prior conception, among other breaches of strict academic discipline. Above all though, one can discern that such writers' view of the distant ancient world has been influenced by theosophical assumptions. The Frances Yates hypothesis of Hermetism and the mighty (operative) Magus as critical historic spur to operative modern science brings comfort to enthusiasts for a remote antiquity, real or imagined. Indeed their ideas and enthusiasm might have earned William Blake's approval for their determination to follow a spiritual vision of life (located in the past, ready to be resurrected, so to speak), indicating to such as he that they may be more in touch "soul-wise" with the Poetic Genius than with the blind god of Reason called "Urizen," who cowers coldly over many of Blake's colorful mythic "prophecies."

Fig. 18.8. *Urizen,* the blind god of reason and law, by William Blake

Much of the interpretative realm of popular archaeology, evinced in the aforementioned magazine and website "Ancient Origins" and many TV documentaries of remote academic worth, derive their basic spin from the explosion of alternative-life theories associated with the 1960s that have found millions of adherents, many of whom are only too keen to puncture the pomposities and social dominance of science. Science seems less friendly these days; it may be typified as something bought and manipulated by governments, with grants extended to scientists useful in either generating private profit or nationalistic dominance. Science is sometimes seen as a killer as well as a healer: a nasty paradox. While to a Lumière or a Meliès, cinema and the camera promised freedom and life, the camera today often means being microwatched by cunning, alien, unwelcome eyes, though we're happy enough to photograph ourselves with no less cunning devices.

One interesting development of relatively recent years is the idea of ancient civilization having something to teach us, not about science necessarily, but how to use basic forms of knowledge effectively, with minimal technology. We are more inclined to see societies of the past that can do this as being "civilized" than were people before the 1960s who knew exactly where the savages were, and how to keep them there.

The fact seems to be that today we are rather agnostic as to the idea of pillars of Enoch being able to encode knowledge from a God-inspired civilization for a future time when the wicked have been obliterated and the pure inherit the earth once more. We obviously cannot accept the myth as it stands, on account of biblical presuppositions about timescales, but we're still intrigued by the general idea, and as long as we are, the mythology of the great source-civilization or culture will continue. Besides, with so many discoveries being made, we're somewhat in the position of a supermarket consumer, able to pick and choose which particular layout of ancient rubble is more significant than another. I read today, for example, that Israeli archaeologists have found remains of a "9,000-year-old Mega-Site" near the town of Motza, not far from

Jerusalem. Apparently, according to the "Ancient Origins" website, the Stone Age discovery "is providing new insights into the origin of urban living and civilization in the Levant." Well, that's a modest expectation in line with archaeological discipline, but there will be those no doubt who will leap upon the basic story and weave a sensational interpretation out of it. The discarded pot of antiquity may find it has many voices in our hungry, nervous age and may be perceived as containing more than the dust and ash of time.

Nevertheless, there is a fundamental aspect of belief in antediluvian knowledge that is not easily dismissed, though many would be happy to do so. We have been taught, and taught over and over, that the "ascent" of Man is a progressive, generally upward affair, at least biologically speaking. It is presumed that early forms of manlike creatures adapted and changed into the being we know today as "Man." The picture, even in thought and religion, is overwhelmingly evolutionary in essence and has borne all kinds of political and social inferences. George Bernard Shaw, familiar with many Theosophists, advocated an ineluctable moral and spiritual evolution, and he obviously felt himself on the leading ranks of such an alleged march to perfection—still a common assumption in Western culture. However, the pillars of Enoch school, if I may invent such a coterie for a moment, are saying something very different; that is, that Man has *devolved,* and devolved from a state that somehow is yet *latent* or, at any rate, partially accessible within us.

This idea of latency has all kinds of possible applications pertinent to a new science of humankind. For example, since it seems to be the case that essential ideas of esoteric religion appear on the surface of history in late antiquity (Sufism being a tenth-century amalgam of late antique esotericism with Islam), it might be argued that it cannot be the case that, as Newton believed, the wisdom of more remote ancestors of wisdom, or patriarchs, was passed down, scattered in abstruse, esoteric forms, seldom understood, but which nonetheless contained gems of pristine scientific truth. If we entertain the idea of latency, then we may suppose the hypothesis of a primal transcendent consciousness being

288 ⌘ Hermetic Philosophy

corrupted (made increasingly inaccessible) but "coming through" from time to time in the experience of what have been called "geniuses" or highly inspired people who have taken the trouble to seek, or who may have suddenly simply *received,* an inspiration. It is natural to accommodate such experiences as coming from "on high," but the language associated with such experience equally suggests "from within."

*Esoteric* means the "inner," to enter into something, gaining "inside knowledge" of . . . the inside: to be *in*itiated. And that inside is, in Blake's terms, what he calls the "worlds of eternity," which are boundless. The process of access may be properly studied, for as my first study of "The Gnostics" shows, explicit recognition of spiritual knowledge recurs through time, especially when people have heightened experience of liberty amid an opposing threat of imminent disaster. Such conditions seem to draw forth formerly unconscious material, which in Jungian terms may then be constellated within the worldview prevailing, with the possibility of "new" (that is, ancient) insight recurring in a changed context.

This idea suggests the possibility of "evolution" *through recognition of devolution,* so that rather than being seen as a romantic, nostalgic view, those lost pillars of Enoch may yet lead us to great heights, so long as our pride can find comfort in the idea, as the "Preacher" of the book Ecclesiastes has it: "There's nothing new under the sun." If we get under the sun, we may find this a fact.

Having now investigated the impact through history of the idea of an antediluvian civilization, repository of higher knowledge, we must now investigate a concomitant of the "antique-is-best" theory; that is, whether "primal knowledge" *has* been preserved in the world's esoteric doctrines, intact or in bits, and whether such knowledge may be reassembled into a form whereby we might recognize what time has lost or deformed.

PART THREE

∾ଈ ଈଵ

# PARADISE
# REGAINED?

# NINETEEN
# Back to the One

Readers will recall antiquarian William Stukeley's view that pristine religion existed before the Flood, and since it came directly from God was scientifically true. However, due to corruption of the pristine religion in distant times its essence has come to us only in fragments, via what Stukeley called the "mysteries." By *mysteries* he meant what today we should call esoteric sodalities, passing on symbolic wisdom in initiatory, mystical, and symbolic forms, with the intention of enlightenment by personal experience of what was formerly hidden or elusive to consciousness. Stukeley believed that Freemasonry's *ultimate* origins probably relied on some such diffusion, transmitted in fragmentary fashion no doubt, but which in his own era promised a fundamental unity of scientific and religious consciousness. It was to be pursued by free beings for the renovation of fallen humanity by pursuit of science and cultivation of the individual mind within a fraternal context.

As we have recognized, Stukeley's was just one of the formulations through history since late antiquity of the essential idea of an all-but-lost, antediluvian, pristine civilization wherein religion and science were once united, where human beings found their highest, essential home in the mind of God, or to use Jesus's mystical phrase, the "kingdom of heaven," accessed by searching within.

I have on numerous occasions humbly asserted a kindred formulation when responding to a now proverbial assumption of "comparative religion" within Western liberal culture. Derived principally from

Theosophy and common enough during the years of my formal education, the assumption boiled down to this: "all religions are basically the same, and say more or less the same thing." Thus, Jesus, the Buddha, Muhammad, Krishna, and Moses were basically all batting for the same team ("Team God," so to speak), but their statements had been twisted and distorted by ignorant followers and self-serving priest craft.

While intended doubtless as a benevolent step forward from the "my God is bigger than your God" arrogation of authority prevalent in fundamentalisms of various hues, the simplistic form of the assumption has its dangers, being based to some degree on wishful thinking. In my experience, people likely to assert confidently that "all religions are basically the same" tend to be people who have never studied world religions in any depth (least of all their own), assuming knowledge of what they have already concluded is "basically the same." What religion is saying usually distills into something along these lines: there is a God who is responsible in some way for the world's existence, and we ought to be kind to one another and do what we can for ourselves, families, and our countries, and avoid causing suffering to others or ignoring others' suffering. Further assumptions include the belief that "we're all equal" (or *ought* to be, whatever "equal" might mean) and that social life is a moral and religious priority, with some postmortem reward for life well lived. Assumptions of this kind are quickly challenged by study of the complex religious traditions of different groups and, it must be said, have been thrown somewhat out of kilter by the recrudescence of antitolerant Jihadism and painful activities of fundamentalist zealots among all of the so-called major religions, perpetrating miseries for others in the "name of God." I well recall the bald statement that opened Steven Runciman's history of the Albigensian Crusade, *The Medieval Manichee* (1947): "Tolerance is a social, not a religious virtue."

While tolerance might be imported into religions and hailed as virtuous by liberally educated clergy, the foundational texts of organized religions, and sustained practices condoned within them, suggest that tolerance is, on the whole, reserved for the perceived righteous, while perceived sinners have much to fear, although "begging for forgiveness"—insofar as such behavior recognizes and reinforces the authority of the judge—may ameliorate severity of sentence. Jesus might well have said that before focusing on the tiny mote in another's eye, one better attend to the glaring beam in one's own, but religions have preoccupied themselves with proscriptions against the motes of others ever since religion was first codified as law in ancient Mesopotamia. The alternative would appear to be anarchy, and it is religion's role in providing authority for the exercise of power that has ensured its survival. Any power that attempts to remove religion's authority for its particular politic (such as communism) simply creates a new "religious" authority cum futuristic, utopian myth, enacted through a mechanical pseudometaphysic of social identity under state control.

My corrective to the "all religions are basically the same" assumption runs like this: that while we can seldom expect religious leaders to agree in much more than "respecting one another's existence"—on grounds that differences among them are held to be axiomatic and nonnegotiable while power, doctrinal integrity, tradition, and influence are at stake—possibilities for concordance take on very different dimensions when we examine the *esoteric,* spiritual traditions sometimes permitted to exist relatively unopposed under the greater religious identity canopies that supervise doctrine for the exoteric faithful.

Thus, taking a broad view, we may see that each global religious grouping has its esoteric formulation (albeit welcome or not).

| | |
|---|---|
| Judaism: | Kabbalah |
| Paganism: | Hermetic "philosophy" and "Magic" |
| Christianity: | Gnosis and "Mysticism" |
| Islam: | Sufism |
| Hinduism: | Vedantic jñāna yoga, Tantrism |
| Mahāyāna Buddhism: | Zen |

Now, while the word *esoteric* is generally supposed to denote obscure, even contrarational beliefs or knowledge likely to be owned by a few and understood only by an "elite"—an interpretation of the word fraught with social bias—the *genuine* meaning of the word *esoteric* is quite specific and is related neither to numbers of adherents nor negative connotations. The Greek *esōterikos* means "inner," while the related noun *esōterion* means an "inner garment." The emphasis is on going beyond appearances, or removing a layer apparent to the eye to reveal what lies within. "The kingdom of heaven is within you" is emphatically an esoteric statement. A cognate Greek verb *terāo* means to "bore through" (like a lathe), and that is actively what is involved in esotericism; that is, getting through to substance beyond appearance. The way is to *go within,* and it is this very going within that we find at the heart of all the esoteric formulations listed above.

The esoteric seeker is led from within.

An essential method common to the above esoteric traditions is profound contemplation, or meditation. That contemplation may begin with eyes open to the world, where one contemplates antecedent causes to what is visible; this practice may give rise to exoteric science: the flight of birds, the passage of tides, the falling of an apple. To the Hermetist, for example, the multiplicity of visible phenomena in the cosmos suggests the fecundity and essential unity of their spiritual source; namely (in Hermetic philosophy), "Mind," which expresses itself in a hierarchy of intelligible levels, of which only one is appreciable to the five senses, the which senses "create" for us what we call the "world," imagined to be solid and therefore real in the ordinary sense of the word. This creation involves the idea of a God or sovereign principle appropriate to such a creation: the more sensual the sense-vision, the more sensual the creator; the more abstract the vision, the more abstract the principle. The esoteric reality beyond sense experience is only appreciable by the eye of the Mind. Investigation of the mind brings spiritual practice into the sphere of science, the investigation of true causes and primary energies.

The more elusive form of contemplation, or meditation, eschews mentation and the visible world altogether. The aim of yoga is to obtain "union," a union obtainable only by cessation of thought and all its categories, such as space and time, and of sense distraction (hence body control is a necessary preliminary). Pico della Mirandola speaks of this negation of the world in his *Oratio* of 1486 when describing the contemplative "happy with no created thing" who ascends to what Pico calls "the solitary darkness of God," which is, for the contemplative, a pure Nothing where the contemplative becomes blissfully one with his spirit, through which experience Man assumes his proper, miraculous "dignity," obscured within the material dimension of being. We find this inward but ascending path of meditation in all of the above listed esoteric traditions, regardless of differences in language used, or the particular religious framework familiar to the contemplative. The aim is essentially, and experientially, one, even though, on return to the sense world the individual mind might choose or be compelled to express inexpressible bliss within mythological language appropriate to his or her "religion." Knowledge retrieved from such experience is shaped by the limitations of the mind temporarily transcended. One man's "Mary" is another man's "Lalita." One man's Krishna, another man's Christ. Indeed, transcendent vision may prove too great for a human receptacle: one man's salvation may be another man's breakdown. Nevertheless, while the way one thinks about such things may necessarily differ, the essence of spiritual experience we shall find mutually recognizable, consistent over time. Esoteric records provide ample evidence for this fact.

My personal view is that it is possible to conceive of a future where the essence of humanity's religious or spiritual life recognizes what is accepted as true in all of the esoteric traditions listed above, in that each of these traditions attempts to open for the individual a path to what Thomas Mann (1875–1955) was himself amazed to find scattered in the Zoroastrian *Avesta,* in Manichaeism, in Hellenism, in Sufism, and in Gnosticism; that is, "a very ancient tradition of human thought, based upon man's truest intuition of himself"—the path to the end goal epitomized in the oracle of Delphi's invitation to "Know yourself." According to the Gnostic *Book of Thomas the Contender* (discovered in Egypt in 1945): "He who has not known himself has known nothing. But he who has known himself has simultaneously achieved knowledge [gnosis] of the depth of the All." This knowledge would constitute the final purpose of religion, whose guides would consist of persons who had achieved the goal, or could at least responsibly point a way with respect to the individual. A path would be repeatable and demonstrable; that is, scientific, though conceivably operating beyond categories currently established as scientific bedrock.

## ESSENTIAL COMMUNION IN ESOTERIC SYSTEMS

Space permits me to indicate only a brief itinerary of what I consider essential insights common to Vedantic jñāna yoga, Christian Gnostic systems, Hermetic philosophies, Jewish Kabbalah, Islamic Sufism, and Zen Buddhism.

Vedantic jñāna yoga of some kind existed in India during late antiquity, taking its philosophy from Advaitist schools that advocated a measure of identification between individual *ātman* (or soul) and supreme creative principle, *Brahman*. The vital principle of jñāna ("knowledge") yoga is that the ordinary self (carnal mind) is blinded by a decline of divine influence from Brahman to the faculties, blinded, that is, to think of itself as sole "self" and essential reality. Man suffers accordingly from lack of union with Brahman, finding his perceptions of the world distorted into illusions. A fall in consciousness is mirrored in the human body by limitations inherent to a series of descending chakras; that is, wheels or centers that radiate living essences to the human structure and that receive distorting sense-impressions, from which the false self and delusory world is constructed. A descending, superior ātman may enlighten, or cleanse them of deficiencies, analogous to the descending Sophia in Gnostic tradition.

We do not know in detail what was practiced in India in late antiquity in this field, though it is arguably the case that in descendant formulations, such as Sabhapaty Swami's *Om. A Vedantic Raj Yoga Philosophy* (published in 1880 in Lahore) remarkable parallels exist with Gnostic systems of second century Syria and Alexandria, including terminology and a concept of "emanations" of descending being.*

A great deal could be learned by expressing the baroque Alexandrian Gnostic universe of emanations, from Bythos (the depth of the Father) to accidental creation of the false ego of the universe (or lord of this world) who is false god or ignorant demiurge not, as is customary, in terms of a model of the cosmos's fall from the plerōma, but rather as a spiritual "map" of the human being from head to genitals and back. If nothing else, one will surely understand what was meant by the ancient microcosm/macrocosm theory (that the human structure mirrors the universe), or the kabbalist legend that primal Man ("Adam Kadmon") once contained the universe in himself, and by extension, one may grasp another way of understanding the too-familiar adage that the kingdom of the heavens is within us. All of this, Blake believed, his culture had severed itself from when embracing reason derived from sense perception alone as master.

*See my *Aleister Crowley in India* (2019), 295–306. For example, in Sabhapaty's system, the Spirit inspects twelve descending "faculties" (chakras), easily comparable to Gnostic emanations. Parallels with the famous sephirotic tree of Hebrew Kabbalah are also striking, from the correspondence of the first sephira, Kether (the crown) with the aperture of Brahma at the crown of the head, then going down in balanced pairs, with Tiphareth (the heart), down to Malkuth (kingdom), or manifest Nature, corresponding to svādishthana and mūlādhāra in the chakra system. Beyond the crown of Kabbalah is the unknowable, limitless Ain Soph, corresponding to Brahman, the unmanifest principle. Of such, we may say, is the human microcosm. The Gnostic demiurge may be equated with the false god, or ego. In Sabhapaty's system, ego is *Jivatma,* which thinks it exists only when separate from *Guru Parmatma* (spirit of Brahman). To paraphrase Jesus, he who loses this sense of self is saved. This also, I think, explains the Gnostic distinction between the psychic and the pneumatic, the one Jivatma, the other in Sabhapaty's terms, *Parmatma,* not separate or two, but *advaita* (literally, "not two"): *one* with God. Note then: "The carnal mind is enmity against God" (Romans 8:7).

Again, as Saint Paul declared, "The carnal mind is enmity against God." Compare with the Hermetic error that initiates the Fall of Man: love of the body. It is the *inside* of the cup that matters, the cup whose cleansing is the spiritual priority of the aspirant to knowledge. Likewise, the white coat does not make the scientist, but the pure mind.

While noting Scholem's alert against "melting down" Hebrew Kabbalah into an undifferentiated gnosis, it is difficult to deny that spiritual encounter with the creator God of the Hebrews' patriarchs and prophets in Kabbalah relies on dynamics shared with other heterodoxies of late antiquity, sufficient to reinforce the idea that Kabbalah involves self-knowledge insights of universal applicability, not entirely differentiated from non-Jewish neighbors.

Briefly, we may observe in kabbalist dynamics an inner, meditative ascent through the sefiroth to the realm of the "mansions" of God and the Throne of divine presence. We observe Kabbalah's maintenance of a spiritual Light above the relativity of creation and the distinction of three parts to the soul: *nephesch, ruach,* and *neschamah,* where the first is related to the body (compare with the Gnostic *hylē*); the second related to life in the sensible, manifest, organic world—that is, emotions and the thinking mind (compare with the Gnostic *psychē*); and the third, a higher faculty accessible to the spiritual world "behind" and above the creation (the Gnostic *pneuma*). In Kabbalah the latter faculty of neschamah requires the will of the individual for its cultivation and realization. These distinctions may usefully be compared to the levels of mind appropriate to ātman and Brahman in jñāna yoga, as well as to the Sufi idea of competition between *ar-Ruh* (the spirit) and *an-nafs* (the soul) for possession of *al-qalb,* the Sufis' essential faculty, the heart. The Sufi hopes that spirit will gain ascendancy over the soul, with the heart transformed into the gold of spirit, inheriting its true destiny as tabernacle for the divine mystery in Man.

We have here, repeated in different religious contexts, the key idea of usurpation, even "impersonation," of a higher by a lower faculty, akin to the jealousy exhibited by the radical Gnostics' demiurge for the spiritual Father and the woeful distance of the imprisoned earth-soul (psychē) from the freedom of the liberated pneuma.

Christian Gnosis, needless to repeat, contains all the above dynamics, told in a number of myth variants of greater or lesser radical content, but always with the idea that the key to Man is self-knowledge in relation to being that transcends the sensible, visible universe.

In the Hermetic tracts we find the essential idea of a Fall of a divine being into a relative and constricting state where he suffers a crapulent incoherence, haunted by a false image of himself reflected in nature, and from which he stands in need of saving by the agency either of a specific being from above (*Mind*), who speaks within himself, or by in some manner answering summons to baptism in the reborn life of mind (Greek: *nous*), which faculty enables vision of the universe beyond three dimensions toward an incorporeal body, sharing in universal Mind of infinite possibilities, able, in the spirit, to see anything, be anywhere—and do anything. The experience of nous is as though having been awakened to an infinitely more marvelous existence, above the world, a being that finds only the manifest cosmos a restriction!

Now, Sufism does not seem to emerge in Islam until the late eighth century, but despite Sufism's adherence to the outward law (*shari'a*), it aims at an inward state of *baqa* (purity beyond the world of the senses or forms), characterized by *haqiqa* (inward truth), whose outward or exoteric expression is the law. Inner ascent is an essential meditative practice to the Sufi gnostic, aspiring to know God by the passing away (*al fana*) of the ego, or false self, by practice of love (*mahabba*) whose goal is gnosis (*ma'rifa*). Again we find ordinary human beings' predicament as one of constraint to passing preoccupations of the day and the pressing in of sense experience, imprisoning the spirit while blinding the individual to the truest identity in God. Fallen humankind subsists in a state of forgetfulness and sleep (like Hermes's drunkenness of the earthbound). The Sufi "waking up" therapy involves performance of the *dhikr:* a mindful recollection, accomplished among the famous whirling dervishes by aid of dance, but recollection may begin simply in chanting the name "Allah" with an inward focusing on the one and only God. The prophet Muhammad is seen by Sufis as "perfect man," exemplar of the possibilities of absorption in the divine will.

Like Sufism, Zen Buddhism is a relative latecomer to the fold, born in China as *Chán* ("Zen" is a Japanese mispronunciation), a melding of aspects of Mahāyāna Buddhism and Taoism (or Daoism) some time in the seventh century CE. Chán is derived from a practice familiar to jñāna yogis—that is *dhyāna*—meaning, broadly, "meditation," to the exclusion of distinction of subject and object, involving conscious destruction of the sense of reality of the manifest world. The meditating Zen Buddhist wants to meditate into the heart of things without dependence on thoughts, ideas, or dogmas. He or she wishes to perceive the true nature of things, looking beyond doctrine to purified consciousness. The metaphysic of Buddhism, of course, contradicts cherished beliefs of Hindu Advaita philosophers, asserting, for example, lack of continued essence (or eternal soul), but the Zen contemplative may say things that would shock orthodox Buddhists who, as he sees it, fail to live in pure reality, in the now of the now. To the Zen practitioner, anything in the world, and especially the creative arts, may bring one to pure consciousness and thus into a frame of mind whereby one can order, or reorder, one's environment harmoniously. Liberation from the bindings of unenlightened mind is the essential aim and any number of means may achieve this over time, including raja yoga practices familiar to Hindu yogis and orthodox Buddhists.

Many will be familiar with the Japanese Zen term *satori,* indicating realization that true awakening did not come to the Buddha through discursive reasoning but in a moment of pure intuition. Thus satori may be equivalent to gnosis as an experience of profound awakening. Another word for satori is *kenshō* (seeing into one's true nature), a major step toward achieving Buddhahood (enlightenment), though some writers would demote the latter term to a glimpse, with satori the more lasting realization of truth.

All in all, we can see that to bring together a thoroughly enlightened Hindu jñāna yogi, Christian Gnostic, pagan Hermetist, Jewish kabbalist, Islamic Sufi, and Zen Buddhist would almost certainly create a kind of remarkably elevated, inwardly consistent "church," though one might wonder whether the individuals had anything original left to say to one another! I suspect social ice might be broken by the words: "What the hell took us so long?"

## RELIGION FOR THE FUTURE

Humanity is in crisis: existential choices must be made. You may agree with me that we need some kind of "religion" at civilization's core, a system universally comprehensible and accessible. Such a system wants organization. The world totters for want of spiritual revolution and updated religious polity, *rooted in antiquity* and agreeable to science. While existing politics are inadequate, a gulf between religion and knowledge (science) is absurd, asking faith to secure more than it properly intends. Of course, you cannot achieve a reordering or rebinding of spiritual practice based on the knowledge aspect of religion in isolation. A gnostic attainment is not within every person's *immediate* grasp; there is, after all, more to religion in this world than spiritual knowledge, as Saint Paul reminds us (1 Corinthians 8:1). The life of simple devotion may get one to the required "space" of perception, it is true, but devotional methods are not for everyone, though they have proved, and continue to prove, popular.

We have spoken of Josephus's two antediluvian pillars, proof against flood and fire. We may ask, *What do these pillars support?* Let us suppose, as an image or model, that they support a tripartite humanity: body, soul, and spirit; the triune aspects of religion.

First, "body"; that is, life in this world. Here religion functions as law and ethics: what is good for us in this world, such guidance to include health and harmony with Nature, including sexual nature. Second, "soul": here we have all the joy, emotions, love, and pleasure of the life of devotion. We may think of festivals and pilgrimage, enthusiasm for spiritual heroes and heroines, saints and prophets, myths and dramatic stories, poetry and song, sacraments of communion, repentance, and renewal, birth, marriage, and death. These two aspects of body and soul should always point quietly to the *third*. At the triangle's apex stands the universal core of conscious spiritual experience of the liberated individual, sovereign of the whole.

Thus, we could imagine every existing religious tradition having a "Path (or College) of Gnostics" (or words to that effect), assembling annually with the colleges or paths of other traditions, sharing studies and discoveries, of themselves and of one another: a civilizing and spiritualizing influence to the world, joined through inner ascent to worlds beyond.

An analogous system may be extended to education, with three stages of development, as we find (largely unexplored) in traditional Freemasonry. First, "Entered Apprentice," teaching infants the basics required of one entering this world of dualities, of dependence on kinship of others, and respect for truth. Second, "Fellow Craft" wherein are taught the seven liberal arts and sciences, gradually ascending the ladder of intellect according to capacity. Then, the third stage, "Master Mason," coming to the limits of merely intellectual knowledge, initiating acquaintance with an ultimate, intelligible, and spiritual cause, requiring the casting off of the old self for raising into the divinity of true wisdom and wholeness of life.

And let us never forget that these three aspects of being mean *nothing* if, when united, they do not issue in *love*—love lived—for love is the fruit that gives meaning to everything else of which we know or is yet unknown. And I do not limit the meaning of love to what is commonly called today "compassion," which suggests, to me at least, something condescending to someone pitiable. I mean burning, positive love in all its radiance, ineffable and intimate with life on earth and worlds beyond.

# TWENTY
# Return of the Lost Pillar

We may now ask: "Has esoteric knowledge *really* come from antediluvian civilization?"

Recall, if you will, our anthropological model for a "brief history of religion." We traced a development from "primitive" conditions of absorption in animistic nature, toward more organized social and agricultural life, and subsequently to city building and temple religion. This model is mirrored somewhat in the first six chapters of Genesis, in which Man moves from unconsciousness (no distinction between self and creation) in Eden's garden (Paradise) to self-consciousness ("they knew they were naked"), and on to the horror of death, with "wild" Cain versus pious Abel with knowledge of agriculture and sacrifice. Cain's son Enoch initiates city life, while divine knowledge is passed from Adam to Seth's descendants, with "God consciousness" exemplified in the Sethite Enoch, whom God "took." According to Josephus, the Sethites' cosmic knowledge was, during a period of corruption, inscribed on pillars to outlast cataclysms.

Consistent with this model we traced a siting of religious consciousness first in nature, then in religion, and subsequently, from about the sixth century BCE onward, sited within the individual soul, leading to esoteric philosophies and practices where the object of religious life moved beyond creation altogether. We then observed, in the late Roman Empire, authoritarian religion commandeering the inner soul relationship, whereafter Western esoteric spirituality was frequently condemned.

On this model, it seems unlikely that esoteric understanding existed in any remote antediluvian or prehistoric civilization, for written evidence points to esoteric systems occurring within late antiquity, building on movements visible from the late sixth and fifth centuries BCE in India, China, Persia, Israel, Egypt, and Greece.

It is arguable, however, that late antiquity's esoteric interpretations of human nature and destiny may represent something of a startling *rediscovery* of spiritual perception lost in remotest times. That loss, mythology associates with Man's Fall from unity with God, or unbroken God-consciousness, to a condition wherein his sole hope lay in redemption by higher being through temporal, revelatory interventions. This "Fall" involved further descents into spiritual corruption that, over millennia, severed human beings from knowledge of essential being, and from knowledge of all kinds, such that seeing a ruin, or hearing a legend, might evoke wonder and nostalgia. Such a pattern of fall followed by revival of hope only served to disquieten sensitive observers further, for a pattern of imminent or future calamity was well established (as we found in Plato's *Timaeus*). Intellectual melancholy and ruminations on the futility of existence would fuel a knowledge-search for transcendence of fundamental conditions from about the sixth to fifth centuries BCE across the historically attestable world. Any spiritual "evolution," then, would represent a struggle against devolution. We have been warned.

Perhaps we attain better understanding of this idea of antediluvian knowledge if we look to William Blake's symbolic reading of the human predicament. Blake speaks of "Poetry, Painting, and Music" as "three powers in Man for conversing with Paradise that the Flood did not sweep away," where the *Flood* meant a fall into materially sensual existence—a flood of time and space. Time and space all but truncate the essentially human from limitlessness imagination, door to infinite and eternal being. Powers of imagination invoked by painting, poetry, and music could restore humanity to true being—what Blake calls the

Poetic Genius, the Hermetic Mind (nous) that creates and perceives simultaneously: the crowning faculty of the human system.

"Conversing with Paradise" goes back to the gospel assertion that the kingdom of heaven is within you. The Fall may be reversed through sacrifice of "old self" and resurrection to eternal worlds, knowledge of which was formerly canceled out by contraction to sense data.

Now, if this kind of thinking is, as the great psychologist Carl Jung frequently asserted with respect to gnosis, Man's truest knowledge of himself, *then it can hardly be something that only emerged in late antiquity!* For human nature did not change in that period, though thoughts may have, of course; rather, we may be seeing in late antiquity and subsequent periods *a reawakening* of ancient knowledge once enjoyed by remote members of our species. The flood, then, may symbolize a break—or indeed many breaks—that have divided us from source, a consciousness that men and women throughout the ages have been convinced we have lost *touch* with, to our detriment, and that our sense of ourselves, and the scope of our knowledge, is painfully deficient so long as we persist in exile from this knowledge of Self beyond ego.

If such be the case, while we may believe in a period of "evolution" leading to our species' appearance (a scenario somewhat difficult to imagine in reality), we may be disposed to consider our species' subsequent history as one characterized as much by *devolution* of consciousness—with occasional interruptions of reawakening—as by some unbroken or progressive ascent. Ascent may turn out to have been the option taken by the few whose efforts have in fact saved the many from themselves—and we may yet fall again. The pillars of Enoch serve to remind us of the stakes involved. We stand on the edge of catastrophe.

Here in the twenty-first century, we may look again to the legend of the lost pillars of Enoch as quintessential symbol for reattaining ancient heritage, a heritage in which it is fully understood how what we consider antithetical worlds of spirit and matter are but perceptions of one system of which we are a part, if only potentially. But insofar as that potential is real, as our myths remind us, it may be elevated as a fact, albeit largely hidden, of our eternal being, and that at some time in the not too distant future, human science may yet regain its wholeness and our religion its true taste.

# Notes

## CHAPTER ONE.
## SAVING KNOWLEDGE FROM CATASTROPHE

1. Josephus, *Antiquities of the Jews,* bk. 1, ch. 2, 3.
2. Herodotus, *The History of Herodotus,* bk. 2, 102–3, 106.
3. Josephus, *Flavii Iosephi opera, editio maior,* book I, chapter 2, 67; Berlin, Weidmann, 6 vols., 1888-1895; edited by Benedikt Niese.
4. See *Manetho, with an English translation by W.G. Waddell,* Harvard, 1964, appendix 1, Pseudo-Manetho, 208n1, citing Richard Reitzenstein, *Poimandres,* Leipzig, Teubner, 1904, 183.

## CHAPTER TWO.
## "SETHITES" IN EGYPT

1. Plato, *Timaeus.*
2. Copenhaver, *Hermetica,* xv.
3. *Manetho,* 208–11.
4. *Manetho, with an English translation by W.G. Waddell,* Harvard, 1964, appendix 1, Pseudo-Manetho, 208n1.
5. Josephus, *Antiquities* (Whiston's numbering), 33–34.

## CHAPTER THREE. ENOCH AND HERMES:
## GUARDIANS OF TRUTH

1. Martelli, "The Alchemical Art of Dyeing," 11n30.
2. Martelli, "The Alchemical Art of Dyeing," 10–11.

3. Pingree, *The Thousands of Abu Ma'shar*, 14–15. See also Ariel Hessayon's excellent summary of medieval and early modern references to Enoch, and identification with Hermes and Idris in "Og King of Bashan, Enoch and the Books of Enoch: Extra-Canonical Texts and Interpretations of Genesis 6:1–4," ch. 1 in *Scripture and Scholarship in Early Modern England,* edited by Ariel Hessayon and Nicholas Keene, 21–24, 28, 36, 39–40. For reference to Abu Ma'shar and the Harranian Sabians, see Green, *The City of the Moon God: Religious Traditions of Harran,* 137.

4. Vassiliev, *Anecdota Graeco-Byzantina,* 196–98, cited in Orlov, "Overshadowed by Enoch's Greatness," 137–58.

5. Orlov, "Overshadowed by Enoch's Greatness," 137–58.

## CHAPTER FOUR.
## A SENSE OF LOSS PERVADES

1. Robinson, *The Nag Hammadi Library in English,* 362–63.

2. Robinson, *The Nag Hammadi Library in English,* 363; Wisse, trans, "Introduction to the Three Steles of Seth," opening paragraph.

3. *Korē Kosmou* (Stobaeus excerpt XXIII, 32), in Scott, *Hermetica* (vol. 1; Shambhala, 1985), 457.

4. *Korē Kosmou* (Stobaeus excerpt XXIII, 4), in Scott, *Hermetica,* 459.

5. *Korē Kosmou* (Stobaeus excerpt XXIII, 5), in Scott, *Hermetica,* 459.

## CHAPTER SEVEN. FROM APOCALYPTIC TO GNOSIS—
## AND BACK TO RELIGION

1. Copenhaver, *Hermetica,* libellus 1, 13b–15a.

2. *Irenaeus Against Heresies,* Bk.I, XXIV, 1-3; *The Ante-Nicene Fathers,* Ed. A. Roberts and J. Donaldson, Vol. 1, Michigan, Eerdmans Publishing, 1981, 348–49.

## CHAPTER EIGHT.
## THE UNITIVE VISION

1. Scholem, *Major Trends in Jewish Mysticism,* 10.

2. Scholem, *Major Trends in Jewish Mysticism,* 21.

3. Yates, *The Occult Philosophy in the Elizabethan Age,* 18.

4. Yates, *The Occult Philosophy in the Elizabethan Age,* 9.

5. Kingsley, "Poimandres," 48.

6. Kingsley, "Poimandres," 44.

## CHAPTER NINE. RESTORING HARMONY: FROM THE SUN TO INFINITY

1. Hirst, *Hidden Riches,* 15.

2. Hirst, *Hidden Riches,* 19.

3. Hirst, *Hidden Riches,* 28.

4. McIntosh and McIntosh, *Fama Fraternitatis 1614–2014,* 46.

## CHAPTER TEN. THE LOST PILLARS OF FREEMASONRY

1. Speth, "Commentary" in *Quatuor Coronatorum Antigrapha: Masonic Reprints,* vol. 2, pt. 2.

2. Texts reproduced in William James Hughan's *The Old Charges of British Freemasons.*

3. Ariel Hessayon summarizes medieval and early modern references to Enoch in "Og King of Bashan, Enoch and the Books of Enoch: Extra-Canonical Texts and Interpretations of Genesis 6:1–4," 1 in *Scripture and Scholarship in Early Modern England,* edited by Ariel Hessayon and Nicholas Keene, 21, 22, 24, 28, 36, 39, 40. On Abu Ma'shar and the Harranian Sabians, see Green, *The City of the Moon God,* 137.

4. Higden, *Polychronicon Ranulphi Higden, Monachi Cestrensis,* ed. Churchill Babington, bk. 2, ch. 5, 231, containing the Latin text and two MS translations of *Polychronicon:* John Trevisa's (ca. 1342–1402) and an anonymous fifteenth-century translator (Harleian MS 2261).

5. Higden, *Polychronicon Ranulphi Higden, Monachi Cestrensis,* 337.

6. Barney, Lewis, Beach, and Berghof, *The Etymologies of Isidore of Seville,* bk. V, ch. 1; Cambridge, 2006.

7. Stevenson, "James Anderson: Man and Mason," 94.

8. *Du Bartas his diuine [divine] Weekes and Workes,* 362–63.

9. *Du Bartas his diuine [divine] Weekes and Workes,* 295.

10. Cryer, *York Mysteries Revealed,* 219.

11. Cryer, *York Mysteries Revealed,* 352.

12. Cryer, *York Mysteries Revealed,* 243–48.
13. Knoop, Jones, and Hamer, *Early Masonic Pamphlets,* 346.
14. Knoop, Jones, and Hamer, *Early Masonic Pamphlets,* 346.
15. Knoop, Jones, and Hamer, *Early Masonic Pamphlets,* 329–31.

## CHAPTER ELEVEN. ESOTERIC MASONRY AND THE MYSTERY OF THE "ACCEPTION"

1. See Churton, *Freemasonry,* 237; also see Churton, *The Invisible History of the Rosicrucians,* 255.
2. Churton, *Freemasonry,* 237–38.
3. Boccaccini, "In Search of the 'Lost' Enoch: The Reception History of Enochic Traditions, from the Fifteenth to the Nineteenth Century," 23. "Hermogenes" is one of the variant forms of Hermes, including "Hermenes" within the body of MS Old Charges.
4. McIntosh and McIntosh, *Fama Fraternitatis 1614–2014,* 46.
5. Renter Wardens Accounts, London Company of Masons Records, Guildhall Library, London; see Churton, *The Magus of Freemasonry,* 189–93. For the argument that the "Accepcon" likely constituted a symbolic form of Freemasonry, see Scanlan, "Nicholas Stone and the Mystery of the Acception." Also compare with Scanlan, "The Mystery of the Acception, 1630–1723: A Fatal Flaw." For an argument that the "Accepcon" was merely a social gathering with little significant spiritual or symbolic content, see Berman, "The Architects of Eighteenth Century English Freemasonry, 1720–1740," 40–45.
6. Anderson, *Constitutions* (1738), 111.
7. Anderson, *Constitutions* (1738), 110.
8. Anderson, *Constitutions* (1738), 99.
9. Knoop and Jones, *The Genesis of Freemasonry,* 146–47.
10. Philalethes, "The Prester of Zoroaster," 81–84.
11. Fludd, *Philosophia Moysaica,* 304.
12. Fludd, *Philosophia Moysaica,* 151–52.
13. Urszula Szulakowska, "Robert Fludd and His Images of the Divine," *The Public Domain Review* (website), September 13, 2011 (publicdomainreview.org).
14. Kvanvig, *Roots of Apocalyptic,* 27.
15. Dee, *Monas Hieroglyphica,* 87, 132–33.
16. Dee, *Monas Hieroglyphica,* 126–27.
17. Clulee, *John Dee's Natural Philosophy,* 91.

18. Dee, *Monas Hieroglyphica,* 122–23.

19. Anderson, *Constitutions,* 24–25.

## CHAPTER TWELVE. THE RETURN OF ENOCH

1. See Churton, *Freemasonry,* 451–64.

2. Sozomen, *The Ecclesiastical History of Sozomen.*

3. See Poole, *Wadham College Books in the Age of John Wilkins (1614–1672),* 12–13.

4. Lee, *Orbis Miraculum,* 370.

5. Jackson, *Rose Croix,* 25–26.

6. Bruce, *Travels to Discover the Source of the Nile,* 1:382–83.

7. Bruce, *Travels to Discover the Source of the Nile,* 1:383.

8. Bruce, *Travels to Discover the Source of the Nile,* 1:379.

9. Bruce, *Travels to Discover the Source of the Nile,* 1:379.

10. Bruce, *Travels to Discover the Source of the Nile,* 1:414–15.

11. Bruce, *Travels to Discover the Source of the Nile,* 1:415.

12. Bruce, *Travels to Discover the Source of the Nile,* 1:416.

13. Bruce, *Travels to Discover the Source of the Nile,* 1:419.

14. Bruce, *Travels to Discover the Source of the Nile,* 1:421.

15. Bruce, *Travels to Discover the Source of the Nile,* 1:498–99.

16. Bruce, *Travels to Discover the Source of the Nile,* 1:499.

17. Bruce, *Travels to Discover the Source of the Nile,* 1:500.

## CHAPTER THIRTEEN.
## ENTER ISAAC NEWTON

1. Desaguliers, *The Newtonian System of the World,* 2.

2. Desaguliers, *The Newtonian System of the World,* 3–4.

3. Draft of Query 23, MS Add. 3970, folio 619r, Portsmouth Collection, Cambridge University Library; cited in White, *Isaac Newton,* 350.

4. White, *Isaac Newton,* 350–51.

5. Keynes MS 33, fol. 5v, Kings College Library; cited in White, *Isaac Newton,* 139–40.

6. Newton to Henry Oldenburg, dated April 26, 1676, MS Add. 9597/2/18/53–54, Cambridge University Library. Published online February 2013 at Newton Project (Newton Catalogue ID: NATP00268).

## CHAPTER FOURTEEN. "A HISTORY OF THE CORRUPTION OF THE SOUL OF MAN"

1. Chambers, *The Metaphysical World of Isaac Newton*, 3.
2. Chambers, *The Metaphysical World of Isaac Newton*, 3, citing Stephen Snobelen, "Isaac Newton (1642–1727): Natural Philosopher, Biblical Scholar and Civil Servant," in *Encyclopedia of the Enlightenment*, ed. Alan Charles Kors (Oxford: Oxford University Press, 2003), 3:172–77.
3. White, *Isaac Newton*, 167.
4. White, *Isaac Newton*, 122.
5. Newton, *Theologiæ Gentilis Origines Philosophicæ*, 13r.
6. Newton, *Theologiæ Gentilis Origines Philosophicæ*, ch. 3, 53v.
7. Chambers, *The Metaphysical World of Isaac Newton*, 197.
8. Newton, "Eirenicum, or Ecclesiastical Polyty Tending to Peace," cited in Chambers, *The Metaphysical World of Isaac Newton*, 205.
9. Miscellaneous draft portions of *Theologiæ Gentilis Origines Philosophicæ*, cited in Chambers, *The Metaphysical World of Isaac Newton*, 217.
10. Quoted in Noorbergen, *Secrets of the Lost Races*, 130–31.
11. Chambers, *The Metaphysical World of Isaac Newton*, 342–45, citing Dobbs, *Janus Faces of Genius*, 187.
12. Newton, "Out of Cudworth."
13. Newton, Miscellaneous Draft Portions of *Theologiæ Gentilis Origines*, ch. 1.

## CHAPTER FIFTEEN. ANTIQUARIANISM: STUKELEY AND BLAKE

1. Stukeley, *Memoirs of Sir Isaac Newton's Life*, 12r–13r.
2. Churton, *Freemasonry: The Reality*, 328–29; cited from Haycock, "Stukeley and the Mysteries," *Freemasonry Today*, issue 5, 1999, 25.

## CHAPTER SEVENTEEN. FROM THE ENLIGHTENMENT TO THEOSOPHY

1. Webb, *The Occult Underground*, 270.
2. Leadbeater and Besant, *Man: Whence, How and Whither*, 249–54.
3. Leadbeater and Besant, *Man: Whence, How and Whither*, 353–495.

# Bibliography

Anderson, James. *The Constitutions Of The Free-Masons, Containing The History, Laws, Charges, Regulations, &C. Of That Most Ancient And Right Worshipful Fraternity.* London: John Senex and John Hooke, 1723. [Revised in 1738; unless otherwise noted, citations are to the 1723 original.]

Barney, Stephen A., W. J. Lewis, J. A. Beach, and Oliver Berghof. *The Etymologies of Isidore of Seville.* With the collaboration of Muriel Hall. Cambridge, UK: University of Cambridge Press, 2006.

Bede. *On Genesis by Bede (the Venerable).* Translated with introduction and notes by Calvin B. Kendall. Liverpool: Liverpool University Press, 2008.

Berman, Richard Andrew. "The Architects of Eighteenth-Century English Freemasonry, 1720–1740." Ph.D. thesis, History, University of Exeter, December 15, 2010, 40–45.

Boccaccini, Gabriele. "In Search of the 'Lost' Enoch: The Reception History of Enochic Traditions, from the Fifteenth to the Nineteenth Century."

Browne, Thomas. *Sir Thomas Browne's Works, Including His Life and Correspondence.* Vol. 2, *Religio Medici-Pseudodoxia Epidemica, Part One,* edited by Simon Wilkin. London: William Pickering, 1835.

Bruce, James. *Travels to Discover the Source of the Nile in the Years 1768–73.* 5 Vols. Edinburgh: J. Ruthven, for G. C. J. and J. Robinson, 1790.

Campanelli, Maurizio, ed. "Premessa" and "Introduzione." *Mercurii Trismegisti Pimander sive De Potestate et Sapientia Dei.* Translated by Marsilio Ficino. Torino, Italy: Nino Aragno, 2011.

Chambers, John. *The Metaphysical World of Isaac Newton: Alchemy, Prophecy, and the Search for Lost Knowledge.* Rochester, Vt.: Inner Traditions, 2018.

Churton, Tobias. *Freemasonry: The Reality.* London: Lewis Masonic, 2007.

———. *Gnostic Philosophy.* Rochester, Vt.: Inner Traditions, 2005.

———. *The Golden Builders*. York Beach, Maine: Weiser, 2004.

———. *The Invisible History of the Rosicrucians*. Rochester, Vt.: Inner Traditions, 2009.

———. *Jerusalem! The Real Life of William Blake*. London: Watkins, 2015.

———. *The Magus of Freemasonry: The Mysterious Life of Elias Ashmole*. Rochester, Vt.: Inner Traditions, 2006.

———. *The Missing Family of Jesus*. London: Watkins, 2010.

———. *The Mysteries of John the Baptist*. Rochester, Vt.: Inner Traditions, 2012.

———. *Occult Paris*. Rochester, Vt.: Inner Traditions, 2016.

Clulee, Nicholas. *John Dee's Natural Philosophy: Between Science and Religion*. London: Routledge, 1988.

Copenhaver, Brian. B., trans. *Hermetica*. Cambridge, UK: Cambridge University Press, 1997.

Cryer, Neville Barker. *The Ark and the Rainbow*. Addlestone, UK: Lewis Masonic, 1996.

———. *York Mysteries Revealed*. Addlestone, UK: Lewis Masonic, 2006.

Dee, John. *Monas Hieroglyphica*. Antwerp: Silvius, 1564.

Desaguliers, John Theophilus. *The Newtonian System of the World: An Allegorical Poem*. Westminster: A. Campbell for J. Roberts, 1728.

Dobbs, Betty Jo Teeter. *Janus Faces of Genius*. Cambridge, UK: Cambridge University Press, 2002.

Du Bartas, Salluste. *Du Bartas His Diuine Weekes and Workes. Translated and dedicated to the King's Most Excellent Maiestie by Josuah Syluester*. London: Humphray Lownes, 1613.

Fludd, Robert. *Philosophia Moysaica*. Gouda: Petrus Rammazenius, 1638.

Green, Tamarah M. *The City of the Moon God: Religious Traditions of Harran*. Leiden, Netherlands: E. J. Brill, 2015.

Herodotus. *The History of Herodotus*. 4 vols. Translated by George Rawlinson. London: John Murray, 1859.

Hessayon, Ariel, and Nicholas Keene, eds. *Scripture and Scholarship in Early Modern England*. London: Routledge, 2006.

Higden, Ranulf. *Polychronicon Ranulphi Higden, Monachi Cestrensis*. Edited by Churchill Babington. London: Her Majesty's Stationery Office, 1869.

Hirst, Désirée. *Hidden Riches: Traditional Symbolism from the Renaissance to Blake*. London: Eyre & Spottiswoode, 1964.

Hortolanus Junr. *Tending to Set Forth a True and Natural Way, to Prepare and Fix Common Mercury into Silver and Gold. Intermix'd With a Discourse*

*Vindicating and Explaining, that famous Universal Medicine of the Ancients, vulgarly called, the Philosophers Stone, Built upon four Natural Principles. An Essay. Written by Hortolanus Junr. Preserved and Published by R.G. M[ichael]. Sendivog[ius]. de Sulph.* [*Novum Lumen Chymicum, II, Treatise on Sulphur*]. *Cùm satis soripsisse putemus, donec aliquis alius veniat, qui totam Receptam, sicut ex lacte conficere caseum, conscribat.* London: J. Mayos, for Rich. Harrison, 1698.

Hughan, William James. *The Old Charges of British Freemasons.* Preface by A. F. A. Woodford. London: Simpkin, Marshall, 1872.

Irenaeus. *Against Heresies.* In *The Anti-Nicene Fathers.* Vol. 1, edited by Alexander Roberts and James Donaldson. Grand Rapids, Mich.: W. B. Eerdmans Publishing, 1981.

Jackson, A. C. F. *Rose Croix: A History of the Ancient and Accepted Rite for England and Wales.* Addlestone, UK: Lewis Masonic, 1980.

James VI. *His Maiesties Poeticall Exercises at Vacant Houres.* Edinburgh: Printed by Robert Walde-graue, printer to the Kings Maiestie, 1591.

Josephus. *Antiquities of the Jews.* Translated by William Whiston. Edinburgh: William P. Nimmo, 1865.

———. *Flavii Iosephi opera, editio maior.* 7 vols, edited by Benedikt Niese. Berlin: Weidmann, 1885–1895. (Benedikt Niese's Greek edition of Josephus's works.)

———. *Flavii Josephi Opera.* Basel: Johann Froben, 1524.

Kingsley, Peter. "Poimandres: The Etymology of the Name and the Origins of the Hermetica." In *From Poimandres to Jacob Böhme: Gnosis, Hermetism and the Christian Tradition,* edited by Roelof van den Broek and Cis van Heertum. Amsterdam: In de Pelikaan, 2000.

Knoop, Douglas, and G. P. Jones. *The Genesis of Freemasonry: An Account of the Rise and Development of Freemasonry in its Operative, Accepted, and Early Speculative Phases.* London: Correspondence Circle, 1978.

Knoop, Douglas, G. P. Jones, and Douglas Hamer. *Early Masonic Pamphlets.* Manchester, UK: University of Manchester, 1945.

Kvanvig, H. S. *Roots of Apocalyptic: The Mesopotamian Background of the Enoch Figure and of the Son of Man.* Neukirchen-Vluyn, Germany: Neukirchener Verlag, 1988.

Leadbeater, C. W., and Annie Besant. *Man: Whence, How and Whither.* Wheaton, Ill.: Theosophical Press, 1913.

Lee, Samuel. *Orbis Miraculum or, the Temple of Solomon, Pourtrayed by*

*Scripture-Light.* London: John Streater, for Giles Calvert, 1659.

Mahé, Jean-Pierre. *Hermès en Haute-Égypte.* 2 vols. Québec: Presses Université Laval, 1978.

Manetho. *Manetho, with an English translation by W. G. Waddell.* Cambridge, Mass.: Harvard University Press, 1964.

Martelli, Matteo. "The Alchemical Art of Dyeing: The Fourfold Division of Alchemy and the Enochian Tradition." In *Laboratories of Art: Alchemy and Art Technology from Antiquity to the 18th Century,* edited by Sven Dupré. London: Springer, 2014.

McIntosh, Christopher, and Donate McIntosh, trans. *Fama Fraternitatis 1614–2014.* N.p.: Vanadis Texts, 2014.

Newton, Isaac. Miscellaneous Draft Portions of *Theologiæ Gentilis Origines.* Translated by Michael Silverthorne. Yahuda MS 16.2. National Library of Israel. Published online at www.newtonproject.ox.ac.uk December 2013.

———. "Out of Cudworth." fN563Z. William Andrews Clark Memorial Library. Published online at www.newtonproject.ox.ac.uk August 2013.

Noorbergen, Rene. *Secrets of the Lost Races.* Brushton, N.Y.: TECH Services, 1977.

Norton, Thomas. *The Ordinall of Alchymy.* 1477. MS 10302. British Library.

Orlov, Andrei A. "Overshadowed by Enoch's Greatness: 'Two Tablets' Traditions from the Book of Giants to *Palaea Historica.*" *Journal for the Study of Judaism* 32 (2001): 137–58.

Philalethes, Eugenius [Thomas Vaughan]. "The Prester of Zoroaster." In *Lumen De Lumine: Or A new Magicall Light discovered, and Communicated to the World,* 81–84. London: H. Blunden, 1651.

Pingree, David. *The Thousands of Abu Ma'shar.* London: Warburg Institute, 1968.

Plato. *Timaeus.* Translated by Benjamin Jowett. London: Macmillan, 1959.

Pletho, Gemistus. *Magika logiatōn apo tou Zōroastrou Magōn* [The Magical Oracles of Zoroaster the Magus]. Paris: Tiletanus, 1538.

Poole, William. *Wadham College Books in the Age of John Wilkins (1614–1672).* Oxford, UK: New College, 2014.

Robinson, James M, ed. *The Nag Hammadi Library in English.* Leiden, Netherlands: E. J. Brill, 1977.

Scanlan, Matthew. "The Mystery of the Acception, 1630–1723: A Fatal Flaw." *Heredom* 11 (2003): 55–112.

———. "Nicholas Stone and the Mystery of the Acception." *Freemasonry Today* 12 (2002).

Scholem, Gershom G. *Major Trends in Jewish Mysticism.* New York: Schocken Books, 1961.

Scott, Walter, trans. *Hermetica.* Boston: Shambhala Press, 1985.

Sozomen. *The Ecclesiastical History of Sozomen, comprising a History of the Church from A.D. 304 to A.D. 440. Translated from the Greek: with a memoir of the Author. Also the Ecclesiastical History of Philostorgius, as epitomised by Photeu Patriarch of Constantinople.* Translated by Edward Walford. London: Henry George Bohn, 1855.

Speth, George William. "Commentary." In *Quatuor Coronatorum Antigrapha, Masonic Reprints.* Vol. 2. Margate: Lodge Quatuor Coronatorum, 1890.

Stevenson, David. "James Anderson: Man and Mason." *Heredom* 10 (2002): 93–138.

———. *The Origins of Freemasonry: Scotland's Century 1590-1710.* Cambridge, UK: Cambridge University Press, 1988.

Stukeley, William. *Memoirs of Sir Isaac Newton's Life.* 1752. MS/142. Royal Society Library, London. Published online at www.newtonproject.ox.ac.uk September 2004.

Vassiliev, A. *Anecdota Graeco-Byzantina.* Moscow: Universitatis Caesareae, 1893.

Webb, James. *The Occult Underground.* La Salle, Ill.: Open Court, 1974.

White, Michael. *Isaac Newton: The Last Sorcerer.* London: 4th Estate, 1987.

Wind, Edgar. *Pagan Mysteries in the Renaissance.* Oxford, UK: Oxford University Press, 1958.

Wisse, Frederik, trans. "Introduction to the Three Steles of Seth." In *The Nag Hammadi Library in English,* edited by James M. Robinson. Leiden, Netherlands: E. J. Brill, 1977.

Yates, Frances A. *Giordano Bruno and the Hermetic Tradition.* London: Routledge & Kegan Paul, 1964.

———. *The Occult Philosophy in the Elizabethan Age.* London: Routledge and Kegan Paul, 1979.

# Index

# BOOKS OF RELATED INTEREST

**Gnostic Philosophy**
From Ancient Persia to Modern Times
*by Tobias Churton*

**The Mysteries of John the Baptist**
His Legacy in Gnosticism, Paganism, and Freemasonry
*by Tobias Churton*

**Aleister Crowley in India**
The Secret Influence of Eastern Mysticism on Magic and the Occult
*by Tobias Churton*

**Deconstructing Gurdjieff**
Biography of a Spiritual Magician
*by Tobias Churton*

**The Spiritual Meaning of the Sixties**
The Magic, Myth, and Music of the Decade That Changed the World
*by Tobias Churton*

**Aleister Crowley in America**
Art, Espionage, and Sex Magick in the New World
*by Tobias Churton*

**Aleister Crowley: The Beast in Berlin**
Art, Sex, and Magick in the Weimar Republic
*by Tobias Churton*

**Occult Paris**
The Lost Magic of the Belle Époque
*by Tobias Churton*

INNER TRADITIONS • BEAR & COMPANY
P.O. Box 388 • Rochester, VT 05767
1-800-246-8648 • www.InnerTraditions.com

Or contact your local bookseller